Pathless Forest

The Quest to Save the World's Largest Flowers

CHRIS THOROGOOD

With illustrations by the author

ALLEN LANE
an imprint of
PENGUIN BOOKS

ALLEN LANE

UK | USA | Canada | Ireland | Australia
India | New Zealand | South Africa

Allen Lane is part of the Penguin Random House group of companies
whose addresses can be found at global.penguinrandomhouse.com

First published 2024

001

Copyright © Chris Thorogood, 2024

The moral right of the author has been asserted

Set in 12/14.75pt Dante MT Std
Typeset by Jouve (UK), Milton Keynes
Printed and bound in Great Britain by Clays Ltd, Elcograf S.p.A.

The authorized representative in the EEA is Penguin Random House Ireland,
Morrison Chambers, 32 Nassau Street, Dublin D02 YH68

A CIP catalogue record for this book is available from the British Library

ISBN: 978–0–241–63262–8

www.greenpenguin.co.uk

Pathless Forest

This book is dedicated to all Rafflesia's faithful
custodians in Southeast Asia

Acknowledgements

My heartfelt thanks go to Adriane Tobias, Pastor Malabrigo Jr., and the team from the University of the Philippines, Los Baños, as well as the many foresters in the Philippines who showed me flowers that changed my world.

Sincere thanks to Joko Witono of the Research Centre for Biosystematics and Evolution, National Research and Innovation Agency of Indonesia (BRIN), and Deki (Septian) Andriki for the magical excursions in Indonesia; and to Deki's extended family for their hospitality. My thanks also to Sofi Mursidawati and Mr Ngatari for the remarkable propagation workshop in Bogor Botanic Garden, Java; and to Agus Susatya and colleagues at the Universitas Bengkulu, Sumatra, for the many thought-provoking discussions.

I owe a debt of thanks to my excellent editor Keith Mansfield who joined the adventures every step of the way from afar, and the whole supportive team at Penguin Random House. The trips to Indonesia were generously sponsored by the Helen Roll Charity.

A book's roots run deep. Thanks to all my loved ones for encouraging me to do what makes me happy. And thank you Simon Hiscock for making me a botanist. As for my lodestars to Southeast Asia – the eight species of *Rafflesia* that pushed me to the brink – any errors are down to them.

Prologue

Rafflesia *is the genus containing the world's largest flowers.*

When we were eight, my friends and I talked about what we wanted to do when we grew up. Our ambitions ranged from athletics and zoo-keeping, to flying to the moon. As we mapped our undetailed lives I realized my own plans were a little unusual: I wanted to spend my life searching for the world's most extraordinary plants.

At night I would sit cross-legged on my bed poring over cherished, dog-eared books. One had foxed, vanilla-scented pages, depicting curious plants in a faraway land. It contained a black and white photograph of a curious flower growing in the rainforests of Southeast Asia. I can still picture it now: an astonishingly large, vaguely grotesque-looking pentagon, draped over the floor like a lumpy great starfish. This was the largest flower in the world, the book told me, spanning over a metre across. I was possessed by it and wanted to see one growing in the wild more than anything. *Rafflesia* had cast its spell on me.

But Southeast Asia may as well have been the moon to me back then. There was no way in which I could see the plants that haunted me from the other side of the planet. So I conjured them up in a pretend rainforest behind my family's back garden. We lived next to an old cemetery, a place reclaimed by nature, where foxes skulked among fallen tombstones netted with ivy and briers. Here I scrambled up yew trees and swung from the branches, pretending I was in the jungle. I made 3D replicas of exotic plants out of papier mâché and clay, all carefully sculpted and painted. Then in a wild corner of the cemetery I staged a life-sized *Rafflesia* model among the mossy branches, and sat on a fallen gravestone, staring at it. This was the closest I could get to an encounter with the world's most magnificent plant. My story put down roots there, in that quiet cemetery in southeast England.

Today I am a botanist. I work at the University of Oxford's Botanic Garden and I have dedicated my life to studying the biology of extraordinary plants such as *Rafflesia*, getting to know them, revealing their secrets. First things first: *Rafflesia* is a parasite that steals its food from other plants. A thief. Parasitic plants make up about 1 per cent of all flowering plants and they're no aberration. In fact they've evolved twelve times – they are all around us. Some abandoned photosynthesis and are completely dependent on other plants, their so-called hosts, for their existence. They have always intrigued me. Their curious leafless forms and ghostly flowers have a spellbinding beauty and their sinister biology animates them somehow – gives them personality. Many parasitic plants are poorly known to science, and most have never even been cultivated. Yes, these botanical enigmas, which are the focus of my research today, still keep me awake at night just as they did when I was a child.

How did such a striking work of nature as *Rafflesia* come to exist?

I have worked with other botanists around the world, seeking to answer this question. Together with Professor Charles Davis and colleagues at Harvard, I have shown that *Rafflesia*, which spends its entire life cycle within the tissues of other plants, exhibits a startling similarity to fungi: they lead secret parallel lives.[1] Fungi are not plants. They belong to their own kingdom, distinct from plants and animals, from which they diverged a billion years ago. And yet, just like fungi, *Rafflesia* exists for most of its life as a microscopic thread, creeping about within the tissues of another plant, sending out 'sinkers' to absorb food. Something like a tapeworm. In the metamorphosis to this hidden existence, genes have gone walkabouts along the way. It is for this reason that the genes needed for photosynthesis are missing in many parasitic plants, meanwhile those encoding certain enzymes are redundant in some fungi; in both cases, they have no need for them, living as they do entirely at the expense of their hosts. There's more: they have also acquired *new* genes by Horizontal Gene Transfers (HGTs) – the rare exchange of genetic material between non-mating organisms. Extinct ancestors of *Rafflesia* have even been shown to possess genes from relatives of the cucumber and carrot due to former associations with these plants: encrypted in their genomes lurk 'DNA fossils' that hint at their evolutionary journey.[2]

But this is a story that goes beyond biology. This is the tale of a man who longed for something, and was drawn to it from the other side of the globe by invisible threads: something that made him recklessly bold. Like Apollo he was struck by an arrow, and he dared; like him too, he was driven to extremes for an unrequited love – and the more he chased the flower that tore at his heart, the more he got rejected by it. Dragged helplessly to heaven through hell and back, he became half-sick with his obsession to find it.

Perhaps as you turn these pages and read how, delirious with sleeplessness, he saw flowers the size of people, personalities in plants, and listened to them speak – you'll wonder if he lost his mind.

God knows, I wondered.

But so it was that, smacking off leeches and hanging off vines, wading through rivers and wrestling the forest, I followed tribes to the very depths of the abyss to find Rafflesia's hidden flowers: dripped blood, sweat and tears on them. And felt something inside me change for ever.

This is the story of a botanist, a flower, and a forester, and how our lives intertwined.

I.

Mr Chris, one day I show you big *Rafflesia* in Indonesia. Yes, Mr Chris visit Bengkulu Selatan and Muara Sahung – we see big flower there together. Big, big flower.

Mr Chris, come to hear my story. My forest – it will be destroyed by people. They do not know how special it is, Mr Chris. The forest is crumbling and soon my children can find *Rafflesia* only on Google.

Come while the forest still exists, Mr Chris. Come soon.

2.

'There are two paths and we must choose one.'

Adriane stares at me expectantly then folds his arms neatly on the table.

'Which one is most likely to take us to the flower?' I ask. I feel like we're solving a riddle.

'The longer one.'

'How long, Adriane?' I drink my green tea down to the clinking ice and hold his gaze. A waiter busies himself taking away our plates of little unfinished pyramids of rice.

'Days. We would need to sleep in the forest.'

'That's OK,' I reassure him. 'I can do that.' I say this a lot out here.

'But there are risks,' he continues, his eyes fixed on mine, impassive. We say nothing for a while, waiting for me to speak.

'What risks?' I finally ask him.

'Someone was shot by an arrow in the forest, not long ago. They died.'

There: we've reached the answer. I nod silently as we trace our fingertips along the shorter route on the map spread out in front of us. It leads to a plant called *Rafflesia leonardi* – one of the forty or so species in the genus *Rafflesia*, which contains the world's largest flowers. Few people have ever set eyes on this plant. It is one of a handful we hope to encounter during the expedition here in the Philippines.

A neural pathway in the non-executive part of my brain has latched on to that longer path and can't shake it off now. There is something deliciously reckless about it, the notion of fleeing tribes and arrows in pursuit of *Rafflesia*. My imagination takes me ducking under branches, tripping over buttress roots, looking back over my shoulder, then jack-knifing to the floor as I narrowly miss taking an arrow to my heart . . .

'Here,' Adriane says, tapping the map, yanking me back into our little street-side restaurant in Los Baños.

He is pointing to a green ink stain of forest spreading along the creases of the eastern seaboard of Luzon Island. As we linger over the map, I wish Adriane would *dare* us to do it, risk everything for the flower. He would – I know he would – just as he knows I would too. Except I am his guest here, and I cannot ask this of him. So, silently, we concede to playing it safe. Relatively speaking that is – for nothing is truly safe on an adventure like this one. I'm not exactly sure what perils await us in the jungle but I'm damned sure of this: whatever path we take, I'll do anything to find that flower.

***

Meet the cast: Adriane is my guide and friend, and together we have been planning this expedition for months. He is twenty-six but looks eighteen. He has short muscly legs, a crop of black hair, and a serious demeanour that softens when someone mentions the place *Kalinga* (I'll return to that); actually the very word makes his eyes flash wild and bright, like a lemur's. Professor Pastor Malabrigo Jr, or 'Pat', is Adriane's boss. He is double Adriane's size (Pat enjoys a beer) and has a big, happy face with high-arched eyebrows that hover permanently somewhere between mirth and surprise. It's impossible not to like him. His knowledge of the flora of the Philippines is unparalleled; he knows every plant.

We'll be accompanied intermittently by Glen, the Philippines' resident expert on dipterocarps – those iconic rainforest trees used for food and medicine by local communities across Southeast Asia – fern specialist Marge, and expert field botanist Ana. Together with the country's knife- and gun-clad foresters and tribes, we are about to bore into the very depths of the Philippines' last green wilderness in pursuit of plants. Later we will join Septian Andriki, known as Deki, in Sumatra – a man who cares deeply about the plight of his rainforests, and Joko Witono, a botanist in Java who holds the key to growing the ungrowable.

Together, our mission is to chart Southeast Asia's most poorly known species of *Rafflesia*, and to conserve them. We will probe their secret lives, and determine where one species ends and another begins: for if we don't know how many exist (and we don't), then how can we possibly protect them?

As the forest burns around us, we'll discover we're in a race against time.

***

My first day in Los Baños, a town sweltering in the folds of Mount Makiling's jungled slopes. Everywhere smells overripe and tropical, like fruit and fried chicken. I am itching to explore the rainforest but there are permits to sort out. Our driver Kuya ('elder brother') Mande is taking us to the offices of the Forestry Department. He pulls up outside our apartment, and Adriane and I hop into the boxy blue Toyota van. On the way to the administration offices, we pass an ever-changing ribbon of life under a torrent of cables: tricycles zooming; children being yanked out of the road; blue flip-flops; blue rooftops; chickens running, chickens frying; two men peeing – each with one hand to the wall; and a politician beaming proudly from triplicate posters, one of them upside down. Smile. Smile. Frown.

We park outside the offices, where a horde of students are crouching on the road. I am introduced to their professor, who is presiding over a blue polythene sheet stretched across the tarmac, on which leaves have been cast about. 'They are identifying figs,' he tells me, pointing to the plastic ocean with green jigsaw pieces floating on its surface.

Watching the students examining their specimens calls forth a memory of teaching undergraduate field botany in Portugal. Every spring for over a decade I taught there, marching sun-frazzled students into the spiny thicket. On the last day of the trip, the other lecturers and I would raid the vegetation to set our students an identification test. We'd arrange the specimens on the hotel's breakfast tables, then watch as the students consulted every leaf and flower. One year, when the test was over, the students decided to carry the magnificent wand-like stem of a *Thapsia* into the town. Some sort of mascot, I suppose. I remember tourists staring as we poured out of our hotel onto the street, brandishing the sturdy, fennel-like sprout of yellow blossom. In the bar that night, I told the students that some plants can be identified by their smell or taste alone. Before I could stop her, Chantelle, one of our livelier students, reached for the *Thapsia* and gnawed off a frond with her teeth, gulping it down with sangria.

'Tastes of nothing,' she said, looking unimpressed, flicking back her hair.

'Chantelle, I'm pretty sure that plant is poisonous!' I said, panicking. I couldn't believe what she'd done.

'Oh my god! How poisonous?' she gasped.

I said I wasn't sure, as the other students picked up their phones and started googling frantically.

'Got it!' announced a more studious student, breathless with the importance of her announcement. She cleared her throat. '*Thapsia* is extremely toxic, even in small doses,' she read, then paused for effect: 'it is also known as the deadly carrot'. She sat back to watch our reaction as Chantelle sprinted to the ladies' room. The following morning, we couldn't assign the symptoms that presented themselves with certainty either to the deadly carrot, or to an excessive quantity of sangria.

***

Adriane sorts the paperwork alongside an administration lady in her mid-sixties with a whisky voice who calls herself his granny. I absorb my surroundings from a sagging sofa in the corner. An eclectic assortment of items including an old propped-up guitar, some mounted butterflies strung to the wall, and last year's Christmas tinsel strewn about the ceiling. Glen wanders over and sits beside me. We talk about our shared love of dipterocarps. These are the trees you sometimes see in rainforest documentaries on TV, filmed from the sky, rising from the canopy like broccoli. Glen tells me they are being used here in Los Baños in computerized models to predict the impacts of climate change. 'That's good,' I say, lamely, as Adriane shuffles paper in the background. We don't talk about how climate change is sending biodiversity into freefall, that the dipterocarps – and all the other indicators – show this; or that we, as botanists, are powerless to change it.

Once the paperwork is in order, Adriane, Glen, and I leave the cool hush of the polished offices to visit the university's arboretum. We walk along a road half repossessed by roots and vines, where birds and insects echo and click about the trees. Glen and Adriane wander side by side, chatting in Tagalog (the national language of the Philippines) a few metres ahead of me. As I shuffle through the leaf litter behind them, something catches my eye along the road-side's scribbled edge: a crescent moon of fallen flowers showering the floor. I pick one up. It has the outline of a parrot's beak and spans the width of my four fingers. Its shapely form alone is intriguing, but the colour – the *colour* – that belongs to another world: it is a shade of turquoise like nothing else. And I do mean turquoise – neither blue nor green. I flip it over with my index finger and peer at it on the palm of my hand. Its surface is minutely dimpled and darker around the edges, like a pool of tropical seawater. Glen and Adriane glance back at me over their shoulders then wander over. Their eyes flit from the flower in my hand to the daft smile on my face.

'Look Chris,' whispers Glen, pointing to the sky, 'there are more!'

Up in the branches above our heads dangles the source of the sublime flowers: a jade vine (*Strongylodon macrobotrys*). I stare at the suspended marvel – a cylinder of claw-shaped blossom that, now I see it from beneath, has a mint-green cast to it. In fact it is almost glowing. I look at Glen and Adriane, lost for words. They laugh. They see this flower almost every day; to them it is no more exotic than a foxglove is to me. I have read that the jade vine's luminous flowers are attractive to bats, but I've not met anyone who has seen the creatures in action to prove this. Standing here among the trees,

I can imagine a bat fluttering in; can almost see it knocking the flowers in front of us.

Last year the jade vine at work pushed out some flowers unenthusiastically against the glasshouse roof at Oxford Botanic Garden. I was excited at the time, as we huddled around the curious blue vision. Well, to see such a striking work of nature anywhere would be special, wouldn't it? But to see one in the wild – that's a gift. Later I learn that we're standing close to where this species was first collected officially, here on the forested slopes of Mount Makiling, during the United States Exploring Expedition led by Charles Wilkes in 1841. Perhaps like me, the nineteenth-century explorers couldn't shake the flowers from their minds – were spellbound by them.

Arboreta I have visited in the past have been clipped, pruned, and mulched – places where nature is managed and bent into shape. Not this one. It feels wild, reclaimed by trees. We pick our way down a root-webbed path and pass a fig tree shooting up into the canopy like an arrow. It has yellow, speckled fruits the size of ping-pong balls, bubbling out of the bark. Oddly, I'm reminded of that lumpy yellow foam that builders use to fill cracks in the wall. I run my fingers over the little golden baubles.

Figs are fascinating. They include some of the earliest domesticated crops and they have been cultivated in some parts of the world for over 11,000 years. But what has always excited me about them is their pollination. First things first: a fig is *not* a fruit, nor is it a flower. Let me explain. Botanically speaking, a fig is a *syconium* – an infolded structure within which the tiny flowers are enclosed – they never see the light of day. So a fig comprises a whole collection of tiny flowers, all crammed into a ball, like seeds in a pumpkin.

There's more: figs are intimately associated with fig wasps – insects they have evolved alongside for 60 million years. The little wasps haul themselves through a tight passageway called an *ostiole*, losing wings and other body parts along the way. I can just make out the ostioles on the specimens in front of me – they look like the bottoms of apples. Upon arrival in the fig's central cavity, the wasps dust themselves down. Pollen they have brought from other figs fertilizes some of the flowers; meanwhile eggs are deposited in others. The flowers that receive eggs nourish the wasps' developing grubs; meanwhile those that receive only pollen develop seeds. Then, a new generation of wasps emerges within the confines of the fig. Wingless males mate with winged females who pick up pollen as they crawl about. The males bite an exit tunnel through which the insects escape; they soon die, while the pollen-laden females zoom off into the wilderness, and the process repeats itself. I can picture it all taking place unseen within the hidden worlds in front of me. I peer up at them, hoping to see a fig wasp fly out. But all I see is a line of ants, marching purposefully to the sky.

A few metres away, the forest floor is spangled with gigantic fallen leaves, snatching light along their sawn edges. They are the shape of oak leaves, only astonishingly large – about 60 centimetres long. I pick one up and it sways about like a sail. It belongs to a nearby tree known as 'antipolo' (*Artocarpus blancoi*), which is found only here in the Philippines and is a distant relative of the fig we have just been admiring. Near it I find the fallen fronds of yet another giant, this time a dipterocarp. These are like triple XL chestnut leaves, the length of my arm. It is as if I have stepped into a wood-land from the Land of the Giants. As we pause for breath beneath the cathedral of over-sized trees, Pat wanders down the path to join us. He slaps me on the back and looks me up and down.

'You're too *thin*, Chris!' he exclaims. 'You need more beer!'

The conversation quickly shifts from beer to *Rafflesia*. Pat whips out his mobile phone and calls a forest ranger in Aurora Province to see if the flower has been seen there recently. An animated exchange in Tagalog follows, after which Pat turns to me, smiles, and says: '*Rafflesia leonardi* has been seen in bud this week.' He pauses. 'If we are lucky,' he continues, 'it will be open when we arrive in two weeks.'

'You have chosen the right time to come here, Chris.' He grins.

As we pick our way quietly out of the netted shade, I feel a surge of adrenaline wash through me. I think they feel it too.

★★★

Later that afternoon, somewhere down a hospital-like corridor, we bang on a green steel door. Adriane and I are standing deep in the bowels of a concrete, municipal-looking building, with plants poking out of the walls and greened over with abandonment. Radio music and cigarette smoke seep through the door as we bash our fists against the metal. Eventually the curator of the herbarium appears, and we file into his kingdom of dried plants, cabinets, and formaldehyde. The air is thick with smoke and the panic of hastily sprayed air freshener. It looks like a locker room, with ranks of floor-to-ceiling metal cases and posters tacked to its doors.

Herbaria are collections of preserved plants stored, catalogued, and arranged systematically. They are magical places, chock-full with botanical treasure, collected over the course of centuries. Each herbarium specimen holds vital information about a plant's whereabouts at a given place and time, when it was in flower, and its DNA. The most important specimens stashed away in these cabinets are the *types*. A type is the definitive go-to specimen for quibbling botanists. Herbaria can assist plant conservation too. Scientists are in a race against time to describe species, to make sense of biodiversity while it still exists. Of the estimated 70,000 plant species still out there waiting to be described, over half may have already been collected and sit waiting in herbaria,[1] pressed for time.

Adriane pulls out a bulging, mushroom-coloured folder from a shelf and places it on a wooden table congested with other, similar-looking folders, and jars of pickled plants; he moves with authority – he knows his way about. The curator leans against the table watching us as Adriane leafs through the folder, pausing at a brown page folded along each side to create a sort of shallow box. Inside this sit two wrinkled black flowers the size of hands. They look like dried mushrooms. Each has a paper label attached to it with string, like a price tag. We peer at the labels, which tell us these *Rafflesia* samples were collected in 1982 from Mount Makiling, just a few miles from where we are standing. The next page is mounted with a photograph of a much larger *Rafflesia*, along with a polyethylene bag containing what looks like a desiccated cabbage.

'*Rafflesia banaoana*,' Adriane whispers. 'This is its bud.'

The curator wanders back to the cabinet and returns with a large, clear plastic bottle in which an enormous brown flower is bobbing in fluid stained the colour of urine. It looks like a monster from the deep.

'The type,' Adriane says, nodding solemnly as we squint at the bottled alien yawning at us from behind the plastic.

I smile, showing my quiet appreciation for what's been shared with me. Then, carefully we return the specimens to their trove. The parade of wizened-brown flowers may not look like much, but I know they're precious.

***

Back at our apartment in Los Baños, our host, a lady called Tita ('aunty') Rose, has rigged up a karaoke bar in the hallway. Tita Rose, who tells us proudly that she is younger than her years, doesn't look a day under seventy-five (she is sixty-one, I find out later). She has cropped grey hair and a square face with kind eyes. She serenades us with love songs, hopping from one slippered foot to the other and staring intently at the screen, while Adriane writes his field report and I push out tweets about the jade vine we saw this morning. After an hour of ballads loud enough to wake the dead, Tita Rose settles on the sofa to watch a travel documentary about Venice.

'*Love* Italy,' she says, pointing to herself.

'Have you been?' I ask her.

'*Never* been. More than *anything*, want go,' she says, then sighs.

'Where would you like to go most in Italy, Tita Rose?'

She pauses to consider this, then nods decisively.

'Bethlehem'.

Later that evening we join Pat and Glen for beer, food, and more karaoke. Pat asks what I'd like to eat. 'Oh I'll eat anything,' I lie, as little bowls of *chicharon bulaklak* (chickens' intestines), *tokwa't baboy* (pigs' ears), and *sisig* (pigs' faces) are passed about. I wash them all down with a beer and a smile. We chat about Leonardo Legaspi Co (known as Leonard), the legendary Filipino botanist and plant taxonomist, after whom *Rafflesia leonardi* was named. I learn that he was Pat's teacher.

'There wasn't a plant he couldn't name,' Pat tells me, then pauses. I detect a quiet sadness clinging to the group. 'Leonard was shot dead on a botanical expedition,' he explains. 'Soldiers in the forest. They mistook him for a rebel.'

We say nothing for a while. Then, sensing the need for a lift in the mood, I tell the party how excited I was to see the jade vine today – how much it means to me to have seen it growing wild, here in the Philippines.

Then Pat beams and says, 'Well, Chris, my friend: our adventure hasn't even started.'

★★★

Let me tell you about my passion for mountains. I've always needed to conquer them. Not for the views, to test my stamina or my endurance – no, none of that. I need to conquer mountains to see *plants*. As a child, I would close my eyes and dream of hauling myself into the cloud forests of Southeast Asia, clambering onto anvils of rock bathed in mist, and spending golden moments with orchids and pitcher plants dangling from the branches. In my early twenties, that dream came true. Like the plant junkie I am, I spent a month feverishly trekking up and down the mountains of Borneo in pursuit of plants, getting skinnier and more wild-eyed by the day. I took a boat down the lazy brown Kinabatangan River, and while the tourists were busy pointing their binoculars at the monkeys and hornbills, I was looking in the other direction: I feigned interest in the orangutans, bluffed astonishment at a crocodile, and pretended I wanted desperately to locate the elephants whose tracks we found in the rainforest like everybody else. But, in truth, all I wanted to see was plants.

So you can imagine my excitement this morning at the prospect of climbing a mountain teeming with pitcher plants and jade vines; a place reputed to contain more woody species than the whole of the United States of America. Mount Makiling is a volcanic cone rising to an elevation of 1,090 metres, with softly forested pleats that pitch gently onto the plains of Laguna. According to legend, the mountain's summit is home to the goddess Maria Makiling. Today, I see a zeppelin of white cloud looming above her roof, as I peer through the mud-dappled window of our driver Kuya Mande's blue van. We pull into a bus stop to pick up Marge, a fellow botanist who will be joining Pat, Adriane and me on the climb today. She clambers into the vehicle, smiling brilliantly.

'The mountain is *incredible*,' she says wide-eyed, smiling. 'But last time I saw *Rafflesia* there, it was still in bud,' she tells me with a furrow between her eyes. 'Perhaps today we will be lucky.'

'I think we will,' I say.

Pat, Marge, and I turn to look out over a tangle of candy-coloured heliconia stems and ragged banana leaves flopping onto the road; Adriane's eyes remain fixed on his phone. Twenty minutes later, we've come as far as the Toyota can take us. Kuya Mande pulls up and we hop out into the hot chaos, then baste ourselves in toxic-smelling insect repellent. We wander over to the entry point, which is shielded by wasp-coloured metal barriers and an assertive-looking guard and an unassertive dog, asleep at his feet. Pat waves all this away with authority, and we are permitted entry, despite the official hiking season being weeks away. We have the whole mountain to ourselves.

The ascent begins with a hard-surfaced path, winding gently up the slope. A warm breeze stirs the canopy and sends down leaves that sway about our heads. Everywhere I look, there is a profusion of vines creeping up the trees, hanging from the branches, and spooling out into the road. Some have even tied themselves in knots. Everything is connected.

Speaking of vines, enter the strangler fig. I stare up at the silvery lattice cascading from the canopy. The web of tributaries seems molten somehow, seeping into the floor like flowing lava. Let me say a few words about this murderous plant. It begins its life of crime in the fork of another tree. After germinating, it sends forth creeping roots that curl around the trunk. They swell like boa constrictors, steadily taking possession. The roots touch down on the rainforest floor, refuelling the struggle. Eventually the encased victim suffocates, and the job is done: the strangler fig has become its own free-standing tree, living on the dead. Cut-throat.

We pause for water at Station Three where, to my delight, we encounter the great leafy parasol of *Amorphophallus longispathaceus* spiralling out of the gloom. I pull the blotchy, pole-like stem towards me and the umbrella of leafy diamonds quivers. From time to time, people ask me how a plant gets its name. Now seems like as good a time as any to dissect a *binomial*. All scientific names are made up of two words that often describe an organism's appearance in some way, a system introduced in the eighteenth century by the Swedish botanist, zoologist, and physician Carl Linnaeus, who later became known as 'the father of modern taxonomy'. Take for example the specimen in front of me. *Amorphophallus* literally means 'distorted penis' (I kid you not). The nineteenth-century Dutch botanists who chose the name must have been referring to the great phallic protrusion in its flowering structure, known as the spadix. *Amorphophallus* is the generic name – it identifies the genus to which the species belongs. The second part – called the specific name – distinguishes the species within that genus. Let's consider *Amorphophallus titanum* – a relative of the plant I am standing with, from the rainforests of Sumatra. *Titanum* means 'of the titans'. So what we have in this case is a *'giant* distorted penis'.

Sweat trickles down my temples as we ascend the mountain's eastern shoulder. The forest has unleashed dark sugary smells, like wet compost in summer. The thicket has become dark and impenetrable, but every now and again we reach a clearing and catch glimpses over the canopy: green drapery, with necklaces of little heart-shaped leaves looping endlessly into the depths. I look down and see a brown snake vanish into the scribble. Adriane looks up at an arthritic branch veiled in fernery. He points to a lipstick vine (*Aeschynanthus*) woven into the green. It is impossible to identify it to species-level from down here, so we turn our attention instead to a stand of *Alpinia* – a relative of root ginger – leaning enthusiastically out of the gloom. It has nodding white flowers with gaping mouths the colour of fire, circling stems, canted with their own effort. Behind the *Alpinia*, apricot-coloured trees have clamped themselves to the earth with great collar-like roots, weaving and folding into the soil. Birds echo about the trees while insects throb and hiss. It is a riot of nature up here on the mountain, and everywhere I look, I see *plants, plants, plants.*

Adriane wanders over to walk beside me.

'Do you like it, Dr Chris?' he asks quietly, looking around him, indicating that he is referring to the forest.

'I do,' I tell him, nodding.

'Then you will *love* Kalinga. In the forest, there is no path. We must make our own,' Adriane says looking at me with his wild, child-like eyes. Then he looks at his feet and whispers, 'The first time I went there and saw *Rafflesia*, I nearly cried.'

Adriane doesn't often speak of his emotions (to me anyway). What is it about the place that haunts him?

A flash of silver. I leave the path and force my way into the thicket to find the winged seed of a Javan cucumber (*Alsomitra macrocarpa*), lodged into a ragged trunk. The papery brown seed is the size of my thumbnail and framed by a shiny boomerang-shaped sail, the consistency of a bee's wing. Javan cucumber produces the largest of all winged seeds – the one I am holding spans the palm of my hand. The seeds are released from *pepos* – fruits the size of footballs strung up in the canopy from which they glide, rising and falling, like butterflies. The geometry of the wing – its upward-swept, twisted shape and trailing aerofoil, give it unparalleled gliding stability. The structure inspired the nineteenth-century aeronautical engineer Igo Etrich, who was fascinated by the seed's prolonged and stable soaring. He built artificial models of it, seeking to emulate its self-stabilizing properties in aircraft.[2] How did it evolve? Flying seeds like the one I am holding enable otherwise-stationary plants to cross vast distances and explore new habitats, which is necessary for the spread and survival of a population in a changing environment. Goodness knows how far this one has drifted.

Technology copying nature, the mimicry of biological structures or processes (known as *biomimetics* in the science biz), is far-reaching. Take self-cleaning paint, for example. The principle of self-cleaning is inspired by the high water-repellence of sacred lotus leaves. The leaves' extreme water-repellence is driven by a combination of microstructures and wax on the leaf surface. As the water beads and rolls off the leaf, it carries dirt particles along with it – a phenomenon called the Lotus Effect.[3]

My own research has also forayed into biomimetics. It began in 2018, when I showed some physicists the giant Amazonian waterlily floating in the heated pond at Oxford Botanic Garden. It's been grown there on and off since the mid-nineteenth century, intriguing people with its monstrous leaves. Waterlilies can unfurl 40 centimetres a day, maxing out at three metres, and sustain the weight of a small child. Incredible. People think I'm exaggerating, but year after year we've proved it: depositing the botanic garden team's bewildered toddlers on the colossal pads, then standing back, clapping. Anyway the physicists asked me how and why the leaves grow so large. I mumbled something about photosynthesis but in truth I was as mystified as they were. So I looked it up. Astonishingly little was known about the mechanics of the thing. For two years we examined the leaves: waded into the water and prodded them, poked them, stacked weights on them and sank them. Then we compared the load-bearing properties of their smaller cousins – the denizens of duck ponds. I waded into those as well, then stank out the office with the smell of pond as we unlocked their mechanical secrets too, using measuring tapes, videography, and mathematical modelling. We even 3D printed them.

This was our discovery: the floating sheet supported by a scaffold of girders produced by the giant Amazonian waterlily has a greater rigidity for a given volume of plant matter than the simple discs of smaller waterlilies. All leaves are restricted mechanically in nature by the expense of maintenance. A larger real estate for photosynthesis is all well and good, but it uses more of a plant's energy to maintain. The structure and load-bearing properties of the giant Amazonian waterlily give it a competitive edge in an environment where it pays to cover a large area, and fast: high strength at low cost.

Away from the glasshouse pond in Oxford, and back in its

natural habitat – the quick-drying ephemeral pools of the Amazon basin – this aquatic monster evolved an advantage in the race among plants for space and light. Its giant leaves unfolded quickly and cheaply to create a mosaic of lily pads, forcing the surrounding plants out of the way, and blocking out their light. The underside of the leaf's flexible (and breathtakingly beautiful) framework can withstand elastic deformation to avoid damage from wading birds. Furthermore, it has minute holes on its surface to drain trapped rainwater, and spikes on its undercarriage push aside the other plants and nibbling fish. An astounding feat of botanical engineering.

Before I float away with the waterlilies, I must return to biomimetics: the remarkable structures in nature that can help us to unlock design challenges in engineering. The physicists and I published our work in *Science Advances*,[4] where we suggested that the form of giant Amazonian waterlilies could inspire the design of giant floating platforms, such as solar panels in the ocean. What better inspiration can there be than a natural floating solar panel, tried and tested by evolution over the course of 100 million years? There's a lot we can learn from plants.

Back in the shrill forest, we pass a string of shacks and a bar, half gobbled-up by trees. These belong to the mountain communities who live in the green twilight. An old woman sits with an audience of children and a yellow dog fidgeting in the dirt. The mutter and *buck* of chickens competes with the hissing trees. Woman, children and dog all turn to stare as we wander past. Beyond the clearing we meet an extraordinary display of rope-like stems knotted with little brown baubles spraying out of the trunk of a tree. Another fig (*Ficus minahassae*). Pat tells me this one has edible fruits; furthermore its sap can be drunk, the leaves have anti-rheumatic properties, and the bark is used to make utensils in some parts of the Philippines. It is a truly multi-purpose tree, we agree, smiling. I scribble all this down in my notebook excitedly and ask what the people we have just passed use the tree for. I'm sure it must have a local use here – for food, medicine, or folklore – that sort of thing.

'To be honest, I think the people here prefer bananas,' Marge tells me with a shrug.

We turn right at a fork and the path becomes wilder. We hobble over a scaffold of slippery, hunched roots, and head deeper into the wilderness. Snatches of sky shift and vanish. Sunshine wanes to broken shards probing the floor, like strobe light, while insects turn up the volume for added effect. Ghost flowers of an unseen jade vine shower the floor like blue confetti. I pick one up and turn it over on the palm of my hand, download its unearthly colours. I'm obsessed by the colours; but I've told you that already.

'We are close now,' Pat tells us. 'This is where it grows.'

The land falls to our right. Vines and tree roots tumble into nothing. Ferns the size of people uncoil in the gloom, like snakes, their outstretched fronds snatching at our feet. I can sense the flower now. This is its place.

Suddenly, an electric frisson runs along my arms, lifting the hairs like static. That's how I know we've found it. 'THERE!' exclaims Pat, pointing to a confusion of vines. We freeze. I follow his eyes along the swarm of tentacles writhing to the floor. And there – there at its source – is a fivefold miracle.

At last.

It looks like one of Ernst Haeckel's creatures, pushing itself up out of the earth. Pat shepherds us towards the fleshy, starfishy thing. *Rafflesia panchoana*: one of the smallest in the genus, no larger than a stretched hand. On closer inspection we find a whole procession of them, each at different stages of development: spent flowers black and glistening, alongside little brown buds like unpolished conkers.

'Little big flowers,' Pat christens them, his eyebrows aflutter.

I crouch to peer at the single open specimen: a box-fresh, pocket *Rafflesia*. It looks solid, powerful; more alive than the surrounding plants. Its otherness is ridiculous. I trace my finger along one of the ear-shaped lobes to know that it's real. It's rough, like woodchip wallpaper, and soapy. In its centre sits a latte-brown disc, singed along the edges; it looks for all the world like crème brûlée. Its petals are the colour of blood. They're showered in a white constellation

21

applied more thickly around the middle, falling and fading over the edges. Like a red galaxy. Mesmerizing.

'Do you know how to sex a *Rafflesia* flower?' Pat asks, breaking the spell. 'You put your finger here,' he says, looking up at me, then cups his hand under the little disk. 'If it is wet and sticky,' he continues, peering into the mechanism of the flower, 'then you know you have a female.' He glances at me again, pauses, then guffaws.

We choreograph photos of the flower, photos of each other with the flower, and photos of each other taking photos of the flower. We can't stop. Then we realize we've forgotten to sniff. Most *Rafflesia* smell awful because they seduce flies (I'll return to that); an encounter is incomplete until you've sniffed. So we take turns to crouch and snuffle the thing, laughing. It smells precisely like bad chicken, but not too strong, we agree nodding, as if we're sampling wine.

We find another freshly opened one that has erupted out of a raised nexus of muddy roots and vines, sitting in the afterbirth of forced earth. It has squashed itself with the effort. Adriane crouches beneath the lopsided vision and stares at it intently, concentrating, like he's shaving in the mirror. I squat beside him and peer at it too. While eight billion people go about their business or sleep, two sit gazing at the world's most striking work of nature. The warped contours have distorted the dispersion of white spots, making patterns in the flow. It reminds me of one of those hidden pictures you have to find in the dots. A code I can't decipher.

It was first officially documented on the mountain under twenty years ago but it must have been here for ages. Yes, thousands of years I should think. Long before people came looking for it, that much is certain. While the forests were being cut down, the fast-food chains were going up, and the world was burning, *Rafflesia* was quietly sending up mysterious flowers, here on this chink of mountain: a constant in the chaos.

The four of us pick our way back down the track without saying much. The further we get from the flower, the deeper it takes root. I can even see it when I blink now. Like obsessions with people,

Adriane with Rafflesia panchoana *on Mount Makiling, Luzon.*

maybe it gets worse after they've gone? I do feel more complete now that I've found it. But it's never enough – I know that. Look, sometimes a plant is like heroin: you feel high on it for a while, but you always need more. Today I met one of the world's smallest *Rafflesia*.

Now I need to find the biggest.

3.

Silken threads dance in and out of existence. Spreading unseen, through the tissue of the forest from an earthen womb. Ramifying, incubating plans. Big plans.

Threads, like traces, barely existing. Embryonic – for now.

My threads. As insubstantial as your thoughts.

4.

If you were to look at it from outer space, Luzon Island would look something like a surfacing whale in profile. Its spine would appear emerald green, marking a forest so vast that you can see it from space too. This is the Sierra Madre: the Philippines' longest mountain range, stretching over 540 kilometres, from the whale's head (Cagayan) to its tail (Quezon). This is a wilderness yet to brush fingers with civilization. Indigenous communities live here who could only be reached by plane or boat, should they need to be, which they don't. Quietly these communities co-exist with monitor lizards the size of people, lizards that creep about the trees; they might pause every now and again to stare up at an eagle soar over the canopy, or a crocodile slink into the mud. The lizards weren't even known about until 2010, and even the range's highest elevation seems uncertain. Somewhere between 1,850 and 1,915 metres, if Google is to be believed. A kingdom as uncharted as the deep sea.

Around the whale's dorsal fin (if I'm not stretching the metaphor too far) lies the Laguna Lake – the Philippines' largest. Zoom in on the edge of the lake, and here you will find three botanists – Pat, Adriane, and me, and their driver Kuya Mande, in a blue van. Two sit staring at their phones, while one gazes out of the window. Slowly they make their way north, right into the very heart of this unfathomable place.

People on bicycles, and ragged banana plants thrusting great fistfuls of green fruit, flicker in and out of view. Haphazardly constructed shacks with corrugated-iron roofs the colour of rust; one of them labelled COSMETIC SURGERY – and for the avoidance of doubt – holding a sign depicting an attractive nurse claiming 'We try our hardest to reach international standards'. A sprawling brown lake forming a constant behind a squiggle of life. Where the water has spilled onto the grass, white birds congregate in a semi-circle around a grazing buffalo – egrets perhaps, I'm not sure. People wearing floral shorts and flip-flops stand in doorways, watching us go by. A day in Luzon.

The road gets steeper and the shanty villages become gobbled up by foliage. A small man wanders beneath the trees; a bag packed with fern leaves is strapped to his back. Nearby, through an open doorway, a woman is sorting a stack of fronds belonging to the same species. Fiddlehead ferns are a staple here in stews. The traffic thins and small children, wearing only shorts, play along the road-side. A pair of brown dogs have coiled themselves clockwise, like bagels. And the plants proliferate.

Those we grow in our homes in temperate places – little potted orchids, palms, ferns, and so on – cover every square inch of the out-doors here. They've been unleashed. Orchids strapped to the trees hold out handfuls of garish pink flowers into the road; epiphytes cling to every branch and telegraph pole with finger-like roots (more on epiphytes shortly); a fern sways gently in the breeze from its half-coconut hammock. All of this happy-looking foliage, conjured out of every orifice by wet warmth, makes temperate houseplants seem somehow sanitized, clinical-looking. Here it's like someone turned up the volume on life. I feel happier just looking at it.

Our destination in the Sierra Madre is the Laguna-Quezon Land Grant, one of two land grants (protected tracts of forest) that belong to the University of the Philippines, Los Baños. Much of the forest that makes up these reserves has been selectively logged for decades, used for *kaingin* (clearing the land by slashing and burning the underbrush then ploughing in the ashes as a fertilizer), or pushed aside for plant-ations and rice paddies. You wouldn't know it to look at it: to the untrained eye these forests here look pristine. And notwithstanding the nicks of human progress, the land grants harbour a bewildering diversity of life. Rare birds such as Worcester's buttonquail (*Turnix worcesteri*) – known locally as *Pugo* – hide in the grasses. The species was known only from historic illustrations until it was spotted in 2009 by a local birdwatching group. Unique lowland rats, civets and fruit bats ping between the trees, while *baboy damo*, or Philippine warty pigs (*Sus philippensis*), seek refuge from bullets and traps. Crab-eating macaques (*Macaca fascicularis*) flutter about the canopy, but you'd be lucky to see one. Gray's monitor lizards (*Varanus olivaceus*) live secretly suspended in the branches too, perhaps acknowledging the terrestrial world every now and again with a sideways glance. I picture all these creatures leading their secret lives in the softly forested hills, as we reach our destination.

The entrance to the Land Grant is framed by a staple-shaped gateway made of artificial tree trunks, on which a plastic-looking hornbill sits staring at no one. The peculiar apparatus would look less out of place in a theme park perhaps – something a rollercoaster might weave under. Or in Jurassic Park. Beside the entrance, little white chalets concertina to the forest's edge; these are where we will sleep. Stepping stones lead from the chalets, over the lawn, to the Land Grant's headquarters – a square building with a turquoise pitched roof and concrete veranda.

We unload the contents of the van onto a rectangle of that tough, papery grass you see everywhere in the tropics; it's beaded with dew. A warm breeze rocks the branches of little trees planted around the edges, from which drooping plants sway to and fro slowly, like sea-weed. Breath from the forest brings wet, mossy smells; scents of hidden life. Pat smiles to his ears as he sees me take it all in and says 'Welcome to my paradise' with an expansive gesture. Pat is the direc-tor of the Land Grant and the site has been slowly but surely transforming under his supervision in recent years. His vision is to generate revenue by making the site a destination for mountaineer-ing, tourism, and recreation, while conserving its internationally important biodiversity. He cares deeply for the place, and its future, I can tell. As he speaks of the countless plants that exist in the forest, the green breeze washes over me and I feel a little frisson of excite-ment about being here in this wild place, like static.

The purpose of my visit is to see the forest and conservation work being done, and to give an online seminar for the University of the Philippines, Los Baños. I give these a lot, but today's feels like an unwelcome distraction from the botanical treasure I know surrounds me. I'm looking forward to having finished the talk so that I can explore.

I log on to the Land Grant's Wi-Fi and check my phone. Among the urgent password expiry notification emails, missed birthdays, and so on, I notice that I've received a text message from Deki in Indonesia:

Maybe he does not understand, or maybe he does. Maybe he is bothered by the flowers, or by us looking.

Curious. I'm not quite sure what to make of it. But I have other things on my mind: a talk to deliver and new forests to explore. I'll decipher it later.

Young people mill about all over the place with pens, notebooks, and an expectant air, as if a class is about to begin. Adriane sits on the low wall of the veranda, staring intently at his laptop. Bystander to all this, I feel unneeded, awkward among so many strangers. So I acquaint myself with the plants.

Plants on plants. Epiphytes live perched on the branches of trees, where they subsist largely on moisture in the air. Rain sluices all the nitrogen they need from the rotting detritus that collects in the fissures of the bark above them. All rainforest plants co-exist in a constant battle fought in slow motion. Speed things up and you'd see them lashing, groping, and fighting their way to the sun. Epiphytes rise above this. Hitchhikers to the light, they are not thieves. No, they take nothing from the other plants; they rent their frugal, soilless place in the sun. And here on this mist-soaked ledge of the Land Grant, every available space writhes with them. I peer at the complicated knot of vegetation in front of me: hundreds of epiphytes spewing from the fork of a deceased tree. From its nucleus sprouts an enormous bird's-nest fern with wavy-edged fronds, held aloft and swaying, like kelp. These are interlaced with the ladder-shaped leaves of another fern I can't name, and, weaving through all of it, a *Hoya* vine. Its glossy leaves are marked messily with what looks like spattered toothpaste. The trees hiss softly with a breeze that billows my T-shirt and stirs the tapestry in front of me, setting the lime-green diamonds aquiver.

Natural beauty touches us in ways we can't comprehend. We've always known that nature is good for us. This has never been more apparent in the wake of a pandemic that deprived so many of us of our *green health*. Doctors are even prescribing green spaces as an effective medical intervention. But scientists have barely scratched the surface of *how* our natural surroundings influence our mental health and well-being. Immersion in nature can feel uplifting. Immersion in a place that sparkles with life – a place where plants grow on other plants – to me that's nirvana.

***

Pat, Adriane, and I have lunch with half a dozen of the Land Grant's foresters, in the criss-crossed shade of a wooden canopy. A few metres away I see torn ribbons of a staghorn fern dribbling out of the fork of a tree; I make a mental note to examine it later. Large platters are brought to us containing pearl-like river snails, boiled river fish, stewed fern, and little heaps of spinach-like vegetables. Scrawny chickens strut aimlessly about our feet and yellow dogs look expectantly at the sky. The food is delicious.

'We're eating like kings,' I say to Pat.

He loves this – his eyes widen and he guffaws heartily. He will repeat this phrase several times in the next day or so. Dessert is an unnatural purple, panna-cotta shaped creation, which I am told is made from the roots of taro (*Colocasia esculenta*) – a large-leaved aroid that is common in the tropics; it's reputed to be one of the earliest cultivated plants. In fact the urgent violet hue derives entirely from the plant; nothing artificial about *this*, my hosts tell me. Eating the fruits of the Land Grant makes me feel attuned to the place, a little more firmly rooted than when I arrived.

A small, nervous lady takes away our plates, as we talk about the expedition stretching in front of us. There are three more species of *Rafflesia* in our sights, and to find them we will need to travel the length and breadth of Luzon – fifteenth largest island in the world. The largest and rarest of all these species, spanning half a metre, will be *Rafflesia banaoana*. It lurks in the depths of Kalinga Province, in a forest so remote that almost no one has been there. Pat tells me that the Banao Tribe are the plant's custodians. He says they avoid the flower because to them it connotes an evil spirit. Quietly ignored, it sends up monstrous blossoms in the half-light, unseen.

'If we find it, you will be the third botanist ever to set eyes on it, my friend,' Pat says, beaming.

'After me and Adriane.' He nods slowly, watching me take this in.

'Chris, you will be the first Westerner to see *Rafflesia banaoana*,' he adds for good measure, smiling, confirming something he reads in my eyes.

His words are so bright, for a moment they blind me like a flash. Suddenly I feel sick with desire to see this plant, to go where no outsider has. I must see it! I can't explain my absurd reaction. Perhaps it's rooted deeply in my culture – in that embarrassing legacy of a Western addiction to being first. First to arrive, find, and conquer. Stalk the land, turn every stone, and leave a mark. Apologize for it later in family-friendly font on museum signs next to foreign objects. Shameful. But I feel it anyway.

Then my mind turns to *not* finding it. To risking everything, getting ten heartbeats from the flower, only to discover it's still in bud, that my plans have come to naught. I do this sometimes: despoil an experience, rob myself of something before it's even happened.

But I won't rest until I've tried.

***

After lunch we wander back to the headquarters where I will give my seminar. But first I am shown a 3D model of the Land Grant, mounted on a table under glass in the corner of the room. I am introduced to Ana, the resident taxonomic botanist, who leans against the model, pointing things out like a geography teacher. Ana is about my age, slim, with long black hair, and eyes like a cat's. She has a sleepy aura that makes me feel calm listening to her. In her slow, American accent she tells me how illegal settlers have burnt and cleared parts of the forest to plant coconuts; we share a knowing look, one that speaks of that inexorable conflict between trees and people in which people always win. I squint at the miniature hills rippling out from the place marked *You are Here*. The label tells me 5,729 hectares, which is just over 57 square kilometres; but I cannot make sense of the scale. I imagine miniature hornbills flying over it, and underneath them, people like ants in a line, vanishing into the pleated hills.

The seminar goes well. Pat is happy with the number of attendees and the feedback we've received. I feel a sense of relief wash over me; like something ticked off, a weight lifted. Now I can focus on what I'm here for. Now I can think about *plants*.

In the evening I drink beer with Pat, Adriane, and five of the foresters out on the headquarters' veranda. We sit on beige plastic chairs at a long, white trestle table, wet from the spray in the breeze. A glossy, sheet-like poster has been hung up to celebrate the foundation of the Land Grant ninety-two years ago. In the photograph on the poster I can make out the veranda on which we are sitting; behind it spills a brown lake I was unaware of, oddly shaped like a curled shark about to launch an attack. Pat presides over a large bucket of ice and beer (he can summon one anywhere, I learn later; even in the depths of a rainforest). The foresters all wear hooded jumpers and baseball caps. They huddle around a phone, intently watching a video I cannot see. Once in a while they all lean back, shout, and slap the table, then quietly lean in again.

'They sleep in hammocks in the forest,' Pat says, as if answering a question I haven't asked.

I nod mutely. I notice one of them is wielding a large gun, but I don't ask what it's for.

Later we assign ourselves rooms in the chalet by the forest. Rain has pooled onto the tiled floor under the window of my bedroom, and the bed feels damp. Wind bothers the trees and flings intentional gusts of rain, like a pack of wild animals shouldering the wall, trying to get in. Oblivious, the crickets chant their two-note song. I write in my journal by torchlight. I call sleep but it just won't come.

***

Heavy-eyed, I'm the last to arrive at the wooden canopy for breakfast at 7 a.m. People surface early in the Philippines. We hand about large bowls of fried tuna, diced swordfish, and rice. I'm seated an arm's length away from the staghorn fern I spotted yesterday. Its jagged fronds flap softly in the swishing breeze. Ana sees me looking at it.

'Beautiful, isn't it?' she says, smiling with her cat's eyes. 'I love them too.'

I agree, and tell her they are a popular houseplant in Britain, but it is difficult to replicate the warm wetness they need to thrive.

'They are hunted,' she continues. I look confused. 'People poach them from the forest to sell them on the internet. The problem got worse during the pandemic when people had no work. They turned to the forest for income. Some of these ferns face extinction here now.'

I had prepared myself for the horrors of logging and deforestation; I've seen it before in Southeast Asia – driven for mile upon mile through palm-oil plantations in Malaysia where the orangutans once swung. But this threat is new and has a truer aim. It goes straight to my heart. I need something to blame – a rich, faceless organization that should know better. But this offender is a person, with needs greater than my own; perhaps I saw him yesterday on the roadside, watching.

Ana plans to take us on a tour of the Land Grant's forests this morning, starting with a conservation garden. After breakfast, we have an hour to kill, so Adriane and I wander to the edge of the forest to examine a rose grape (*Medinilla magnifica*) we spotted from the van as we arrived. I've seen one before – of course I have; it's sold in florists and grown in conservatories the world over. But this one is *wild*, and that makes it special. We stand staring at the spectacle. Its square stems arch upwards out of the moss, sending forth great cabbage-like leaves at intervals. But it's the flowers that earn the name *magnifica*. They hang at eye-level in fat bunches the colour of strawberry ice-cream. We watch them swing back and forth heavily in the breeze, the blue hills flickering behind them, simmering with cloud.

More! Just metres away, another species of rose grape (*Medinilla teysmannii*) is flinging out white blossom in the spiny thicket. Its budding stems splay out like open handfuls of pearls. Even the ripening fruits are demanding attention: cream berries the size of marbles, each daubed fuchsia-pink at one end. Extraordinary. Adriane seems more excited by this one and spends some time trying to position it for a photograph, willing its stubborn stems into submission. Somewhat drunk on rose grapes, we weave through the thicket behind the chalets, down to the lake I saw yesterday on the map. It's a perfect mirror of the cloudy sky. Softly forested hills recede into banks of orange mud spattered with grasses. A jetty of planks leads to three pergola-like huts with green corrugated-iron roofs, stationed at odd angles to one another. Against this serene backdrop, a drama unfolds.

Ana looks harassed. She appears to be herding bikers, each clad in an assortment of boots, helmets, and baseball caps, laughing loudly and revving their engines by the water's edge. Intriguing.

'Riders. They patrol the forest,' Ana explains over the pulsing roar. 'I need photographs of them for an online marketing campaign. To market the Land Grant for recreation.'

'I *see*,' I nod, thinking perhaps I don't.

'Foreigner!' shouts one of the riders, beckoning me into the throng.

Ana ushers everyone onto the jetty. The riders part with their bikes and we all form a line, clomping along the planks towards one of the little huts. Three of the riders go to the other side of the lake where yellow boats are moored. They row to the hut and wait for us there as we clip into orange life jackets. Then we file onto the boats, take our seats, and row aimlessly onto the lake, into the jetty, and one another. Ana captures all this for her mysterious marketing campaign while we fall about laughing at the ridiculousness of it.

Next we must 'admire nature and drink coffee'. Sounds idyllic. Coffee is dispensed from large thermos flasks on the wooden canopy where we had breakfast. I feel warm, gratifying caffeine course through my veins. Once all our cups are filled, Ana picks five riders and beckons them to one side. Then she leads us down the canopy's wooden steps to a patch of bare clay next to a chicken coop, dappled by tropical-looking foliage. Here she choreographs a photo next to a jade vine hanging from the thicket. Shutterclick.

'Admire it,' instructs Ana.

Not difficult; it is the most prolific one I have seen. Searing blue flowers scatter the red clay all around our feet. The riders disperse hesitantly around the luminous stalactite, unsure whether to look at the blossom or Ana's camera. Shutterclick. As I study their faces, the moment also becomes a still in my mind; fixed in colour.

I have always painted plants and people. I absorb colours and shadows from the world around me, hold on to them, then set them free. The medium I choose depends on the subject. This particular moment will be released in graphite. These men's faces will be borne in a swirl of dust, then built up layer upon layer, until they are alive beneath my fingers. I might breathe life into the flowers using

Foresters from the Land Grant with a jade vine in the Sierra Madre, Luzon.

graphite too – a feather-soft touch – any harder than this and they will fall into the shade. I need them to shine.

★★★

The conservation garden is about eight metres by five and enclosed by wire mesh on all sides like an aviary. It smells of moss and summer rain. Ana ushers Adriane and me inside, while Kuya Dante – one of the foresters who has joined us – stands outside gazing at the trees. The trodden-earth floor is carpeted thickly in creeping ferns and tradescantia. It's impossible not to step on them. Little orchids have been strapped to the side of the enclosure and whip-like vines of *Hoya* escape through the mesh. One is carrying an upside-down umbrella of rose-pink flowers. Then I notice a sprawling *Nepenthes* pitcher plant clutching a solitary apple-coloured pitcher. I feel that sparkle of excitement *Nepenthes* always gives me.

'I don't think he is happy,' Ana warns, as I leap excitedly to the far corner of the enclosure.

'Oh, he's not so bad,' I reply, parroting her use of gender, as I inspect the leaves, stems, and shapely pitcher. I've seen far worse in centrally heated houses. People grow *Nepenthes* in pots and baskets all over the world as botanical curiosities, but in the Philippines they are native. They belong here in this damp, mossy place where everything grows on everything else.

'Can we see them growing wild in the Land Grant?' I ask. My heart beats a little faster. A picture forms in my mind. Long ropes of *Nepenthes* festooning ferny banks; pitchers dangling. Me in the middle.

'No, Chris,' she replies. 'They only grow at the far end of the reserve.'

I feel a sense of urgency now, sharpened by the prospect of not seeing them.

'Don't *worry*, Chris. We will see them in Kalinga,' Adriane says a little impatiently, but smiling. A playful breeze wafts through the enclosure and jostles the greenery. I draw it in; absorb the tiny droplets sent from all the plants in the forest, like a thousand promises.

Nepenthes is remarkable. A killer motivated by poverty. Risen from poverty – rain-washed slopes and swamps where every ounce of nitrogen was leeched – it had to find a way to survive, and it did it by hunting. Charles Darwin was fascinated by carnivorous plants such as *Nepenthes*. Like so much science, it happened by accident. During a holiday in Sussex in the summer of 1860, Darwin noticed the remains of insects plastered to the leaves of sundews – distant relatives of *Nepenthes* that grow in nutrient-poor bogs, moors, marshes, and so on. Curious to know the agent of these massacres, he collected plants to perform experiments on. He poked and prodded them, flicked them, blew on them, then fed them scraps of meat, glass, and goodness knows what else. And watched. By the end of the summer, he revealed the sundews' dark secret: their glistening tentacles are a snare, attracting insect prey, then curling inwards to suffocate their hapless victims. Darwin dedicated years of experimental work to carnivorous plants; indeed he wrote a whole book on them.[5] And they've inspired generations since.

They certainly inspired me. I read about the Victorian plant hunters' encounters with them, as a child, rapt; imagined it was me who had stumbled across them. Some of the books I found contained vivid descriptions of how the plants trapped their prey, described 'insects plummeting' and 'suffocating to death'. What child wouldn't be enthralled by that? I joined the Carnivorous Plant Society when I was twelve and submitted my little black and white illustrations to their quarterly newsletter. I grew the plants too. I staged an old fish tank on my bedroom windowsill and heated it with a pad, designed for reptiles and amphibians, which slotted underneath. No reptile or amphibian ever saw this tank – that would have been a bloodbath. No, this Little Shop of Horrors was for *plants*. I crammed it with Venus flytraps, sundews, and *Nepenthes*. I coaxed them out of little mossy baskets, and trained them around branches. Every time I lifted the lid, damp, leafy smells filled the air; it was like entering a different world. I'd collect woodlice and beetles from the back garden and drop them into the leafy jaws, feeding the plants and my obsession.

They inspire me still. Plant predators are a focus of my research at Oxford Botanic Garden. I am interested in their evolutionary origins, once a source of contention among botanists. Some couldn't believe that the killer instinct could have evolved multiple times among plants, but it did. It's written into their DNA. Still, it's astonishing that pitcher plants such as *Nepenthes* – those that employ leafy pitfalls to trap prey – evolved at least six times independently. This phenomenon is called *convergent evolution*: a process by which distantly related organisms evolved similar traits in response to a common environmental pressure. It has happened across the tree of life; I'll share an example: in the Arid House at the Botanic Garden we have a tree-sized cactus and a seemingly identical euphorbia, standing two metres apart. One originated in the Americas; the other in Africa. When I show visitors and students these, they nod confidently at the cactus but look enquiringly at me when I christen the other euphorbia. '*Surely* that's also a cactus,' they say, but it's not. Both the cactus and the euphorbia were shaped by millions of years of drought. Both arrived at the same solution to a shared problem, but they did it independently, on different continents. A coincidence of evolution.

Back to my killer. Like a flower, the pitcher of *Nepenthes* attracts insects with the sickly promise of nectar, but this is no reward; this is bait. Insects crawl all over the trap, feeding dizzily, high on sugar. But tiptoe onto the peristome (the slippery rim), and they're doomed. Condensed rainwater on the peristome's surface makes it slippery, and the insects aquaplane into a pool of digestive fluid. There's more. The fluid is *viscoelastic* – it has a sticky, stretchy property to it, like strings of saliva. The more the insect struggles, the further it's dragged into the abyss. Even if it did manage to crawl out, the sodden creature would slide straight back down again because the interior wall is covered in a layer of slippery wax. It's hopeless. The miserable winged thing drowns and rots in a puddle of nitrogen – just as the plant requires. Never a free meal in nature.

How did this cruel trick evolve? I'm often asked this. It's a question I've sought to answer with fellow scientists. In 2017 my colleague Ulrike Bauer, from the University of Bristol, and I examined the surfaces of *Nepenthes* pitchers, and related plants, using electron microscopy – a technique used to obtain high-resolution images of tissues and cells. Under the high-powered microscope, a black and white forest of stalked tentacles and branches blossomed like coral polyps. We observed that Darwin's sundews, *Nepenthes*, and a distant relative of both these plants called *Plumbago* all possessed similar structures. Why?

Glands – secreting structures – are a key piece in the jigsaw of *Nepenthes* evolution. Many non-carnivorous plants like *Plumbago* produce glands for various reasons: stickiness as a form of defence against predators, or to secrete excess salt, for example. Let's suppose, tens of millions of years ago, a hypothetical plant with sticky glands ensnared insects; they may have decomposed there, releasing nitrogen, to the benefit of the plant. This plant would hold a *selective advantage* over other plants – in other words, be more likely to survive and produce offspring. Over the course of generations, random mutations would conceive new traits favourable to entrapment – a greater level of stickiness, for example; this, in turn, would confer a greater selective advantage. Now let's suppose that just by chance, a sticky leaf, like that of a sundew, fused along one side to form a vessel. It's easily done: random mutations cause leaves to fuse in this way from time to time in other plants; we see them sometimes in potted *Codiaeum* plants in the glasshouses. A vessel may have been a more efficient trap – a better receptacle for holding on to precious nitrogen. Two final pieces in the jigsaw: first, DNA tells us that sundews and *Nepenthes* are genetically related. They evolved from a common ancestor, many millions of years ago. Second, the sticky fluid of a sundew is chemically similar to the viscoelastic fluid in *Nepenthes*. Both retained this trait on their separate paths, a journey called *divergent* evolution. That's how a sticky leaf became a deadly trap.

My friend Ulrike spent months observing *Nepenthes* in Borneo. She noticed that on occasions ants – a frequent victim – scuttled about the pitcher with abandon. But at other times they fell like lemmings over a cliff. It seemed they only aquaplaned perilously when conditions were wet. Humidity changes fast in the tropics. If the traps were wet all the time, would the plants fare better? Determined to find out, Ulrike dragged a hospital drip into the depths of a Bornean swamp and rigged it up to the plants, infusing them with water throughout the day (these are the lengths to which a scientist will go to answer her question). And her curious discovery was this: when permanently wet, the pitchers don't catch more ants over time; they trap *fewer*. How? The answer to the paradox lies in the ants' behaviour. Ant colonies send out foraging scouts. When a scout identifies food, it recruits fellow workers using pheromone trails. But if a scout is captured by the plant, it cannot broadcast its discovery. By sparing a few scout ants when conditions are dry, *Nepenthes* invests in the possibility of a batch-capture event – a blowout – when the mist returns. The plant makes a high-odds bet that the ants will orchestrate their own mass murder.

Returning to the trip to Borneo in my early twenties, I was struck by the diversity of pitcher geometries. Goblets and flagons, flasks and jars – why would they vary so much if they all served the same purpose? *Nepenthes* grow in different habitats across their range – from lowland swamps to mist-filled forests. Each habitat has its own unique fauna. Perhaps little tweaks and adjustments in geometry during the course of evolution enabled dietary shifts. Made-to-order pitchers. Darwin knew all about such things. During a visit to the Galápagos Islands on the voyage of HMS *Beagle*, he observed that finches had different beak shapes for probing different food sources – insects or seeds, for example. A common ancestor arrived on the Galápagos two million years ago and proliferated into fifteen species, each adapted to a different niche. I ask my first-year undergraduate biology students if they're aware of Darwin's finches and most of them are. It's textbook. Well, a similar process shaped *Nepenthes*, I tell them.

Perhaps the most remarkable *Nepenthes* are those that evolved toilets (I kid you not). Picture this: a tree shrew (a furtive, squirrel-like creature) clambers onto a pitcher. He glances around surreptitiously as he finds his balance, clinging to the seat, shuffling. Then carefully he leans into position, licking nectar from the pitcher lid with his rear end hovering over the pitcher's orifice. He pauses, and squints. Then he dumps a steaming great turd, right into the pitcher's fluid with a plunk. This provides the plant with much-needed nitrogen; as every gardener knows, plants thrive on manure. Ulrike spent several wet, miserable weeks in a tin shed on Mount Mulu in Borneo, setting up secret cameras to capture the event. That's commitment.

Meanwhile, another form of *Nepenthes* produces delicate flutes that dangle from the branches. Watch one for long enough, and you'd see a bat flutter to it and crawl in. It's a snug fit. It even has a railing to cling on to – a purpose-built nesting box. All day long the bat holes up with its young, plopping away. Rented accommodation. Scientists have shown that each of these *Nepenthes* possesses dimensions tailored to match the size and shape of their mammalian visitors.[6-8] In environments such as cool mountain slopes where insects may be scarce, it wouldn't pay to invest in an energetically expensive pitcher: a shift in diet was needed. Natural selection sought a new path for an existing structure – a volte-face known in evolutionary biology as *co-option*.

We know little about the behaviour of most *Nepenthes*. Regardless of what they catch, they possess a mathematical beauty. Sometimes I find myself staring at them for minutes at a time, trying to solve them with my eyes. In recent years I've been collaborating with a leading professor of applied mathematics, Alain Goriely, and his team. Using specimens grown in the glasshouses at Oxford Botanic Garden, we're seeking to understand how peristome geometry influences prey capture. Every month we congregate around the little collection of vines fleeing their pots and baskets, pressing their miscellany of curious balloons and chalices to the glass. We ask them questions such as 'What do *you* feed on in nature?' to which the answers lie waiting in a faraway land – like where I'm standing now. Alain tilts one between his fingers, peers at it intently, then muses over its angles with his French accent and a little wry smile you'd easily miss. We chant words such as *isotropic, anisotropic*, and *coefficients of friction*; words that somehow exist outside the human mind. I sever a pitcher from its vine, which we ruminate on over coffee at a wooden table, trade ideas about, while punters shriek and plash down the River Cherwell behind us. Then my collaborators spirit it away in a shoebox to the other side of Oxford, where they shuffle symbols around it. This is our quest to decode nature's beautiful, deadly enigma.

When I sat cross-legged on my bed peering at picture books years ago, it all seemed so simple: a tubular leaf that insects tumbled into. But there is so much more to these plants than that; so much more to discover still.

As I said, remarkable.

We pick our way out of the cage-like structure, and our conversation returns to the forests of Kalinga. Adriane's eyes reflect the trees as he talks of the many tribes living in the wild mountains there. 'And a tattoo artist,' he adds.

I look at him quizzically, thinking I've misunderstood. He explains that body art called *Batok*, symbolic of power, has been an ancient tradition among Kalinga people since the sixteenth century. He says there is an old woman who knows how to do *Batok*, and that people travel for days to Kalinga just to see her. We plan to travel for days to reach Kalinga too, but for something else entirely.

Something inside me that has quickened has been set in motion, and will not be stopped. Like a cancer, stealing its vigour in stages, cell by cell; setting down roots then growing stealthily, thread-like.

Like a parasite.

5.

Mount Makiling was not my first encounter with *Rafflesia*. That was in Borneo. On that same febrile adventure of my early twenties, spent chasing plants up and down the mountains – something fixed in me then. And seeing *Rafflesia* on Mount Makiling a few days ago took my mind back to it: down a wild path, to a parcel of forest guarded by reeds where it lay hiding. A long-closed door to my childhood reopened, reminding me what wonder feels like. Like it was yesterday, I remember stroking its warted petals in the uncertain light while my local guide looked on, smiling. Seeing *Rafflesia* for the first time, barely out of my teens, held a mirror up to my childhood. One in which an odd boy knelt at the altar to a phantom flower – a fire-coloured effigy – and divined it in the forests of his dreams.

Today, that place in Borneo is fenced off, signposted and ticketed. The world's wildest plant has been captured like a caged beast. With so many tourists now, it had to be this way, I suppose. Announced on Facebook, shared, liked, forgotten. Existing in pixels around the world, everywhere and nowhere; in the ether, in The Cloud. As Deki said in one of his text messages once: one day it may exist only there.

But to find the rarest species of *Rafflesia* in the Philippines, you have to go to the very depths of the forest; machete your way through a serpent-ridden place ruled by nature. A place less trodden than the moon.

In the forest, there is no path.

I'll come to know that soon; once we've gone to the edge of the map.

Then stepped right off it, into oblivion.

★★★

Six hundred kilometres south of Kalinga, back in the Sierra Madre's Land Grant, we're on a gentle warm-up for the expedition. Ana, Kuya Mande, and another forester called Kuya Chester are tasked with leading Adriane and me into the Sierra Madre's mossy wilderness.

We start at the tip of the lake. A dirt track has been carved here to form jagged orange cliffs crested with interlocking grey trees. Climbing stems crawl up their trunks like centipedes. They belong to a plant called *Pothoidium lobbianum*, a member of the aroid family (Araceae) that also includes well-known examples such as Swiss cheese plants, peace lilies, and anthuriums. It also contains a 'giant distorted penis', but I've told you about that already. *Pothoidium* is different to all of these; it looks like an infinite fern frond laddering into the sky. Apparently it is used here to make fishing traps. I don't know what sort of traps, but I imagine a basket-like contraption woven from the lattice-like stems. Nearby, another tree is embraced by a satin pothos (*Scindapsus pictus*), which is widespread across tropical Asia, and cultivated as an attractive houseplant elsewhere. The shield-shaped leaves are clamped to the bark, following its contours, and the colour of green and silver leopard print.

Ana takes us through a 'jade vine alley', which is paradoxically one of the few places I've seen here that's bereft of jade vines. 'They have not been planted yet,' she says, addressing my unspoken question. Meanwhile, Adriane plucks a small apple-like fruit from a shaking branch.

'What's this, Dr Chris?' he asks me.

'A sort of custard apple?' I say, knowing it isn't, reaching for the least ridiculous suggestion.

'A sort of *Elephant* apple,' he replies, dismantling it with his pianist hands. '*Dillenia philippinensis*'.

Half correct, then? Not even close. *Dillenia* belongs to its own family, the Dilleniaceae – which bears no relation to an apple,

44

custard or otherwise – and this particular species grows only here in the Philippines. Little wonder I didn't know it. The interior is glistening green and spiralled like a shell, with a counter-clockwise crown of red tentacles. Odd.

'Try it,' Adriane says, his eyebrows arched permissively.

It tastes tart and green, like an under-ripe berry. Ana guides us through what she calls her *Medinilla* and Aroid gardens, pointing out this and that on the green-spattered slopes. We crush an arrow-shaped leaf that smells of citrus, then follow a snaking path of grey stones edged with bamboo logs which, in places, have rooted and sent up ambitious shoots. I'm not surprised. Anything would root and regenerate in these conditions given the chance. We admire a little ditch choked with peace lilies and a giant taro (*Alocasia macrorrhizos*). Its pleated leaves are the size of small cars. Kuya Mande leans against a tree with one arm and stares at it, looking bored.

Next, the path leads us through a thicket of ferns with a familiar scent, like cardboard, into a wild ginger garden. We clamber up the slope to admire an unnamed ginger thrusting red, cone-like structures from the ground. They're still earthy from the journey up. Then Adriane becomes ecstatic about an epiphytic ginger (*Hedychium philippinense*) we see leaning out of a tree.

'Look!' he says, hopping about. Flame-like reflections of the flowers flash about his eyes as he strokes it and takes photographs. It doesn't excite me much, but you have to engage with what excites other botanists; we each have our favourites.

You'd be forgiven for wondering why we are peering at a dead orchid. I wondered myself a moment ago. But if you were to zoom in, and in, and in, you'd see why. Peeking out of the withered knot gleam little tooth-like flowers, each smaller than a pea. The plant was collected from the depths of the Land Grant and strapped to this tree here for conservation purposes; no one has identified it yet (it is a species of *Agrostophyllum*, Ana tells me later). We spot another orchid called *Phalaenopsis lueddemanniana*, clinging to a branch like a koala. The plant's lurid flowers glow pink in the dappled shade. This is a relative of the popular moth orchids we buy in

45

supermarkets and petrol stations in the Northern Hemisphere; a houseplant that thrives on neglect. To see a *Phalaenopsis* in the wild, you can appreciate why. This one seems to be doing just fine on fresh air. As we leave the orchid garden we spot a Christmas orchid (*Calanthe triplicata*). Its cloud of white flowers reminds me of the butterfly orchids I've seen in British grasslands and the forests of Japan; only these flowers aren't quite butterflies; no, these are fleeing their stem like an armful of doves.

The hills above the conservation garden have been planted with an orchard of elephant apple trees that are an important local crop. Adriane tells me the flowers do not last long, and they are worth looking for. We push through bunches of papery, hazel-like leaves to find them. Eventually we spot one on a branch above our heads and I pull the branch down for us to admire the flower. It has the form and dimensions of a magnolia, with five white petals, pleated like satin sheets, and cerise pollen-bearing stamens and spine-like structures, all pouring out of the centre like a frozen fountain. The sum of its parts is like an exquisite work of patisserie, only more perfect.

As well as for food, plants are used for traditional medicines here in the Philippines, just as they are across the world. In Southeast Asia, rather than competing with modern medicine, plant-based medicine is being introduced into primary healthcare as a readily available and inexpensive alternative to mainstream pharmaceuticals. Tribes are especially knowledgeable when it comes to herbal remedies. Instead of clinical trials, they've relied on trial and error, close observation, and a body of knowledge handed down through the generations. The Subanen, or 'River People', in Dumingag, in the south of the Philippines, believe that plants like humans hold spirits that must be respected. They say their knowledge of herbal remedies is brought to them through a dream.[9]

As with so many plants, the discoveries of various *Rafflesia* species are often bestowed casually upon Western explorers; indigenous communities in the forest knew about the plants long before. Across Southeast Asia, *Rafflesia* has been used by people for centuries. In Malaysia the flower is often called *bunga patma*, referring to fertility, and the buds are reputedly prescribed after childbirth to reduce bleeding, and they restore the figure. In Thailand, the so-called 'flowers of plenty' grant magical powers that confer invulnerability; some also believe the flowers emerge to hold Buddha's feet at birth. And, as Pat told me earlier today, in Kalinga the local people believe the plant possesses an evil spirit.

There is a growing danger of erosion of traditional knowledge like this, worldwide; we risk losing not just plants, but also the bio-cultural diversity that has grown alongside them for thousands of years. In our mission to become more connected and aligned, striving to see the world one way – digitizing everything – we are losing some of the richness of our existence in nature. At the very least we should appreciate and document our collective knowledge of plants where this has not been done; learn from those who understand the ways of nature better than anyone. Otherwise, as Richard Deverell, Director of Kew, put it to me, 'We risk burning down the library before we've even read the books'.

★★★

On a rocky slope in northern Iraq, 8,000 kilometres away, an old woman called Fariha stoops painfully, pulling weeds out of the dry earth against a backdrop of saw-tooth mountain peaks in a pristine sky. She wears an *abayah*, a long black cloak, over olive-grey trousers, and a white and blue silken scarf wrapped tightly around her head. Her face is a web of wrinkles. She squints as she labours in the dazzling morning sun, stacking the plants between sheets of newspaper in a basket. She spots the stems of locoweed sprawling among the stones. *Good*, she thinks. That will clear up the eczema flare-up of her neighbour's daughter, little Aram. A pair of youths ride by on a motorcycle, paying her no attention as she shakes earth from the stems; the bikes leave a cloud of white dust in their wake. Slowly she picks her way back down the broken hillside, crablike, in the shimmering heat.

By the time she returns home to the little house of reeds and clay later that morning, she has filled her basket with no fewer than twelve medicinal herbs. *Afiaa alik*, she tells herself with a small sigh – a job well done, as she lowers herself arthritically into her chair in the blue shade. She pops a *Zlabia* into her mouth in reward. The plants' prickles and wilting fronds flop over the rim of the basket on the stony ground beside her. Then she closes her eyes to the sun and listens to her two daughters, chatting inside. The two women kneel on the cool stone floor surrounded by large pans of flour, little mountains of herbs, and various pastes. They are making *Khubz tannour*, traditional flatbreads. Fariha's eleven-year-old granddaughter watches them, wide-eyed, crouching beside a row of green melons, the size of beach balls, leaning against the rough white wall. Fariha's son bought these from the roadside earlier today, then thumbed a lift home with them on the back of a pickup truck – they're too heavy to carry on foot. Melons are a delicacy here in summer, and a source of water in a place where this is precious.

Fariha and her family value all these things: the medicinal herbs, the flour, and the melons. Above all, they value *plants*. They are attuned to their land and its green riches; their lives are closely intertwined with plants and always have been. None more so than Farid, who is Fariha's husband. Later this afternoon, he will take the bundles of herbs Fariha collected and hang them up to dry from the ceiling of the ramshackle shop at the souk in the pale hillside village. The shop has been handed down through his family for centuries, along with the knowledge of the plants it sells. Some of the stems, roots, and bark he knows he will need to decoct fresh today; these he will boil in his small copper cauldron, infusing the minty-green air with rich and earthy smells. Outside his shop, a jumble of grass-like salad onions and white root vegetables are heaped atop crates and sandbags with spidery Arabic lettering. Inside, in the cool shade, Farid sits on a stool in the shadows, presiding over his kingdom of brass bowls and hessian sacks brimming with dried herbs, seeds, and powders.

Farid is a herbalist, an *attar*. Herbal medicine is a trade Farid was first taught by his father, which he has since refined over sixty years of collecting, decocting, and dispensing. He knows every plant in this land and has no need for books or the internet. People come to him with their little complaints, looking to him and his bundles of herbs expectantly for the answer. Rashes and bruises; gifts and gossip; poisonous plants, poisonous people – they all come to his door. Goodness knows he's seen it all, he chuckles, when it comes to complaints. Today he sold packets of *Kaisoom* leaves to six customers seeking a repellent to ward off the mosquitoes that assail sleepers here, *inshallah*; yesterday he prepared a gargle made from *Khotma Wardy* for his nephew who is suffering from toothache; last week a young mother visited him, complaining of a child with a fever, so he picked leaves from his potted Cassia bush to make a paste for her. When fresh wild-tulip bulbs are available, his wife harvests them so he can grind them up for an age-old painkiller recipe. And *heel hwaia* (heavens above), last year he dispensed enough *Lesan Althour* to cure an army when the school had an outbreak of lice, thanks to the evil eye. Useful plants are all around him and he notices them. Even the plantain that grows as a roadside weed after winter rainfall has its uses – for chest infections and to restore lost appetite. Yes, Farid has seen it all when it comes to people's complaints. But in plants, he sees *magic*. You might call him a wizard.

People have always performed magic with plants here. Iraq's yellow patchwork of deserts, plateaus, and mountains were the stage for the domestication of crops by some of the earliest human civilizations. They managed to coax edible plants out of a land that turns to dust in summer. Temperatures ripen at a sweltering 50°C in Iraq, and, unsurprisingly, deserts blanket much of the region. Nomads and camels drag their feet over the vast stretches of sand and little else that form Al Khali, 'The Empty Quarter'. Petrol-blue haze shimmers around the rocks as camel spiders scuttle into the shadows; floury orange clouds fall over the land like an uncomfortably hot quilt; and people look up to the sky for rain that never comes.

And yet, the country has a rich flora. Ancestral food plants including the almond, apricot, barley, grape, lentil, pistachio, pomegranate, walnut, and wheat came from this barren land; they still grow in some remnant mountain forests. Traditional herbal medicine in Iraq can be traced back to the Sumerian (4000–1970 BCE) and

Babylonian and Assyrian periods (1970–549 BCE) respectively. Urban and rural communities still depend on this rich heritage of knowledge, handed down the generations. In fact, in some districts, traditional herbal medicine is the only healthcare system. To people here, plants and people like Farid who know how to use them are not a lifestyle; they are a lifeline.

Rana Ibrahim taught me this. One summer she visited me, at Oxford Botanic Garden, carrying three black leather-bound books under her arm. 'These were the work of my father,' she told me, heavily laying each one side by side on the table in the library. I leafed through one of them, picking out black and white pictures of plants I recognized. Rana peered at the text and recited the names one by one in consonant-heavy Arabic.

Rana's father was called Abdul Jaleel Ibrahim Al-Quragheely. He was born in 1934 in Baghdad and was appointed to the Ministry of Higher Education as an agricultural engineer. That's where he met her mother, Nazik Saeed Al-Jarrah, a biology teacher.

'They had seven children. They shared their passion for natural history with each of us,' Rana told me earnestly.

Abdul Jaleel ran a large farm near Radwaniyah in central Iraq where he cultivated hundreds of medicinal herbs. He treated his own diabetes using the plants he grew, and the seed of an idea was planted: he wouldn't just solve his own medical problems; no, he would solve everyone's. He set up a community practice in traditional herbal medicine. He cleared half the family home to dedicate the premises to the preparation of medicines and decoctions, and put a sign above the door: *Al-Ashab*. At a time of war, when people relied on herbal medicine, they came in their hundreds, queuing up for pungent remedies, emollients, and poultices. The practice grew in popularity and importance, eventually serving the whole of the Karkh region in Baghdad. In time he became known as 'the Doctor of Al-Ashab'.

'But then his practice was hit by an explosion,' Rana continued, gathering pace. 'His work – his records, his plants – all of it, destroyed.' She looked at me levelly, then paused before continuing, 'But my father, he was *committed* to serving his community. So he set up a new practice in Mansour, Baghdad.'

Undeterred, Abdul Jaleel compiled comprehensive records of hundreds of plants and their traditional use in remedies, Rana went on to tell me. Every customer was prescribed a plant. Every plant told a story. He scribbled them all down in these treasured books.

Abdul Jaleel was killed during a terrorist attack on Al-Yousifia in 2009. But his flora, and the wealth of knowledge and cultural heritage they contained, survive. They were bequeathed to Rana in 2011 in Syria – the only safe meeting point at that time – by her mother, for safekeeping in Oxford.

'One day I hope my father's life work will be published, so that his work will live on, *inshallah*,' Rana said, with a solemn nod.

That's when I stepped in.

Working with a friend and botanist, Shahina Ghazanfar, at Kew, we successfully sought funds to translate, authenticate, edit, and illustrate Abdul Jaleel's work. Shahina was formerly an associate professor in Oman, where she documented the medicinal properties of plants, and is a leading expert on Middle Eastern floras. She has still, wise eyes and a calm temperament, and she listened carefully to Rana's story. Then we set to work. Word by word, the translation from Arabic into English that we commissioned brought into focus a colourful apothecary of tonics, salves, anthelmintics, and aphrodisiacs made from plants. You name a complaint and there was a plant reputed to cure it. Some were symbolic, for example the rose of Jericho, thought to bring luck to pregnant women because the plant unfurls like new life when soaked in water. Others were cosmetic, for example sprigs of *Artemisia* used to make hair ointments. Some spoke of superstition, for example bitter apples, strung up like tinsel, to protect against the evil eye. Meanwhile the smoke from burning Syrian rue seed was said to drive away epidemics. Symbols, promises, warnings; knowledge of herbal medicine handed down a thousand times, tested by time, and frozen in Abdul Jaleel's herbal remedy books.

Yes, every plant tells a story.

★★★

We enter the mouth of the Santa Clara Forest. I hear it hissing softly as we approach. Kuya Dante leads the way, stooping under a curtain of fronds and vines. A light mist swims through the trees and everything is slick from last night's rain. It is different to a temperate woodland, more three-dimensional. Rangy saplings topped with green flourishes top out all over the place, and vines spiral in and out of them like barbed wire. We trudge through a soft mantle of fallen leaves, which in places is scarcely visible for plants. A mewing bird cuts above the insects' drone; one zooms past us but the canopy is too dense to identify it. Most of the long-pointed, oval-shaped leaves we pass look the same too; a botanist should never say such a thing, but they do. The first distinctive plant we encounter is a wild pepper (*Piper*). Its leaves splay horizontally from knotted twigs. The flowers are borne in catkin-like structures the length of a finger, which stand vertically and arch at the tips, like rearing snakes.

It becomes darker, almost black in places. Mosses and *Hoya* leaves consume the trees, and ferns grope our legs. Ana spots an agarwood (*Aquilaria*) sapling in the wet gloom. Its leaves look like all the others, but a mature tree is sought after here. In fact people would kill for one, Adriane tells me, blinking, brushing away a tentacle of wet hair hanging in his eyes. Agarwood is one of the most expensive natural raw materials in the world. But it isn't a timber tree; it's the perfume it yields that is highly prized. The resinous wood is only produced when the tree becomes infected with a particular fungus; the perfume is the result of a resistance response to that infection. Nearby, we spot a shrub known in Tagalog as *Talyantan* – a species of *Leea*. It is a distant relative of the grape. Cream and violet flowers bubble up from its stem like foam.

We head deeper in. Marching silently, we push low-hanging branches out of the way that smack back defiantly, and pull snagging briers from our hair and clothes. We pass rattans – climbing palms that are common across the closed-canopy old-growth rainforests of Southeast Asia. Yellow thorns march angrily up their stems. Then we enter a hall of towering pandans (*Pandanus*). They look like over-sized yuccas. The enormous sword-shaped leaves

52

force through the vegetation, each serrated like a breadknife, and arching with its own weight. Tough fibres from the leaves are used in the Philippines to make *bayong*, traditional woven baskets. The plants seem prehistoric, like something a dinosaur might graze upon.

The forest breathes in rain. I stroke the soggy fur of a fern crozier (*Cyathea*) nuzzling my thigh, like an animal demanding attention. The vegetation thins a little and zinc sky shines through the broken canopy. We pause to admire the complicated geometry of forked ferns (*Dicranopteris*) crawling up the bank. They have a symmetry that reminds me of those folded cut-out snowflakes made by children. The fronds are sometimes used to make chair seats and mats. Then Adriane spots a *Bulbophyllum* orchid on a mossy branch above us. Its flowers hang like goldfish. Nearby, Ana points out the curious hunched leaves of *Hoya imbricata*. They are clamped to the branches like algae-encrusted limpets in the receding tide. Kuya Dante finds another *Hoya* too (*H. mariae*). This one is in flower: a solitary, fleshy, star-like structure, caramel-coloured, held on a slender stalk, seemingly afloat. I have a *Hoya* vine at home in my kitchen; just an ordinary one (*H. carnosa*), but I love it. Every summer its night-flowering blossoms fill the entire house with a heavy smell somewhere between honey and chocolate. The nocturnal flowers of *Hoya* release their perfume at dusk to draw in moths like the moon. I wonder which exotic moth will visit this one here tonight, unseen.

Falling leaves erase our path, and the forest's personality changes again, as filaments of light of a particular softness filter through the trees. Perhaps I am changing too. Mine is a mind easily distracted – in most compartments of my life the shortness of my attention span borders on heroic; but here things are different. I'm suddenly intensely aware of every lichen, branch, and leaf. I can almost sense the sap surging, pulsing through the living, breathing web. And then, as if I summoned it by thought: a gift.

I shriek with excitement at the sight of it at my feet. An ant plant (*Myrmecodia tuberosa*). It must have dropped out of the canopy to the floor, unmoored from tethered life, like a beached marine animal. A fallen star. It is remarkably intact, considering its journey. Its papery-brown stem has the proportions of a balloon, channelled all over, and violently thorny, like a pufferfish. We crouch to examine the spiny thing. I stroke it gingerly, as you might a sea urchin. Suddenly the line of ants that was marching purposefully over its surface abandon their orderly queues and start a riot. I can't help but smile as they wave their arms angrily at me. This is *exactly* how they should behave. Evolution in action.

I'll explain: ant plants and ants are a manifestation of an evolutionary crossroad that was set in motion 100 million years ago when the flowering plants were rising to dominance. The ants' nest is inside the plant – its stem is their home. If I was to slice it open, I would see a labyrinth of hollow galleries, like honeycomb, which connect to the outside world via little punctured entrance holes. As every child who has prodded an ants' nest with a stick will attest, its occupants object violently to an intrusion. Out they come, arms waving, biting and stinging determinedly! A resident ant army that behaves in this way can serve a plant well if their vitriol is directed towards a herbivore. Yes, ants will stop at nothing to protect their home, and therein lies the foundation for this ecological quid pro quo: patrolled accommodation.

Ant plants have been cultivated at Oxford Botanic Garden for decades. Camilla Huxley-Lambrick, a former scientist of the university, dedicated years of research to them and collected specimens in the 1970s and 1980s. They still lurk in corners of the glasshouses today, like hedgehogs crouched in pots, waving leafy flags at curious passers-by. Guillaume Chomicki is another authority on the plants who worked in Oxford. He examined ant plants for his PhD with Professor Susanne Renner, who was the former Director of Munich Botanic Garden and a formidable botanist. I co-authored a paper[10] with them both years ago on an ant plant called *Squamellaria* from Fiji – a distant relative of the specimen we are crouching next to in the Philippines. Guillaume carried out his fieldwork in Fiji, hauling himself up trees, creeping along branches, and chasing ants. His fascinating discovery was that the ants were *farming* the plants. Furtively they harvest the seeds from their unripe fruits, before the birds can discover them. They cart them off to fissures in the tree's bark, dragging the seeds to safety and planting them there. Then they wait. A small group of worker ants patrols the germinating seedlings, tends them, and protects them from predators. Once a seedling has swelled to the size of a thumbnail, an entrance hole expands on its surface. Ants shuttle in and out of this and defecate in the hallway, fertilizing the seedling. As the plant matures, it rewards its occupants with droplets of nutritious nectar only the ants know how to find. The ants farm specimens of different ages simultaneously; unoccupied plants are always available to let when a new home is needed.[11]

Some ants even tend plots of fungi, deep within the plants' chambers. They offer the fungi leafy detritus, defecate on them, and nibble off bits periodically, for a snack. Meanwhile in the Amazon, ants have been observed harvesting mycelia (the network of threads by which fungi grow), and the hairs of their host plant, to construct an elaborate trap. They sever hairs along the plant's stems, clearing a path, then regurgitate glue to bind them back together, creating a series of vaults in which to hide, with their jaws poking out of little cut-out holes. The fungal mycelium, manipulated by the ants, pervades the structure and reinforces it. They wait. An unsuspecting locust lands, and the ants leap out of their tunnels, ambushing their prey. They grasp its legs, sting it, and stretch it to death. Then they carry it to a pouch – a garrison provided by the ant plant – where they carve it up.[12] An artifice perfected by tens of millions of years of evolution.

Yes, ants were hunting, farming, and making civilizations long before we were.

Back in the forest, Kuya Mande scoops up the volatile plant. Ants pour out angrily, but he seems oblivious. We cart off our prize to the conservation garden; it would perish if we left it on the forest floor. On the way back, Ana and Adriane teach me sayings in Tagalog.

'Gutom na *gutom* na ako,' they say – 'I'm famished'.

I repeat the expression to Pat when we arrive at headquarters. He laughs and slaps me hard on the back. 'Then we will eat like kings,

Kuya Dante with an ant plant at the Land Grant in the Sierra Madre, Luzon.

my friend!' We hoist up our trophy ant plant to show him. He can see how happy it has made me, I can tell.

'What a special place this is,' I say, adding, 'the only thing it's missing is *Rafflesia*!'

'But there is *Tetrastigma* here at the Land Grant,' Pat says, pointing vaguely to the forest with a smile so broad his ears wiggle. *Tetrastigma* is the vine *Rafflesia* grows on; its host. I know what he is thinking.

'We could graft *Rafflesia* on to the vine at the Land Grant!' I exclaim.

'Yes,' he says, his eyes shining.

If we achieved this, we would be the first people outside of Bogor Botanic Garden in Indonesia to propagate *Rafflesia*. I ponder on this as we pack our cases to leave the Sierra Madre after lunch. *Rafflesia* appears in the International Union for Conservation of Nature (IUCN) Red List: a spectrum of wildlife moving closer to the edge of the precipice, losing the fight with extinction. Like so many plants in Southeast Asia, *Rafflesia* is threatened by habitat destruction. But *Rafflesia* is at particular risk because it cannot be grown in botanic gardens, or stored in seed banks – efforts that might otherwise safeguard its existence as the trees fall around it. Growing *Rafflesia* at the Land Grant would be a radical advance in our efforts to conserve the plant. It would be radical full stop.

We haul our bags to the van where Kuya Mande is waiting patiently for us, and I say goodbye to Pat and Ana, who will stay on at the Land Grant for the next few days as Adriane and I head south to Quezon Province.

Outside the headquarters building, the Wi-Fi kicks in. Reconnected with the digital world, I remember that strange text message I received from Deki earlier. As I try to make sense of his riddle, I notice he has also attached a photograph to the cryptic words, which is now downloading slowly. It seems to depict a collection of orange, ball-like *Rafflesia* buds, rolling along the floor. The largest of them has split in half in a peculiar way; it seems to be smiling, like a Halloween pumpkin. How strange. Then my blood runs cold. As the picture comes into focus, I realize all of them have been slashed violently with a knife.

6.

The forest is sick.

Sekedai Cup. Mystical to the people, mystical to Bengkulu. Mr Chris. People come to it. Sit with the cup, spend time and take selfies.

But they harm the cup. Sometimes they harm the forest. No more forest, no more cup. It is also called a Ghost Bowl.

7.

Under a torrent of interlocking cables and vines swooping into the road, Kuya Mande, Adriane, and I drive through San Pablo looking for a place to stay. Multicoloured flags and bunting have been strung up to every building, as if a festival is afoot. Roadside shops banged together from corrugated metal broadcast mysterious combinations of wares such as 'SMART 5G & ALE' and 'CARWASH & WATERGIRL'. One has a red awning, featuring the words 'BANG BANG' with a cartoon explosion. I can't decipher any of this violent advertisement, but Adriane has nodded off so I make my assumptions. I ask Kuya Mande if we have reached the Municipality of Dolores and he nods silently, but I'm unsure if he has understood. So I sit quietly with my head against the window, and watch the sun step out of the sky.

Mount Banahaw appears. At first I'm uncertain; I just see shards of mountain flickering through the trees and houses over the blaze, like a face in the flame. Then the unmistakable grey mass rises out of the earth, pushing the world above, like Everest. Mount Banahaw is an active volcano rising to 2,170 metres, with a summit blown out by a screaming crater, 3.5 kilometres across and 210 metres deep. It looks taller than it is because of the flatness of the surrounding plains. The mountain is rich in biodiversity: thousands of species of plant, fungus, and animal stitching together lives on its warm, forested slopes. This generosity of life extends to a high number of *point endemics* too – species found nowhere else. An entomologist here in the Philippines told me that years ago researchers heard the call of an endemic cicada on the mountain's summit; it sounded uncannily like a screaming baby. They initially feared '*tiyanak*' – an evil spirit. The call has never been recorded electronically; beyond Banahaw's summit, it exists only in human memory.

Nearly 140 tree species make up the green felted foothills of the mountain. For context, there are just sixty in the whole of the UK. Some of the trees have significant cultural value, for Mount Banahaw is a sacred place – a 'promised land' in the Philippines. The Kinabuhayan River, which frills around its foot, bestows healing powers: thousands flock there to kneel and light candles, perform rituals among the trees, and bathe in the miracle water. This is a special place for plants and people; a place steeped in mystery.

The closer we get, the less of the mountain I see. The road becomes swallowed up by vegetation that lashes and smacks the van. Adriane Googles his phone, looking for places we can stay for the night. San Pablo with its strange little shops and signs gives way to villages lost in leafy clouds, where families congregate: several men fixing a bike, women in purple T-shirts frying chicken; children kicking a ball around, laughing. We try four guesthouses but they're all full, and the options are dwindling. Adriane crouches next to my seat, at the front of the van, directing Kuya Mande to the last guest-house on the mountain using the map on his phone.

The dirt track peters out at a blocky chalet next to a rutted square where milky-chocolate puddles have collected. I slam shut the vehicle door, and warm, wet air wraps around me like a blanket. Sunset is nigh but the crickets persist with their violent shaking sounds, like maracas. Adriane dashes about to look for someone to make enquiries about beds for the night, as Kuya Mande and I wait silently by the van. He returns with raised eyebrows and a shrug, and declares the place abandoned. Saying nothing, we wander over to a concrete veranda overlooking the forest before making the long drive back to Los Baños where we're confident we'll finally find a bed for the night. We gaze over dozing hills framed by tree ferns and watch a frozen tide of cloud pour over the horizon. By the time we leave, the insects have exhausted themselves, and their volume recedes to soft white noise.

I wake up from a deep sleep, alone in the van, on the side of the road. It's the dead of night. I could be anywhere. So could the bag containing all my earthly belongings, it seems. As my eyes adjust to the darkness, electric yellow light pools along the pavement, spot-lighting tropical-looking foliage glinting like knives. I feel alert, and all the little hairs along my arms stand on end. A face appears, lit white from beneath. It freezes, slowly looks up, meets my eyes.

It's Adriane with his phone. He slides open the door, sucking in warm air and the smell of night.

'Adriane!' I exclaim a little more abruptly than I had intended. 'Where were you?'

'Why?' he says simply.

He often answers my questions this way. It transpires that he and Kuya Mande have found somewhere to stay for the night on the outskirts of Los Baños. I hop out and follow Adriane to the room. It is small and white with a single bed, a bucket of water to wash with in the corner, and an air-conditioning unit humming industriously. Adriane seems nervous, I think because we have to share a bed; I assure him this is fine, and we arrange ourselves top and tail. Adri-ane studies his phone under the blanket and I sleep soundly for the first time since I arrived a week ago.

We wake at 8 a.m. – late by Filipino standards. The thought of driving back to Mount Banahaw is too much; anyway Kuya Mande and his van have vanished. Adriane and I agree to have a rest day. I sort through the fragments of my suspended life: journal, camera charger, adapters, antimalarial tablets, and so on; marshal my exist-ence. After bathing with a bucket of cold water, we wander over to the small café belonging to our lodgings, for breakfast. We eat pork and rice, chased down with little cups of instant coffee; worshippers in a mosque chant morning prayer somewhere in the distance. Adri-ane taps on his laptop as I watch an impossibly large dragonfly hang motionless in the air, rise and repeat, as if someone is controlling it like a drone.

Clouds shift around the summit of Mount Makiling in the dis-tance; I think I can make out the shoulder we climbed over to see the little flowers of *Rafflesia panchoana*. It sounds odd, I know, but it feels a part of me now somehow. I once read somewhere that every time you breathe, you absorb a number of molecules so vast the sum total contains twenty-three digits. When I breathed in *Rafflesia* on Mount Makiling I absorbed it. And now I'm carrying it inside me like a promise.

★★★

'Urine pots,' says Adriane.

I look at him blankly.

'We need urine sample pots,' he repeats.

We are standing in a pharmacy looking for makeshift laboratory materials to collect *Rafflesia* samples for DNA analysis. A fortnight ago, I shipped a crate here containing equipment vials and reagents, but it was held up at customs so we need to improvise. The urine pots look conveniently like the Falcon tubes I had planned for us to use anyway. Next we require scalpels and ethyl alcohol to preserve the samples. We find great vats of it in the first-aid section. Finally we need whisky, Adriane tells me (which, oddly, is also sold in the first-aid section).

'I'm sure the ethyl alcohol is purer,' I suggest.

'The whisky is for gifts, Dr Chris,' he says. 'A bottle for the tribe, and another for Tita Rose.'

The woman at the check-out desk says nothing as she scans thirty urine sample pots plus several litres of alcohol. We sweep it all into a cardboard box and cart it back to our accommodation on a tricycle (a motorcycle attached to a passenger cab). Adriane hangs off the back of the bike, shouting to the driver in Tagalog over the buzzing drone, while I sit in the passenger cab, crouched like a spider over our box of combustibles. I hope no one lights a cigarette.

★★★

It is the weekend, and Kuya Mande has the day off (this must be why he vanished), so we have a new driver, propitiously called Kuya Darwin. He has dark skin and missing teeth. We are returning to Mount Banahaw. It's a week into the expedition and our mission is to document a rare and poorly understood species of *Rafflesia* called

R. banahawensis. It grows only on this mountain and few people have seen it.

Rangy coconut palms glisten as we drive under the fierce morning sun. We pass pyramids of pineapple and jackfruit, and a green sign instructing 'Slow down, accident prone area', leaning precariously because someone has driven into it.

After an hour, overlapping grey triangles of mountain rise around us on all sides. We pass Mount San Cristobal, which I must have missed last time we passed it; perhaps I was dozing. San Cristobal is Banahaw's alter ego – known here as the Devil's mountain, and believed to emanate negative energy. I'm not surprised, looking at it. Denuded of its blanket of forest, the mountain's contours are unnaturally sharp, like a starved person's. Unlike the deferred catastrophe of climate change, deforestation is a fait accompli in many lowland parts of Southeast Asia. Still, most mountains at least support vestiges of ancient forest; a gift we were given that we've not yet squandered. So to be confronted with San Cristobal's bare slopes is disturbing. When I see things like this, I wish dearly we could turn back the clock, do things better; probably what people will say about what we're doing to the planet now in years to come. They will be our judge.

You can't just turn up at a mountain in the Philippines and expect to climb. Most are closed to the public and require written permission. Even then, there are no guarantees. It's especially complicated if you're foreign – a word I've heard a lot these last few days. Adriane is mooting contingency plans and I feel twitchy about the very real prospect of being turned away from a potentially life-changing encounter with a plant.

We pull up at Barangay Kinabuhayan, a ramshackle village nestled at the foot of Mount Banahaw. A vault of grey trees, straight as spears, shoots up into the green. A board nailed to a tree has painted on it an evil eye, watching a green tin hut; a group of young men in shorts and flip-flops sit beside the hut, watching us. Adriane hops out and talks to the men at the makeshift checkpoint, who lean in to peer at his phone at intervals. I see surprise written on Adriane's features at something that has just been said; the group laughs.

Then the man in the group with authority stands and ushers Kuya Darwin to park the van.

We're in.

Julius is his name, and he will be our guide. He's in his mid-thirties, I think, slim, with smooth dark skin and bony hands like my own. He's wearing a blue, red, and white polo shirt, with a circular logo across the breast emblazoned 'police', and jeans and flip-flops. Most people wear flip-flops here regardless of what they do, or where they go. He tells Adriane he saw *Rafflesia* in the forest only yesterday, and starts scrolling his phone to show us a photograph. I can't believe what I am hearing; perhaps he's mistaken. As I've said, *Rafflesia* is rare and unpredictable and this just seems too good to be true. But sure enough, his photograph depicts the preposterous steak-red flower. Excitement sparkles around us like glitter. Beaming like a lunatic, I put my arm around Adriane – 'It's here!' I whisper. He smiles awkwardly, but for just a second I see his face light up too.

We have to walk the length of Barangay Kinabuhayan to reach the foot of the mountain. Julius stops at a shack to buy three cigarettes. The vendor says something in Tagalog, to which he, Adriane, and Julius turn to look at me. Adriane explains that the man is warning that by association with me, the foreigner, Julius will have a nosebleed today. I'm unsure what to make of this so I say nothing.

As we wander, Adriane shows me a bristly-looking plant leaning out of a hedge, which he tells me is used here for scrubbing pans. We pluck a handful of its scabrid leaves, then he crouches to the ground, looks up at me, and demonstrates how they can be used to clean muddy shoes. I copy him, scouring the dirt from my boots. Just like in Iraq, and so many parts of the world, plants mean much more than just beautiful scenery to exist against; here they are a way of life.

People go about their business in miniature under Mount Banahaw's great wall. Formless clouds boil around its summit. We pass low-slung shacks containing neatly stacked jars and tins, smoke creeping through the trees, and camel-coloured dogs nibbling themselves. Julius leads us to the mouth of a trench-like path carved into the hill. At the threshold of the forest, knuckles of vine look polished from wear, and little fragments of litter – Coke cans, crisp packets, and so on – glint in the soil like embers. It is a protected landscape, but like every place frequented by people, it has scars.

We enter the forest. Bass clef *hiss*, treble clef *chirp*. Steep mossy banks splashed with vibrant ferns rise up on either side of us. The base of the path is so narrow in places it is hard to walk without stumbling up the sides. Trees interlock overhead to form a dappled green cylinder. The air feels heavier than it ought, and sweat dribbles down my back. It is claustrophobic, dark, and close. A punishing place. The climb is instantly exhausting but our singular focus draws us up like an invisible rope. We couldn't go back now if we wanted to.

We pause to rest after just twenty minutes. Julius leans against a tree, and lights one of his rationed cigarettes with one hand, the other lodged in his pocket. Adriane checks his phone, but there is no reception; we have left the human realm. Nature is in charge now. As we wait for our hearts to slacken, I examine a patch of vibrant green vegetation. Outstretched branches of ferns and lycophytes fan over cushions of moss: flowerless, spore-producing plants. Plants born in a land before time.

★★★

Look around. You can probably see a plant somewhere nearby, perhaps in a pot, or through the window. What you see is a living descendant of something that appeared underwater, hundreds of millions of years ago. Something as obscure as it was profound. Something that would change how our planet functions and rewrite the history of existence. The dawn of *plants*. Plants configured the climate, changed the soil, created habitats, and drove the evolution of millions of species. Everything humans are doing, in reverse.

If you've ever been pond-dipping, you'll have seen a tail of algae drooping from your net. 'Algae' is an artificial term to describe all the simple (I might say slimy) plants that tend to occur in water and lack true roots, stems, leaves, and specialized reproductive structures such as flowers and seeds. Your pond net may have contained a particular alga called a stonewort (a charophyte). I remember holding one up and peering at the dripping tentacle as an undergraduate student, a little unimpressed. It's not beautiful. But this unprepossessing pondweed has *stamina*. As the dinosaurs thundered through its ponds, glaciers reorganized the land and the earth recast itself around it, the stonewort soldiered on, uninterrupted. Age before beauty.

Fossil stoneworts of the early Devonian age similar to the specimen I peered at as a student have been found in Scotland's Rhynie Chert. The Rhynie Chert is a sedimentary deposit dating back 410 million years that captures a whole ecosystem of early plants, fungi, and animals, frozen in deep time. It is a place of pilgrimage for scientists examining the early evolution of plants. Their eyes light up when you mention the place. Specimens unearthed there show us that stoneworts remained virtually unchanged for hundreds of millions of years. We, as a species, have existed 0.05 per cent of the time stoneworts have been lurking in ponds. Yet this fraction of the stoneworts' existence, the Anthropocene – an epoch of implacable human impact – poses their greatest risk of extinction.

Land plants – most of those we see around us today – probably evolved from the lineage that contains the stoneworts. It's difficult to know exactly how land plants as we know them came to be. If paleobotanists don't agree on much, they agree on that. Paleobotanists are the scientists who examine fossils; read the rock. But the early fossil record is much too sparse to decipher clearly; it's like trying to read music with most of the notes missing. And it doesn't help that even the relationship among the four main lineages of plant that still exist today, hornworts, liverworts, mosses, and vascular plants ('plants with plumbing') – the latter three of which are all jostling for position in front of me – remains unresolved.

Scientists have long used living and fossil species to piece together the scraps of evidence available. Now they also analyse DNA using advanced statistical analyses. The paleontologist Philip Donoghue and his team used these to build a time machine. They dived deep into evolutionary time using a *molecular clock* – an approach used to examine mutation rates to predict when particular life forms diverged along separate lines. Surprisingly, their work showed that plants crept out of the water 500 million years ago, during the Cambrian Period – about the same time as the emergence of the first land animals.[13] This was far earlier than previously understood, and necessitated a rethink of how and when plants dominated the land. They also challenged an orthodoxy prescribing that land plants evolved from liverworts – the frilly, seaweed-like plants that you often see sprawling over wet rocks and earth. Liverworts lack stomata, the pores through which oxygen diffuses in other plants. This had long led scientists to believe that liverworts must be primitive, and that mosses were more likely to be closer relatives of the 'higher' land plants. But Philip and his colleagues' work showed that the clock didn't just stop at liverworts. No, liverworts and mosses are sisters; *together*, they are the likely cousins of the land plants we see all around us.[14] This means that liverworts are not missing the features such as stomata because they never evolved them. Rather, they probably evolved and then lost them. The ancestral land plant was much more complex than mosses and liverworts. And decades of work by scientists invested solely in the liverwort *Marchantia* – heralded as the blue-chip living ancestor – might arguably have been invested better elsewhere.

Time marched on. Mosses and liverworts formed vast green continents of carpet that drove down levels of carbon dioxide, and laid down soil. They breathed life over the earth. New types of vegetation sprouted among them, and strange creatures slunk furtively out of the mud. Exactly how complex plants evolved from this carpet of mosses and liverworts is unclear. *Cooksonia* is one of the best examples of a fossil plant showing a transition from the 'lower plants' (hornworts, liverworts, mosses) to the vascular plants – those plumbed to the ground – with systems for transporting water and nutrients. Digital reconstructions depict oceans of *Cooksonia* waving branched tentacles, holding up little brown cups asking for rain.

One of the plants on the bank in front of me here in the Philippines is a lycophyte. It has lime-green, ferny foliage pressed into flat fingers that splay over the moss. Lycophytes are some of the most ancient vascular plants alive. They were among the first to possess roots, stems, and true leaves, fuelling a fight to the light. Marching across the earth, they shot out of the warm, wet swamps, like dominoes in reverse, to form the first forests. One of the largest was *Sigillaria*, a vaguely yucca-like thing with fat, scaly stems, crowned with spiky foliage, which could rise to over 30 metres in just a few years.

The lycophytes jostled for position with ferns, which appeared about 400 million years ago, and are still going strong. I can see several species of them from where I'm standing. As the ferns took possession of the forest, goliaths such as *Sigillaria* abdicated, and their descendants shrank into submission. I shake hands with the fingery fronds of the small specimen in front of me and watch it nod back. For 425 million years its ancestors have been passing down their genes, evading extinction as the plants around them lost the battle with existence. Assuming each plant lives for twenty years, that's 21 million repeats of itself.

Step out of the prehistoric lycophyte and fern prairies, 300 million years ago, and you'd look up into a vaguely more familiar canopy. Besides trees such as ferns and lycophytes, new plants were appearing. Crucially, they were able to conquer drier habitats than their ancestors: they sowed the seeds of change. 'A seed is a little box with a plant inside' was a definition proffered by the renowned botanist Edred John Henry Corner. He taught it to Simon Hiscock, my former PhD supervisor, who taught it to me. These little boxes with plants inside enabled dormancy and long-distance dispersal, freeing plants from the water. This saw the rise of the gymnosperms (literally 'naked seed' plants), a lineage of seed plants that today includes conifers, cycads, gingko, and some oddities such as desert-dwelling *Welwitschia*. They emerged in the Carboniferous and they still dominate some habitats. The early, flowerless forests they formed locked up vast volumes of carbon in the form of fallen leaves and branches. Curious lizard-, snake-, and crocodile-like amphibians slithered into existence among these new productive forests that sprang up all over the place. Carboniferous (literally 'coal-bearing') refers to the extensive coal deposits that formed from the plant matter produced during this geologic period. Today, nearly

40 per cent of the electricity we use worldwide comes from the coal produced by plant matter laid down by those first seed plants. Important fossils are often preserved within the coal. Some of them hold clues about how early plants evolved. In a box of fossils destined for the rubbish bin a few years ago at Oxford University's Department of Plant Sciences, a whole new rooting system was unearthed. My good friend Sandy Hetherington, a paleobotanist, discovered it.[15] Peering down the microscope at the nearly scrapped fossil lycophyte, he saw something astonishing: branched rootlets, as fine as fuzz, frozen in motion. This observation turned on its head a century and a half's steadfast belief that these plants lacked such organs: it's not that the branched rootlets weren't there – it's that we hadn't noticed them. A discerning paleobotanist knows that absence of evidence isn't evidence of absence.

Dinosaurs went extinct over 66 million years ago; still, we have a far better idea of what they looked like than we do of the first flowering plants they tramped about on. Flowers are the sex organs of a lineage of plants called angiosperms, which changed the face of our planet once again. There are close to 300,000 species of them, and they make up most of the diversity of plants that exist today. Darwin described the sudden appearance of flowers in the fossil record as 'an abominable mystery' and, more than a century later, scientists still haven't solved it adequately. Early flower fossils are controversial and subject to interpretation; some are just a couple of millimetres across and there has been much debate over whether they appeared in the Cretaceous or, as some suggest, earlier on, in the Jurassic. There is some consensus that early flowers may have looked something like a magnolia. *Archaeanthus* is one of the better-preserved examples. Reconstructions of it depict a simple white flower and corn-on-the-cob structure clasping tightly packed fruits. The first flowering plants enlisted insects and other animals for their pollen and seed dispersal, and this was probably key to their success. Scientists have also suggested that a higher density of leaf veins, driving more efficient photosynthesis, may also have played a part in their rise to dominance.[16] Today flowering plants make up 96 per cent of the world's vegetation.

The flowering plants that exist are a living library for scientists to explore. Before the 1990s, the evolutionary relationships among flowering plants were often at best unconfirmed and at worst hopelessly wrong. DNA sequencing enabled the first objective classification, and it unearthed some big surprises (literally, in the case of *Rafflesia*). The Angiosperm Phylogeny Group (APG) is an international team of botanists who work towards a consensus on the taxonomy of flowering plants. The flowering-plant family tree they produced has been updated four times, most recently in 2016. Herbaria, field guides, and botanic garden beds across the globe had to be reshuffled to keep in step.

Taxonomic changes can be controversial. Take, for example, when rosemary became sage. DNA data showed that the genus to which rosemary belongs (*Rosmarinus*) had to be absorbed into that to which sage belongs (*Salvia*) to be truly reflective of the plants' relatedness.[17] To ignore the data would hinder science: how can we objectively group plants, their pharmacological uses, and their horticultural needs, if we don't follow the evidence? On the other hand, continuing to recognize the genus *Rosmarinus* would mean changing the name of over 700 species of *Salvia*. There was no way around it. *Rosmarinus officinalis* was rechristened *Salvia rosmarinus*.

As I said, *Rafflesia* was the biggest surprise of all. Unsure what to do with it, taxonomists lumped it with other parasitic plants that live inside their hosts, such as a curious yellow plant called *Cytinus* (which I shall return to). A team of scientists in the United States, including Charles Davis, examined several genes from *Rafflesia*, and showed that it evolved from within the spurge family (Euphorbiaceae).[18] Astonishingly, most spurges and their relatives produce minute flowers. The data estimated an eighty-fold expansion in flower size, one of the most dramatic examples of size evolution ever reported. Perhaps gigantism evolved in response to fly pollination. *Rafflesia* is a phantom corpse: it mimics rotting meat in appearance and smell to attract flies, duping them with the false promise of a reward to secure cross-fertilization. In nature, larger corpses draw in more flies because they are better resources for their maggots to feed on; it makes sense to live large when you play dead. Actually, deceit is rife in the plant kingdom – from advertising nectar where there is none, to the chemical mimicry of phero- mones, to confuse sex-crazed male bees into trying to mate with a flower. Yes, white lies spring up all over the plant kingdom; but *Rafflesia* wins the prize for the biggest.

One of the mosses in front of me is clutching little spore- producing structures, as fine as hair. I smile as they call forth memories of teaching undergraduate biology back in Oxford.

In plants, sexual reproduction – brought about through cross- fertilization – isn't the only means of reproduction in the same way as it is in most animals. It is a bolt-on to asexual reproduction – the generation of identical offspring involving a single parent, also known as cloning. Sexual reproduction is a change agent, it gener- ates variation upon which natural selection can act. Asexual reproduction yields assuredness – it can happen without a mate. Both sexual and asexual reproduction feature in the same life cycle in plants – they alternate in phases; which is the dominant phase changes as we go up the evolutionary scale. This shift was fund- amental to how plants took charge of the land.

'Understand *this*, and you can conquer anything in plant biology,' Simon Hiscock and I tell the first-year biology undergraduate stu- dents huddling around a trestle table in a corner of the Botanic Garden. The tables are bestrewn with fronds and Petri dishes stuffed with liverworts and moss we've raided from the glasshouses.

'The *Alternation of Generations*,' Simon says, pausing for effect.

They nod and scribble it down. Simon taught me the Alternation of Generations twenty years ago; today, we are teaching them.

'We, as humans, are diploid,' he continues. 'This means our cells have two complete sets of chromosomes – each of our parents con- tributed a chromosome to each pair.'

The students nod harder, showing us they know this already. Chromosomes are the threadlike structures that contain our DNA and they all learned this before they arrived in Oxford.

'Only our sperm and egg cells are *haploid* – they contain just a single set of chromosomes,' we continue.

Things are more complicated in plants. Both haploid and diploid phases can dominate a plant's life cycle, and this is the crux of what the students need to understand today.

'Everything you can see here is haploid,' we explain as the students pass around Petri dishes of moss and liverwort, bobbing their heads in turn as they peer at the miniature parasols, like a slow Mexican wave. What they are looking at is analogous to a human's sperm and egg cells, only in mosses and liverworts the sexual phase is not reduced to single cells, it is a free-living organism, a dominant part of the life cycle. Meiotic cell divisions bloom in their minds' eyes as the students digest this. One or two shuffle their feet, looking bored. A duck wanders over expecting to be fed and I see a student secretly offer it a piece of liverwort.

'But everything you can see *here* is diploid,' Simon continues, now waving around a wand-like fern frond. 'In this plant, the haploid phase is small and short-lived. The diploid phase has become dominant. This is the case for most of the plants we see around us.'

'And *this*? *This* one is a seed plant,' I chime in, holding a potted cycad to the sky. 'The mosses, liverworts and ferns all produced spores which needed water to develop their haploid generation. But the evolution of pollen and seeds enabled transport by wind or animal couriers. It unmoored them from the water.'

One by one, we show them examples of plants alternating between haploid and diploid life forms, and their scribbling gathers pace. The plants on the table are just the living descendants – a shutterclick in evolution. We encourage the students to reimagine fallen forests, plants frozen in stone – to see through time. By the time we get to double fertilization in flowering plants, they are writing furiously, willing 500 million years of evolution explained in three hours to stick.

Back in the mountain thicket, I stare at the living fossils in front of me and they lose scale – the little canopy of ferns and lycophytes arching over the moss becomes a miniature forest of its own, lost in time. Steadily these organisms have surrendered their secrets to us. They have plenty to share still, I'm sure. Perhaps the plants that first breathed life over the earth can help us in the Anthropocene, our hour of need; a trice in their time. If we can deduce how climate change influenced life in the distant past, we might predict patterns in a changing world, and see further into the future; dig deeper for the solutions that might lie beneath the earth, to the quagmire we're making above it. Reconfigure the climate, restore the soil, recreate the habitats, and avert the extinctions. Reset the clock and reverse what we've done.

★★★

We pass a wooden shack in a clearing. Crops have been planted among the trees; it would be unclear where the forest ends and the smallholding begins but for the noise – the insects wane the moment the forest recedes. Julius stops to talk to the farmer and Adriane and I rest on a shelf of earth. We sit silently, taking in the view that swoops down over the green globes of trees and rests on folded blue hills. My body is tired but my mind is clear, focused. *Rafflesia* is within reach. We've seen the photograph on Julius's phone. Even if we hadn't, I know it's there; it's pulling us like a magnet.

We press on, our bags jostling heavily, wiping the sweat from our brows. Giant grasses well up around us as we approach another smallholding, seemingly abandoned, lost in leaves. Breadfruits have been stacked in a pyramid at the foot of a tree. One is smashed and blackening with rot like an overripe avocado. We look up and see them growing, great brown orbs the size of watermelons in the tree, which would surely kill a man should they fall. Adriane and I admire an epiphytic orchid clasping the fork of a sapling, half consumed by trusses of lichen and moss.

We slip back into the forest. Shadows and *hisssh*; warm earth with rich smells, like espresso coffee; filaments of leaf-tempered light. We become subsumed by trees. Just a few minutes in, Julius stops. He points to the floor and turns to look at us, waiting for a reaction. Pushing out of the leafy viscera at our feet is a bud.

Rafflesia.

As if in prayer, Adriane and I drop to our knees. Gently, I brush my fingers over the strange orange effusion. It is warm, and as full of promise as an egg. Its closed petals are glossy and taut, like the skin of an aubergine. Clenched into a fist this way, it looks as though

73

it might respond to my touch, burst open in a trice. *Sentient.* I visualize the hollow interior of the pregnant flower, and the intricate architecture it contains, beneath my fingers. I look about to trace its host – lifeline to the forest. I see it, like an umbilical cord, shooting up into the gloom. Then we sit in silence with the half-formed marvel. As I trace the palm of my hand over the flower, I feel my mind follow it like a current, through the vine, and out into the web of the forest. Now we are connected, the flower and me.

'Where is the open one, the flower you saw yesterday?' Adriane asks Julius excitedly, jolting me out of my metaphysical forest. Just a few metres from the bud, Julius points down again. We follow his line of sight to the ground, our hearts pounding, and see this: a withered, black flower.

Hope shrivels inside me like a dying poppy. Twenty-four hours after Julius found the *Rafflesia* flower, it is no more. Powerless, mortal, and bereft of its being. Now it looks like the cache of leafy detritus it's framed in. The forest is taking it back.

Julius and Adriane look disappointed too. 'It's OK,' I say, but my voice sounds small. 'You can't expect to find *Rafflesia* every time, we know that.'

Adriane nods in wordless agreement. But finding *R. panchoana* on Mount Makiling last week made me bold. I should have known it wouldn't be as simple as walking up a mountain track for half a day. But more than anything I *wanted* to find it. It's all I wanted. To have missed it by a day hurts like a fist.

We weave our way silently down the mountain, stooping under branches, and emerging in a steamy clearing that stinks of piss and horseshit. Back at the tin hut, we sit and wait for Kuya Darwin to appear. Julius and his friends kindly offer me sugared coffee from a thermos which I sip as I watch a young man in white gumboots push a reluctant horse laden with sacks of potatoes into the village.

'*Rafflesia* is magnificent,' I say to Julius for no reason at all. Then, feeling an urge to qualify this and cover the silence, I add, 'I hope it grows here for a long time to come.'

'Shouldbe. Shouldbe,' he repeats vaguely to the air, then turns and stares at the mountain.

8.

Chris is patient. Nine months it takes a hand to make a flower. Nine months.

9.

'We can't continue. It's not safe,' Pat announces to Ana, Adriane, and me, from the front seat of the van, still looking ahead. 'Even without a foreigner,' he adds. 'We will rest for the night and continue at dawn.'

Bandits hide along the road to the Sierra Madre, he goes on to explain, and there is a risk of kidnap. By extension I'm an added risk, I suspect, but this isn't said aloud. The populations of *Rafflesia* we are examining are flung across all of Luzon, and we must cover vast distances by road to reach them all.

We stop for grilled fish and beer in the sticky heat at a roadside café, from where we resume our ordinary lives for an hour; Pat appears to be giving an online tutorial to his students, while Adriane prepares for a future forestry class; a pleat of concentration forms between his eyes as he stares intently at his laptop. I scroll through photos I have taken on my phone, depicting softly forested hills. Dopamine and tiredness wash through me gently. It's 3 a.m. by the time we reach the town of Santiago, where we spend the night in a windowless dormitory. Still, we have no need for windows because we rise just three hours later to continue on our journey to the Amro River Basin, unwashed and heavy-eyed.

The Aurora Province, in east-central Luzon, is our next destination: a storm-washed crescent of forest smiling at the sea. We're waved through a military checkpoint along a pale road that plunges into an ocean of reeds and tree ferns. Where the road steepens, blood-red tracks have been slashed into the verge leading to half-baked constructions and other loose ends of life in the trees. The land levels out through ranks of palms and banana plants, into the Casiguran Sound: a dimpled grey sea with traditional boats holding complicated sails, in front of a snout of forested rock I initially mistake for an island.

We stop at the market in Casiguran for supplies; aside from coconuts there will be little to eat or drink once we arrive, Pat tells us. Adriane and Ana take the lead and I follow, observing everything. Politicians smile benevolently from posters over hordes of stallholders herding chickens and rolling fruit. We enter a dark maze inside a municipal-looking building. Dissonant notes of rotten fruit and bleach creep through a labyrinth of stalls and boxes. People shout loudly, fish scream silently, and severed animal heads stare at no one. Ana and Adriane barter over some chicken while I wait patiently next to a pile of sacks with pictures of lions on them (pet food?). Stacked cartons contain purple-painted eggs; I wonder if they're for Easter, but their colour indicates that they are salted, I learn later. We trundle back to the van, sagging with bottled water, chicken parts, and glowing eggs. The food couldn't possibly stay cool, but that can't be helped; anyway we're all too tired to care.

★★★

A hornbill glides over a continent of mountains, unseen. It watches four botanists clamber out of a van, fifty metres below. The Amro River Protected Landscape we're stepping into is one of five designated reserves in the Aurora Province. I'm told that Asian water monitor lizards (*Varanus salvator*) live here – prehistoric-looking reptiles that tiptoe about the forests; they occur across Southeast Asia and I've encountered them before on my adventures. The trees are colossal: relatives of dipterocarps, *Shorea*, soar from the canopy. They are recorded to reach heights of 80 metres; the very tallest trees in Britain are specimen conifers that top out at just 61 metres. One other giant hides in the depths here too. One that few people have seen.

Rafflesia leonardi is our target today. Other botanists have lumped this rare species with the one that grows in the Kalinga Province that Pat told me about last week, *R. banaoana* – seen by almost no one. But Pat and Adriane know these plants better than anyone. They know they're different. The aim of our research is to show this scientifically, get to know each of the plants' intricacies, their secrets. It is important for their conservation that we do; for if we cannot adequately quantify the biodiversity that exists then how can we protect it?

We unpack the van. Behind us, the Amro River sluices over a broad, pebbly rise strewn with boulders, down a concrete ramp. Beyond the fury stretches a glassy lagoon.

'We will bathe in this later,' Adriane whispers in his soft, mono-tone voice, as we help Kuya Mande unload boxes of sample tubes. I look out over the bank of straggling roots beneath softly forested mountains from which slow-motion clouds are exploding.

'Do you think we'll find it?' I ask Adriane without context, as we haul the supplies inside. He knows I'm referring to *Rafflesia*. He pauses to scan the horizon, as if he sees the answer written there, but says nothing.

I am introduced to Max, the reserve's superintendent, by the river, in the striped shade of a green metal hut without sides. Max has a firm handshake and an air of no-nonsense; a man in charge.

'What do you think of my forest?' he asks me with an upward glance and a slight wave to the hills.

'I like it very much,' I tell him.

'Please,' he says, ushering us all to the table. 'Join us for breakfast.'

We sit at the table on which little plastic dishes of meat and rice have already been set. I hope they don't contain intestines or pigs' faces – *chicharon* or *sisig*.

'Today we have *chicharon* and *sisig*,' Max says beaming.

I'd sell my soul for a bowl of cereal. But I opt for a third, unannounced dish of river fish in banana and coconut milk, which turns out to be delicious. We share coffee from a thermos while I stare out at an assertive dragonfly. A couple of foresters wander over to greet us, and Pat speaks to them and Max about the *Rafflesia* population that grows here. From the drip-feed of translations I'm offered, I deduce that the hike to the plant is either 4 kilometres or

15 kilometres long, and will take either five hours or a day. We wander back to the lodge to prepare for the unknown.

I'm trawling an empty inner well for energy after the long drives and forest treks which, including rest days, span almost two weeks now. I'm doing a poor job of hiding it. Waspish thoughts crawl around my brain and I've become sullen, retreating into journal writing for hours at a time. We bathe with buckets of cold water – we've not had hot water for days now – and the shock clears my head. But when I look down, I realize I've lost weight. My ribs are sharper and my body is no longer my own. My beard has grown too, it's curling. As we towel dry and dress facing away from one another, I notice we're all starting to look different. Indelible mud and scratches mark our skin and we ignore them; hair hangs wetly in our eyes and we let it; our dark eyes reflect the forest. We're getting wilder.

Five foresters, four botanists, three dogs. The foresters wear baseball caps and gumboots, and carry machetes in wooden cases strung to their waists. One is also holding a bouquet of palm leaves; I'm unsure what these are for. The leader of the pack is Danillo, a tall, dark-skinned man, who has blood-red teeth – the consequence of a life spent chewing betel nut (an ancient tradition here). He marches us in a band towards the green horizon, across a plain of warm wet grass that smells of stewed tea. The dogs nose at fallen coconuts that litter the ground and orange termite mounds rising out of the earth like miniature lost continents. The morning sun is hot and I can feel my pulse in my ears; rivulets of sweat carrying insect repellent and sun cream smart my eyes: little seeds of discomfort starting to send out roots.

In a sea-green light we crawl through a tunnel of reeds that delivers us to the mouth of the forest. Sky and land evaporate; we're bereft of the markers of space and time now. We pull ourselves up the scarp using trees for poles. We pause halfway up the slope to allow our hearts to slacken. Already I feel exhausted. Half a mile into the trek; half a world away from home. I look up at the plants that are unfamiliar to me. I stare down at the hands that are no longer my own. For a moment I have the strangest perception that the forest is mocking me for squaring up to it, for thinking I could just breeze in like this and it would disclose its secrets. I may not have meant to, but I've started a war.

***

Rafflesia's cousin *Cytinus* taught me to think like a plant. I learnt it years ago, collecting samples of it in southern Portugal for research. Scientists formerly considered this Mediterranean parasite to be a close relative of *Rafflesia*. But, unbeknownst to them, the plants were disobeying their looks-based classification system, refusing to follow the rules. Sequencing the plants' DNA finally exposed them. They were not blood relatives at all – by chance alone, they had evolved the same fugitive existence: a plant-within-a-plant. Re-enter: convergent evolution.

Cytinus hides on a thistled slope, a sandy place minted by storms and sea. Every year for a decade I visited, while teaching under-graduate field botany. I forced through vicious gorses in the shimmery heat to find it. I *knew* that wind-beaten slab of Portugal intimately. Like a goatherd, I belonged to the place, could identify all of its plants by their smell alone: the demanding, parsley-like tang of *Margotia*; the pelargonium scent of camphor thyme; the sticky, pine-like smell of gum rockrose, its leaves as bright as glass. All of them whispered to me and I listened.

I pushed my feet into the dimpled sand, pausing to relieve myself in the grey shade of a pine, darkening the earth at its foot. Little insects whined intermittently about the gorse. I watched a moth-like bird zoom off in the sun dazzle and disappear into the willowy thicket of a *Halimium* bush, and I followed it. Then, crunching through the cindery dead leaves, I saw my prize. Like embers: little yellow and red sprouts of *Cytinus* announced themselves, called to me through the ashes. I parted spiteful branches to get to them. *There.* I smiled, stroked them, sniffed them, and drew their musty perfume into my bloodstream.

Sun between the clouds.

I sat for a while watching the flowers glow and my skin darken. Yes, like a goatherd, I belonged to that place.

80

Here in the Philippines I am foreign. My skin is pale and sensitive – it overreacts to every scratch and snare. People stare at me wherever I go. I can't read their thoughts and they can't read mine. I can't read the land either. Although I am an experienced field botanist, at times I can barely name a single plant in this savage forest. Like someone learning a language, I can't call forth the words I need, I flounder, embarrass myself, and make simple mistakes. A stranger in the forest. Yes, foreign.

★★★

We join an old logging road at the hill's summit. The reserve was designated a protected landscape in 2000 but the road was still used to fell trees as late as 2010 I am told. Intricate ferns that smell of wet cardboard form a broken mantle rising over our heads; Danillo has to slash them down with his knife where they have repossessed the track. We push our way into a clearing of crooked reeds looking out over mountain prisms grazing the sky, where we pause to take photos. Pink Philippine ground orchids (*Spathoglottis plicata*) shine in the grass like jewels. Then the mist swims in.

At first it is insubstantial, like steam, but it draws strength, blotting out land and sky. Danillo and I reach a temple of trees where we each lean against a trunk, and wait for the others in silence. Rain conspires with the mist, at first tapping the leaves above like plastic, then piercing the canopy like an overflowing bath pouring through floorboards. It slices the trees like knives and makes the leaves dance. I blink out empty-tasting rivulets that tickle my nostrils and mouth. Adriane and Ana appear with tendrils of hair plastered to their faces, followed by Pat and the other foresters, all shiny-wet. As we wait for the rain to pass, Pat points to a concrete pillar that was put here by the foresters as a boundary to the reserve a few years ago. I can't comprehend how anyone could bring anything so heavy through the punitive forest we've wrestled to get here. Pat translates my astonishment and the foresters nod silently.

The storm passes and we head deeper in, crossing a ferny ridge bisecting the trees. Forested kingdoms rise powerfully either side of us like a reflection, over which tree ferns stand watch: nature admiring itself. The ferns remind me of crinoids (sea lilies) – creatures that stand like sentinels along the deep-sea mounts, patiently watching marine snow fall. They live in places where clocks and calendars have no meaning. *Eternity in an hour*. These 'underwater trees' with their upswept umbrellas are in fact animals: distant relatives of starfish that first appeared in the seas of the mid-Cambrian, 300 million years before the arrival of dinosaurs. Time moving through seas and forests at different speeds; sending up branched monuments then taking them back. Yes, ferns do remind me of crinoids.

The dogs get under our feet and Danillo gives one of them a violent kick, but it's unbothered. It doesn't even yelp. Adriane and Ana clamber side by side, chatting. Pat lags behind the group. He doesn't seem his ebullient self today and I ask him if he is all right.

'I have very bad acid reflux, Chris,' he tells me. 'Very, very bad.'

He looks wan. I offer him water, but this won't help, he tells me dolefully. Panic blooms inside me like a thistle; should one of us fall seriously ill here, we'd have little chance of receiving medical assistance. Under tree cover, even a helicopter wouldn't find us. I start to feel faintly sick as I wonder if this is my fault. The expedition wouldn't be taking place if I wasn't here, that's for certain: it is the product of my obsession to find *Rafflesia*. Another shower patters the leaves and a strange-sounding bird laughs dementedly somewhere. The forest wants me to know it's winning.

Combs of forked fern splay out over everything and we can't see our feet. Slowly we pull ourselves over the ridge using hanging branches for balance. The land angles up, then falls away in front of us, and we have to swing from an overhanging tree to clear a void. We haul ourselves over the yellow mud using our hands and feet, tripping and stumbling over knotted roots as we go.

Beads of water have collected on the bronze leaves of a vigorous shrub I can't put a name to, and hang from the tips of reeds and grasses. Everything is sleek-wet. Rain drenches my socks, making my footsteps heavier. But on the crest of a ridge, where everything glistens, we find the first wild *Nepenthes* (*N. gracilliflora*) of the expedition, and for an instant all hardship evaporates. We huddle to form an audience around the clutch of pitchers suspended in the sodden furze. No one needs to point out that it's special. I step forward to hold one, and the congregation watches expectantly, as if it's about to perform a trick; one of the foresters takes a photo of me with it on his phone, but I hardly notice. I twist the pear-green eggshell this way and that, and peer at the gossamer veins netted on its surface. Its mouth is waxed over like bloom on a grape, and tiny water droplets have collected around its contours, sparkling like broken glass. Liquid the colour of green tea sloshes around its throat and I see the remains of winged things there: its prey. I'm reminded of my first encounter with a wild *Nepenthes* on Mount Kinabalu in Borneo seventeen years ago, of that same giddy feeling you get when you drive over a speed bump – as if you've dipped and left your stomach behind. The Bornean species were magnificent, yes. But this one has its own artless beauty – there's nothing bombastic about it: sleek and symmetrical, with keen attention paid to balance. *Art Nouveau.*

Reluctantly we leave the *Nepenthes*; I expect to find more to dream over, but we don't. We do, however, find the curious yellow flowering structures of a wild ginger lighting the misty forest like candles. Each has the form of a miniature pineapple, with white and pink flowers sticking out like tongues. Next we see an outlandishly large gesneriad, holding candelabras of kitten-soft leaves. I pull back one of the leaves and find a cluster of white, orchid-like flowers with a crystalline surface, glinting like fresh snow. It belongs to a family of plants that have tiptoed onto kitchen tables and windowsills around the world by dint of their lustrous, low maintenance flowers – African violets (*Streptocarpus*), for example. Plants with va-va-voom.

As if reading my mind, a further two wild houseplant relatives announce themselves: a begonia with lopsided jigsaw-shaped leaves, and above it, a green velvet taro (*Alocasia micholitziana*) with flopping great fronds, emerald green, slashed with zinc-white stripes like a zebra's. They each look exuberant next to the other, mortal vegetation, almost obscenely so – as if living was easier for being beautiful. (Like people.) I pause to take photos of each of them and

83

then one of a solitary rattan (a climbing palm like the one we found on the Land Grant the other day), for a colleague at the Royal Botanic Gardens, Kew. It brandishes its thorns like knives, daring me to touch them.

We reach a sort of precipice from where the land rising behind us swoops beneath our feet; now we can see the forest we've been trekking through from above. We inch along the ledge with our backs to the cliff. My palms are clammy; one misstep could lead to a broken limb or worse – the expedition could be called off. We take it in turns, cheering one another on as we each clear the drop, laughing wide-eyed at our recklessness. Pat crosses last, and this time a silent anxiety grips the party as he edges to safety. I notice bruise-like circles framing his eyes and his brow sleeked with sweat. I hope he's all right.

Danillo indicates that we're about to reach the spot. There is a ringing sound, like tinnitus. We penetrate a cat's cradle of lianas – blue as arteries in the half-light – and use the finger-thick loops for footholds. Leafy detritus dislodges and showers us from above, as we push through the rope. I'm spat out the other side to see Danillo point blankly at a complex cylinder of roots writhing out of the earth like a hydrothermal vent. My eyes follow his outstretched arm to a football-sized *Rafflesia* bud lodged in the vinework, two metres from the ground. Not a flower; a bud. I feel like I'm falling. We have travelled for days, risked kidnap, broken limbs, and the loss of our sanity, to see a flower. *And it's not here.*

The others crawl out of the lattice, dusting themselves down. 'IT'S IN BUD!' I blurt, pointing as Danillo did; he's still staring at it mutely. We drop our bags and assess the situation. Pat, seeming to regain stamina from the dilemma, orders the men up and down the slope to find an open flower.

Five foresters tear through the forest like men possessed, and three dogs follow them. Four botanists watch their mission disintegrate, and one plant laughs at them. Its petals clench shut defiantly, overlapping in circles to form a smirk, with dimpled eyes – yes, it *wants* to withhold its secrets from us; that's blissfully clear to me now. We listen with bated breath to the foresters' calls echoing about the trees. If there is one *Rafflesia* bud there may be more. My heart pounds in my chest. Surely they will find an open flower.

They don't. Pat drops disconsolately against the ferny bank, looking defeated. I offer him water in the hope it might quell his acid reflux.

'Only beer will help me now,' he whimpers, which initially I take in jest, but he's not smiling.

A beam of light falls through the canopy and holds the bud for a moment, spotlighting the source of our trouble. Adriane stands watching it solemnly. I wander over to join him and brush my fingers over its leathern folds. *Why are you hiding from us?*

The pain is visceral. It stabs me like knives from my ankles up. Then I realize I'm standing in a colony of giant ants that have launched a raid up my legs and arms. Each is fearsomely large – about half the length of a small finger – and they seem to be doing forward-rolls in their efforts to bite me through my clothes. I smack them off in a frenzy then start hopping around the *Rafflesia* bud; the rest of the group watch curiously as if I'm performing some strange ritual dance around the plant.

Once I've mastered calm, and we've taken photographs and measurements of the bud in its habitat, we decide to break for lunch. The foresters make a clearing in the trees and light a fire to ward off biting insects. Then we share cold rice and *adobo* (pork stew) wrapped in tinfoil, which we eat with our hands, using pleated palm leaves for plates, as monkeys shake the trees above us. I offer 'wet wipes' (packets of cleansing tissue) from my bag that I was given on a former expedition to Japan and which seem remarkably evergreen (notwithstanding their questionable environmental credentials). The group seem mesmerized by these; we each sit wiping our arms and brows for several minutes. As the group chats in Tagalog through the smoke, I turn over a flat piece of sandstone through curiosity (half a life spent exploring rock pools has taught me that fascinating things live in such places); an astonishingly large worm appears. The snake-like creature has milk-and white-chocolate stripes that shimmer green like a peacock. It looks vaguely grotesque, even to a biologist. As if insulted by the thought, it begins sucking itself into the wet clay like spaghetti and vanishes.

On the return journey the forest takes on an intense green complexion and it's quieter in the wake of the rain. Weary failure enshrouds us. Pat pulls himself heavily through the wet moats of ferns and Adriane stares at the floor. Disappointment makes my feet heavier; I stumble over hunched roots and tripwire grass, mumbling words of embarrassment as I hold up the group behind me. I know it was there. I could almost feel it watching, mocking. I've got no proof – the foresters searched high and low for an open flower and found nothing; but still, I know it was there.

Then something conciliatory appears: a peace offering from the forest.

Fallen flowers the shape of doves spangle the floor. Ana scans the canopy, and points skyward, her cat's eyes shining brightly.

'Look,' she says in her soothing voice.

Above us hangs a jade vine we've not yet seen yet on the expedition, *Strongylodon elmeri*. Its colour is the same ethereal blue possessed by the jade vine we saw on Mount Makiling; only here the flowers have arranged themselves in concentric rings to form a perfect sphere. The chandelier is held by a long, cable-like tendril, which vanishes somewhere up in the leafy chaos. It glows like neon through the gloom, lighting the forest, and I swear – I *swear* – I've never seen anything so beautiful. I scramble up the steep grassy scarp to take a closer look, however it's hanging metres above our heads. I can't get to it, but I *must*. Ana points to a smaller specimen she'd spotted that's within easier reach. Frenzied now, I switch direction and haul myself up into the fork of a tree to get to it. I lean out of the eaves and pull the unearthly flowers towards me with an outstretched arm as the group looks on below. They appear vaguely concerned, as if I'm walking a tightrope, but I can't worry about that now. And *there*. For a glorious moment, I have it in my grasp, fragile as a bird. A ball of flowers that shines so brightly it almost leaves a trace of colour in its wake.

Like all held birds, it flees. I let go, and in a rush of leaves and twigs I fall through the sky. Down, down, down I go, brought back to earth with eight gasps and a *thump*. Later I will discover a bruise an equally impressive, if less beautiful, shade of blue.

By the time we reach the lodge, the clouds are blushing, and the river winks a hundred suns. We wade in, fully clothed. The silky surface belies the water's strength, and it pulls insistently, ballooning my trousers. Pat and Ana lather themselves and I face the other way in discretion, against the current. Pat feels better, he says, but he looks tired. Adriane is standing motionless and looks deep in thought, like he is solving a puzzle with his eyes. Perhaps, like me, they still see leafy chaos when they close their eyes. I look out over the watchful forest as the water pummels my legs, and think about its secrets; the fleeting curiosities that lurk there unseen. From a distance it looks so serene. *Benign.* I squint and see the trees release a man who starts to walk along the river's pebbly beach. He's carrying a giant palm leaf over his head. I wonder what it's for. People here know things I'll never know.

★★★

We rise before dawn, rousing ourselves with buckets of cold water in the dark. It's pouring with rain and the boots I left outside the lodge are sodden. I force them on and squelch my way to the tin hut to say goodbye to Max. Rain pours from the corrugated canopy in long lines; like fifty people pissing from the roof. With one eye still on the hills, Max tells me about the challenges of running the reserve. Water pools around my feet as I listen. He speaks of conflicts between indigenous tribes and people who live in the villages; of hardship; of guns. 'But they know how to care for the forest,' he says acceptingly. 'They take what they need, nothing more.' Back on the road, we pass a toothless man pulling a reluctant buffalo along the road by a thin cord. His face is as riven as the trees. Life looks hard.

We reach the Department of Environment and Natural Resources where we make plans for the next trek. I'm introduced to the lady in charge, called Mercy, who nods assuredly when Pat explains that I work at the University of Oxford Botanic Garden.

'Yes, yes, Oxford, USA,' she replies. She goes on to explain that to see *Rafflesia* here, we will need to travel by motorcycle for an hour to reach the forest; we will trek from there with a team of foresters.

She has lived here her whole life, and still she's never seen this species in flower.

Our riders have assembled by the side of the road, and stand leaning against their bikes. Flip-flops; no helmets. With the authority of a gym teacher, Mercy pairs up the five of us (herself included). I am assigned George, who is wearing a back-to-front baseball cap and a Colgate smile. As we clamber onto the bikes, I'm told to hold on tightly, as if our two bodies are one (unfortunate for George because I've not bathed properly in days). As we jolt along a rutted track, splashing through puddles, warm air washes over me like a balm. We reach a milky-brown stream that's too deep to cross, so we hop off and wade through as the riders grapple with their bikes, bumping and floating over the current.

We leave the bikes by a river hissing urgently over a stony flat. The riders metamorphose into foresters, preparing for the work ahead with bonhomie, adjusting one another's bags and fastening knives to their belts. On expeditions I've accompanied elsewhere in the world, we've worn military-style clothing and mosquito nets; here many of the riders and foresters simply wear shorts and T-shirts. They're intimate with the forest.

We march through a small coconut plantation in the damp heat. The trees are ubiquitous here; the Philippines is the second-largest producer of coconut in the world, after Indonesia. Sprouts are shooting up from the fallen shells between the widely spaced trees. At the end of the plantation, the forest rises above us like a black wall. I hear it whisper before we arrive. Irwin, the chief forester, leading the way, is slim, in his early thirties, and wears combat shorts and a blue T-shirt, with an XXL machete in a wooden case slung over his hip. He takes us along an obscure path reclaimed by nature, pausing every so often to assess a blockage, ducking under python-thick vines and slashing at vegetation. There are ten of us, but it's impossible to see more than one other person at any time because of the forest's density. Irwin stops occasionally with one arm leaning on a tree, and cries like an animal, waiting for the forester at the rear to echo his call.

Strange fungi appear in globules, goblets, antlers, and shells.

A farrago of them springs up all over the place from the entrails of the forest – rotting pockets, branches, stumps, and so on. A log straddling the track we must clamber over has issued a succession of discs, held palm-side up. They're the colour of honey, emblazoned with concentric black and white rings. They remind me of 'peacock's-tail' – a seaweed you often see when snorkelling, fanning out of the rock. An inestimable diversity of fungi exists in this forest, I'm sure of it.

We congregate by an unusual, glossy-leafed *Medinilla* sprouting at eye level from the fork of a tree. The beetroot-pink flowers have outgrown their lolling stalk. None of us can assign the plant a name.

'Probably new,' Pat says nodding once.

It isn't new to science, we discover later, but it is rare. We head deeper into the forest, through deeply cut moats with mossed walls rising steeply, crossing sandy streams, and sloshing into muddy ditches. A bird whistles, sounding uncannily like a person.

We rest periodically to wait for one another or admire the view. Irwin lights a cigarette and the pair of us gaze through a gap in the trees over a wild gulf of forest folding into dove-grey clouds. A fire-crackle above us precedes an almighty snap, and then an enormous branch drops from the canopy, an arm's length from our heads. It falls like a thunderbolt through a storm of leaves. Irwin and I look at one another in consternation; had it struck our heads, I think it might have killed us.

The track vanishes in a gallery of trees. Irwin and his co-pilot hack a tunnel through the mesh, balancing themselves using the poles of *Angiopteris* ferns holding up fronds the size of house roofs. It's cooler up here, wherever we may be, for all views have vanished – but the trek feels more demanding. Vegetation covers every dimension, blotting out earth and sky, disorienting us in a green blur.

In the forest, there is no path.

We cut across a shallow stream that mirrors a ribbon of sky but not quite; arching branches try to conceal it. Irwin tells me he hears a hornbill; he cranes his head as if he is listening to it call from the earth. I can just discern the cadence above the layers of sound: a sort of scream, broken like laughter. I think I heard this yesterday too, but I didn't know what it was then. I feel better for knowing; like I'm learning the forest's language, becoming more connected to the place.

'It's somewhere around here,' Irwin then says vaguely to the floor, scanning left and right. Vines loop in and out of the earth like serpents. I know he means *Rafflesia*. What else could compel ten people to ride and trek for hours, through terrain like this, in the punishing heat?

Buds.

This time they're not even close to opening; the largest are only the size of tennis balls. Dozens of them are bubbling up from the floor among the pencil-thick vines crawling in and out of the leaf litter. I crouch to examine them. They're so young the petals are still concealed by shiny black bracts; just one seems to be glinting red like burning coal. It looks charged, potent.

'Where are their leaves, Sir?' Irwin asks earnestly, crouching beside me, peering at the ground. I explain that they don't need them.

'They're thieves, you see,' I tell him. 'They steal their food from this vine – this one, here.'

He nods slowly with his eyes still fixed to the floor, then casually stands to light a cigarette. He sends a long blue plume up into the trees. The others catch up, their satiny clothes clinging wetly from the many rivers we've crossed to get here.

'Well?' Pat whispers, his eyebrows raised in question.

I shake my head. 'Not today, Pat,' I say. 'Not today.'

We shuffle around the shrine of buds in an arc. Those closest crouch to stroke them, look along the vines and then up into the trees, as if making a plea to the forest. No one says much. Then Mercy takes command of the situation, snapping us out of our confoundment, ushering us in different directions. We fan out, surveying the leaf litter like a forensics squad. But it's no use; I already know that. There are no flowers to be found here. They're not ready to disclose their secrets to us yet. I understand that now, and for the first time in days, I feel something unfamiliar, almost like calm. I'm starting to think like the forest.

★★★

The river washes away the dregs of disappointment. In a line, we spider over slimy rocks, through the plunge pools, then up the grassy bank the other side. The foresters know an old man who lives in the trees who'll prepare a meal for us here.

Rudy is sixty-four years of age, he tells me, 'But this?' he says pointing to his groin. 'This is twenty-four. Still strong.' Then he laughs violently. He cuts open a coconut for me to drink; it's refreshing.

'Does England have coconut trees?' he asks me. 'No, then what about bananas?'

'No rivers, either?' he continues, gesturing to the gentle *hish* of the water we can hear behind us.

'We have those,' I assure him, relieved to find common ground.

'I am sixty-four,' he repeats, 'and every day I bathe in the river and drink one of these [pointing to the coconut] before taking my morning coffee.' He nods proudly.

I notice a row of children watching us from a glassless window at the top of the wooden hut. The stragglers of the group appear with armfuls of branches, including the probably new *Medinilla*, and sit wearily on the tree stumps scattered among the piles of coconuts. Pleasant smells emanate from the open-fronted hut, where Rudy's wife and three other women stand stirring bowls on a long wooden table. I'm invited to eat banana mixed with coconut, salt, and river water; a simple dish, but delicious. Then we're given bowls of pork with vegetables. The meat is fattier than I'm used to; there's usually a dog at hand to help me out of a situation such as this, but I can't see one. I do my best to chew and swallow as much as I can so as not to appear rude. Rudy entertains us as we eat.

'I made this,' he says, lifting a baseball cap from its hat stand. I'm confused because the hat is branded and clearly not handcrafted, then I realize he is referring to the wooden hat stand. It is a large erect penis, chiselled to perfection. We share coffee from a thermos and I ask Pat how he is feeling today.

'My gut is not so good still, Chris,' he laments. I ask if there is anything I can do to help.

'No, no,' he says forlornly. 'What I need now is an enormous burp.'

Before we leave, Rudy asks if he can have his photograph taken with the American.

***

George seems more comfortable talking on the way back. We shout over the roar of the bike and the breeze, pausing our conversation to cross a stream, then picking up where we left off. 'Life is simple here,' he tells me. 'It's just farming, eating, farming, and eating.'

We pass ever-changing stripes of earth and plant, red splashed green; a woman pouring a blue plastic bowl of water out of the front door; a cat with a smashed face.

'My parents ran a fruit stall when I was a kid. We were hard up.' He continues. 'My brothers and I would climb the trees in our neighbour's yard to steal mangoes,' he laughs. 'We got caught once and the guy chased us through the trees.'

His hair blows back into my face and our clothes ripple in the breeze. 'But life is hard as a forester. Tree poachers threaten to kill you all the time. But I'm used to that now. Anyway. It's my job.'

I feel guilty that privately I'd felt slightly envious of these men's uncomplicated lives in the trees. They experience hardships I can't comprehend, I know that now. I cover the silence by telling George that much of my work is spent in front of a computer; that it's not just spent travelling the globe, looking at plants. He laughs politely.

Kuya Mande is waiting with the vehicle by the roadside. I feel a weightlessness on dismounting from the motorcycle, as if the world has stilled. As we say our thanks and goodbyes to Mercy and her foresters, I feel a slight heaviness around my throat. I realize I've become attached to these people in a short space of time.

'Come back,' Mercy says simply.

We change our clothes at a roadside shack, taking it in turns to use the windowless room full of sacks and boxes. An old woman with a face like tree bark sits with her granddaughter across the road, watching us troop back and forth to the van. She calls me over in broken English, gives me a searching look, then asks me to guess her age.

She looks a hundred.

'Sixty,' I say.

'Eighty-five,' she barters.

I raise my eyebrows in polite astonishment.

'Happiness is the key to eternal youth,' she concludes, nodding. Then she orders her granddaughter to take a photograph of me sitting with her. I swap seats with the girl and put my arm around the old lady's shoulder.

'I'll never forget the day the foreigner came to visit,' she says shaking her head. 'Never forget it.'

10.

Today I rescue big lizard from forest. Forest burns but I sit with him, pay him attention. Later I take him to his new home, on bike. Take him to Bengkulu Selatan – special forest where he be happy. Fifteen hours it will take me.

II.

Time marches on. The vines, my creeping domicile, inch their way up into the canopy then scatter their leaves back down onto the earth. They grow and I grow with them, like thoughts along a nerve. Together we listen to the rain drumming the pipework every afternoon. But it'll take more than rain to lure me out. I'll wait a little longer. Even a thief can't steal time.

12.

There are several ways I might die here.

I drag myself through a tunnel of vines leading deeper into the abyss. It's so narrow, I can't even see behind me. Sharp smells fill my nostrils: sap, the reek of my own sweat, and something else – I don't know what. My rucksack snags the roof of the passage, and as I try to yank it free, the earth angles up to my chin with a jolt. I couldn't turn back if I wanted to: the die is cast. A few metres ahead, Kuya Missan, of the Banao Tribe, slashes a way through the trees and, blindly, I follow him. Fragments of leaf and stem leave a broken trail in the wake of his machete. A vengeful creeper fights back, lashing my face, marking me.

As I was saying: several ways I might die. A Philippine cobra, capable of accurately spitting one of the most toxic venoms of all cobras at a target three metres away, is one. An antivenin exists for this snake; still, I don't fancy my chances of getting that here. The Philippine pit viper – a tree-dwelling serpent, so well-camouflaged you might miss it but for its bloodshot eyes – is another. No antivenin for that, no, it would just knock me flat.

Or, more likely than a deadly snakebite, I might simply turn left instead of right: take a wrong turn, then disappear into the green. And who would find me? In a place so remote, no one's bothered putting it on the map? A place where you'd be buried in leaves within days, crept over by vines, then sucked into the underworld without trace. Like a crime scene.

Several ways to die, but it'll all be worth it, if we're successful. It is what I want. It is *all* I want. To find the unfindable.

As you know, *Rafflesia* has possessed me, and taken a part of my spirit.

Might it take a life?

★★★

It began with a change in the wind. I lay awake listening to it rattling the shutters, flinging rain at the roof like fingers clattering a keyboard. *Ratta-tat-tat-tat*. The whisper of a storm, the start of a crescendo. That's how the real adventure began.

By the time we got up bleary-eyed in the dark, it was raining so hard it looked as though the water was shooting up from the ground. It rains like this here in Southeast Asia sometimes. Now Adriane and I are sitting quietly among the boxes of supplies in the hallway of Tita Rose's house, where we've been staying the last few days. We watch the rain through the open doorway, and listen to it hiss. We stare at the unbroken glassy columns, gilded by electric light, exploding like firecrackers over the threshold and pooling out onto the tiles.

Kuya Mande arrives a little after 4 a.m. with a towel wrapped around his head, and we plash our way over to his blue van, hurling boxes into the back by street light in a wet panic. Then we clamber into the vehicle, slam shut the sliding door behind us, and shake the rain from our hair like wild dogs. Kuya Mande stops down the road in Los Baños to pick up Pat, then Ana, and the five of us set off into the night. I hope we haven't forgotten anything. Because, as I said: where we're heading, that could mean life or death.

By dawn, the artillery-fire rain on the roof of the van subsides to fitful gusts, and out of the wet blur comes into focus a stereoscope of blue-faded billboards. Attractive people announce austere things with glee: self-control, and 'anti-sexy clothing', for example. I've given up trying to make sense of all this. Hastily clad shanty towns overhang the road, and under a distant concertina of grey hills: the sea. The humid sun casts a pink stillness over the dimpled water like a spell.

We stop at a service station outside Manila for breakfast. It smells of rain, petrol, and chip fat. We slip into a crowd of people with blue and white face coverings. The five of us stand staring up at illuminated photos of platters on the wall above. I ask Ana which might be the least oily option.

'That one,' she says squinting, pointing to a picture of a bowl of noodle soup.

A large wooden bowl arrives with a raw-looking ball of floating dough. We carry our food on plastic brown trays to the table. As we arrange ourselves and do away with face coverings, Pat gives Adriane a friendly clap on the back, like a father would his son. We eat hungrily. I ask Pat how long the drive north to Kalinga will take.

'Twenty hours,' he says, flicking his eyes up briefly to the ceiling, and chuckling in a way that wiggles his ears.

I take this absurdly long forecast in gest, on account of his laughter, but then I realize from the others' faces that he isn't joking. However, I'm oddly reassured by the long journey. The expedition has been intense and I need time to think.

Back on the road we pass mile upon mile of motorway and fields – really it could be anywhere. But after a few hours, the city gives way to roadside villages teeming with people, and beyond them, brilliant paddy fields that step into the sky; we're back in Southeast Asia. I see a fisherman cast his net across a muddy stream. He's wearing a red, broad-brimmed hat, and sits staring intently at the water. I wonder what worries him.

At the edge of a village, a gang of military policemen wave us down. I slink into my seat in anticipation (foreigners attract unwanted attention here), but Pat tells Kuya Mande to ignore them. Kuya Mande accelerates, leaving the policemen running after us along the road, waving angrily. From a distance they remind me of those ants we found patrolling the Land Grant, but I keep this to myself.

Next we pass a funeral procession, although at first I don't realize it's this. An ordinary-looking silver car sprinkled with white flowers precedes a crowd of about seventy people wearing colourful shorts, T-shirts, and flip-flops. Some have formed breakout groups who walk together, chatting, while a sand-coloured dog trots in step, looking sideways at them. I hear lively music too – from where I am unsure – and someone is blowing a whistle repeatedly, but the procession continues. It is so unlike the solemnities of a funeral back home; so perversely full of life. How different things are here.

An arc of camel-brown hills dissects the land from the sky. The hills here are denuded of life; I could be in the Sierra Nevada. One or two lonely trees weave skyward out of the bankrupt land; the trees remember a forest here, not so long ago. Before I was born, for sure, but just a heartbeat ago in geological time. Millions of years in the making, gone in a trice.

The Philippines hold about 5 per cent of the world's plant species – extraordinary given the land area of 300,000 square kilometres.[19] Like some coral reefs, great tracts were smashed up then burnt to the ground, and countless species were lost before we even knew they existed. I feel faintly sick as I look out over the barren hills – mile upon mile of them – and I ask Pat what happened here, casually, covering my anxiety.

'A century ago, rainforests covered most of the Philippines. Most of it has gone, and only a fraction of what remains is original, old-growth forest.' Pat says this still looking ahead, without emotion.

The 7,100 islands that make up the Philippines were partially, if not wholly, covered with forest at the start of the twentieth century. Between 1903 and 2001, 16 million hectares of forest burned to the ground,[20] and with them went an inestimable loss of life. Today, less than 10 per cent of the original forests are left standing.[21] Chilling figures roll off his tongue, desensitized from decades spent teaching hopeful new generations of foresters. Since this wholesale deforestation, the ecological consequences have been dire: drought, accelerated soil erosion, and massive flooding of low-lying regions. Most of the remaining forests are defined as secondary forests – those that regenerated after the original trees fell like dominoes; they appear intact, but they retain a human fingerprint. They never fully recover.

I was dimly aware of the scale of deforestation here, but seeing it with my own eyes is violently different. As I look out over the bald hills, I imagine horrors: can see people cutting the trees down in front of me – can hear the chainsaws, smell the smoke. Like in a nightmare, I shout at them to stop; to tell them that what they're doing – what *we're* doing – is irreversible. How easily things could have been different. Decades later, I, like you, am their judge. Just as future generations will be ours.

Now there is that new, less perceptible, but all-pervading threat of climate change looming in the sky. Adriane told me earlier about vast tracts of forests he's seen here in Luzon, devastated by fire; something on a scale not seen here before. Not even close. Biodiversity in free fall in one of the world's most species-rich places. Yes, nature has been either erased without apology, or pushed to one side – shunted into reserves, protected areas, and so on. We've become purblind to the devastation. The so-called 'shifting baseline syndrome' describes how, over time, knowledge is lost about the state of the natural world, because people don't perceive the changes that are taking place. Our perceptions are out of kilter with the reality because of a generational amnesia.[22] We're each of us born into a world gone wrong, but it's the only world we've known.

The Philippines is the centre of diversity for the world's *Rafflesia*: more species occur on this sprinkling of islands than anywhere else. Most of them occur on mountains. I've long considered this to be of some obscure ecological importance. But now I wonder if it is just an artefact of the near-annihilation of lowland forests. How many *Rafflesia* species were lost without anyone even knowing they existed?

My mind turns to Deki's beloved forests in Indonesia, and his desperation to save *Rafflesia*. For his grandchildren, he says, but what about beyond them? Is our innate inability to see beyond two generations part of the problem? Man's big strategic plan with no vision. Borrow now, pay later.

I don't know. Perhaps *Rafflesia* playing God with my life – ushering me over continents, dragging me slavishly through forests and driving me to my knees – goes beyond one man's need to find something extraordinary and tell the world. Perhaps this is a calling: to help save *Rafflesia* while there is still time?

The brown conveyor belt continues, hour after hour. At first I stare at the gaunt hills with a sort of morbid fascination – almost a sick pleasure I can't explain; like scratching an insect bite until it bleeds. But then, as we drive past mile after brown mile of the naked hills, I close my eyes and shut it out. Just as we all do. Just as we always have.

Adriane creeps up from the back of the vehicle and sits beside me, jolting me out of my funk. We compare notes we've written during the expedition, like kids matching homework. Every field botanist keeps a diary of one sort or another – captures the world in plants. Adriane's contains neat, closely written blocks of text with little clouds of numbers annotating intricate diagrams. Although I pride myself on neatness in most compartments of my life, my diary tells a different story. Scribbled leaves, unmoored from the margins, sprawl across the page and fight for space with the text. The text, too, is impulsive. Buried in cerebral botanical language (tomentose, strigose, serrate, and so on) hide written portraits of the people we encounter: actors they remind me of, tropes, accents, impersonations – that sort of thing. Adriane flicks through the pages slowly, apparently missing these, but pauses when he spots a cartoon *Rafflesia* bud smirking back at him.

'Do you think we'll find an open one this time?' I ask.

'Yes,' he replies presciently, not looking up, in a voice as clear and bright as glass. Now, pictures of the flower crowd in on me. Absurdly large cabbage-like buds unfurl heavily behind my eyes, moving, glowing, as if powered by supernatural forces. But I hold my excitement away from me. When something means that much to you, it isn't safe to indulge it, I know.

We stop at a roadside café for lunch, parking under the canopy of a large, exotic-looking tree. Opposite the café, desert-brown hills fold and repeat over the horizon. Inside, a long table is piled high with a diversity of fruits, milkshakes, rice, and stews, all arranged on a jigsaw of tropical foliage. We order papaya milkshakes and various forms of stew. I congratulate myself for choosing a vegetarian option, only to realize upon finishing it that what I mistook for gherkins was tripe.

Over lunch we discuss the journey – how many hours ago we set off, and the work still in store. Adriane stirs his milkshake with his straw for some time without drinking while I leaf through the various brochures, fliers, and booklets that are scattered across the table, all written in Tagalog. I can barely decipher any of them but for some reason my eye is drawn to a page depicting a forest, upon which are inscribed the words *Lahat ng gubat ay may ahas* in disquieting red font. I peer at the curious, harsh-looking script on the page and look to Adriane for the answer. A line forms between his eyes as he looks at me and says, 'In every forest there is a snake.'

Twelve hours into the journey, the worn-out hills give way to patches of green – vestiges of a former forest. On the horizon, a jagged blue wall of mountains rises like a kingdom in the clouds. The hills on either side of the road are green, but even here they've been mostly scraped of trees. We pass two old ladies walking hand in hand along the road, one with a brimmed hat, the other with an orange and white towel on her head. Next we see an old man with a seamed face, sitting on a riverbank beside the road. He looks pre-occupied as he pokes the water slowly with a long stick. A row of dangling, strange-looking fish have been strung up about the branches behind him. As we drive past I realize they are in fact dead frogs, pegged up like socks.

I stare vacantly at a dazzling reef of cloud that forms a purple negative image when I blink. I am tired, almost to the point of delusional, it seems. Maybe it's the antimalarial tablets, I don't know. Look, I'm a logical person. I like facts, *science*, patterns in the flow. But these last few days, my thought processes have been knocked. Don't laugh but of all the things I possess here, which are few, the most precious to me in this moment is a towel we bought at a roadside street market yesterday (there are no towels where we are heading). A soft grey one – polyester I think. I can't for the life of me explain why, but wrapping it around me on the journey brings inordinate comfort. Children develop strong attachments to blankets and towels, so perhaps this is some sort of age regression induced by sleeplessness? I once read that Sigmund Freud considered age regression to be an unconscious defence mechanism to ward off trauma. Perhaps it's that.

I must have nodded off. It is 5.30 p.m., according to my phone, and as I rouse the sun is setting behind the ragged banana leaves. Cars and people have vanished and the character of the land has changed too – large clumps of grasses are spraying out onto the road; it's wilder here. Pat turns when he realizes I have come to, and tells me that we will need to stop overnight at the next town, Tabuk.

'The roads to the forest are *too* bad to cross at night,' he says emphatically, wagging an admonishing finger at the darkening road. '*Too* dangerous.'

We spend the night at the office of the Department of Environment and Natural Resources after Adriane has made the pleading arrangements on his phone. The lady he speaks with tells him that the Banao Tribe (the indigenous community with whom we'll be staying) was expecting us this evening, and they have prepared food especially; but this cannot be helped.

We park the van outside a blocky, municipal building and make our way wearily up a concrete stairway where aimless insects drift through the electric light like lost souls. Inside, a long wooden table has been set with hands of miniature bananas, a great pyramid of rice, and a cauldron of *adobo*. The turquoise walls are plastered with vague commands such as 'Reuse scrap!' and 'Make a change!'

I'm introduced to a small lady with a high, sighing voice, and a middle-aged man with an anxious face. '*Sir!*' the lady exclaims repeatedly (with emphasis on the *r*), recognizing Pat from his last visit over a decade ago, she says. Then she tells me I will be the first foreigner ever to set foot in the Balbalasang–Balbalan (the forest that is our destination in Kalinga). With a keen look, she asks me where I'm from. She and the man seem surprised to learn I'm British. They peer at me with curiosity, seemingly fascinated by my beard. Perhaps they don't think I look like a botanist, that I don't fit the template. Or, perhaps, it is indeed because I am perfectly foreign.

Pat sends Adriane out with a lad (who seems to appear from

nowhere) to buy beer (which seems always to appear from some-where), while the rest of us pull up mushroom-coloured plastic chairs around the table.

'He is too anxious,' Pat says, shaking his head then resting a hand on the table. I know he is referring to Adriane.

'When he's not looking,' he says, turning his head left and right to look at invisible spies, 'I put brandy in his coffee.' Then he nods, looking at each of us with raised eyebrows. We laugh and vow not to disclose this secret to Adriane.

Adriane and the lad return with a box of twenty-five bottles of beer and a berg of ice that has to be smashed against the wall.

'Balbalasang–Balbalan has not been botanized,' Pat announces with a beam that waggles his ears slightly. 'Just about everything you will see there will be new.' He sits back, nodding like a Buddha as I take this in.

Everything new. Words so potent, they charge the air. I can't believe I am going to this place. Really I can't. We've talked about trekking Kalinga's wildest forests for so long, written permits, planned outrageous adventures and then cancelled them because of the pandemic – it doesn't feel real to me. Adriane snaps opens another beer; he does this each time I've not quite finished a bottle, under Pat's watchful tutelage. Combined with the excitement it makes a heady confection. Dizzy.

Conversation turns to the Banao Tribe. We talk about the tribe's exemplary forest-management practices. Every time a tree is felled, I'm told, a tribal elder's permission must first be sought; then, 100 new saplings must be planted in its place. So sagacious. So *simple*! A rare example of kindness to the land.

We sleep on the floor, fully clothed, in the sticky heat. Only, despite my exhaustion, I cannot sleep. My senses swarm: Kuya Mande snoring fitfully; crickets chanting softly through an open door to the stars; and a procession of images dancing through my mind. I think of the endless ranks of deforested hills we passed on the journey here – the unspeakable devastation. Then I try to picture the *everything-new* forests of Balbalasang–Balbalan. A wild place where nature's greatest works form unseen. I find *Rafflesia* blooming there in my mind's eye, like a premonition.

But a man who has never set foot in a place like that can never truly understand it, picture it properly – he just sees what he already knows. Visions are like memories: half-invented. The reality is beyond imagination. He cannot fight like an animal, hate and love like a madman, and go to heaven and hell and back, for something he's only dreamed of.

Later I'll learn that. Once I've gone into the abyss.

***

Our alarms sound at 4 a.m., just an hour after I drifted off. I feel anaesthetized and faintly nauseous with fatigue. We take it in turns to wash with a bucket of cold water, then move about slowly and robotically, organizing our supplies and quietly fussing over this and that. Adriane and I crouch beside the box containing the sample tubes, labelling and apportioning them to rucksacks. Ana sits staring through the open door at nothing; she looks as tired as I am.

We leave under an ink sky. The moon breathes light over the tree-tops and the land feels sentient, watchful. Wild packs of dogs trot aimlessly through the night, their eyes glowing in the headlights. They look like wolves. For all I know, they could be.

The new sun burns red through a V in the land, like a rising phoenix. Pinnacles of dreamland form along the skyline: mountain silhouettes on a bed of glowing cloud. I see a farmer standing, staring at the spectacle. I wonder if he does this every day.

An ugly metal bridge crosses the Chico River, which forks into a complicated labyrinth of streams weaving around little islands strewn with blond grass and shingle. Into the grey and yellow marbled ravine bed, forested hills drop steeply. And beyond this, autumnal-looking honeyed light creeps down the hills.

Up and up. We dip into dark, wet thickets where large branches draped in assorted ferns form forests within forests. Wild torrents pour over ramparts of mossed rock, splashing onto the road like burst pipes. Brilliant ferns spatter the rusted earth along the bank.

Above us to our left, softly forested mountain walls become half-swallowed by cloud, and to our right, the land falls into the air.

After a steep rise, we become lost in mist, like white noise, and the view vanishes. When it reappears, we gasp in astonishment at the beauty: a procession of mythic peaks, each rising higher than the last, marching up the horizon. Their Euclidean forms seem not quite real. The sun – now a gleaming orb in the translucent blue sky – glances over their soaring peaks, and pours light down the near-vertical hillsides. Each fold of mountain shades the next like a row of parasols, while silver-edged clouds cast sharp shadows on the unbroken walls of forest. Kuya Mande stares immutably forward, while Pat, Ana, Adriane, and I all gaze 90 degrees to the right, in synchrony, each of us spellbound by what looks back at us. 'Kalinga,' Adriane says absolutely, with his rare seraphic smile. And at last I understand.

Something has changed in me here in the Philippines – taken a hold – bedded deeper on each excursion we've made, heading into the unknown. First, *Rafflesia panchoana*, glowing in the dark halls of the forest on Mount Makiling, lighting the way like a star. A small miracle; a harbinger. Then *R. banahawensis* on the sacred Mount Banahaw, and *R. leonardi*, deep in the heart of the Sierra Madre. That cruel passage of pain and possibility, of *aching* to see flowers – one that led only to hard-clenched buds, like false promises. Like fists.

Yes, something deep inside me – hidden, growing, like a parasite; feeding on premonitions and ungranted wishes. And now, there's an even bigger promise at stake: the votive *Rafflesia banaoana* – possessing the largest flowers of all Luzon and one of the largest in the world – seen by almost no one.

God, I must see it – not to see it after all we've endured is unthinkable! An obsession is growing inside me like a tumour. Making me thin. Making me sick. I feel that wild hope rise inside me again, and I have to breathe deeply to hold it down.

Of course feelings like that can only be held back for so long.

★★★

Kalinga is absurdly different, like another country. I wrap my towel around me and watch us inch forward in space and back in time. No telegraph poles, wires, or petrol stations. Even the ubiquitous politicians smiling down from posters haven't made it up here. Just wild hills, valleys, and endless acres of green. Nature in charge.

I forget what day it is. Monday, I think. I wonder what events are unfolding outside these forests, in the other realm. Half a world away people will be setting their alarms ahead of the working week. In a world where tides rise and fall, where countless millions of online messages are sent every minute, where 250 babies have been born since you started reading this page. And another species will be lost before you finish it.

Yes, we set off for Kalinga on Saturday so today must be Monday. Anyway, time moves differently here, as I've said.

Three great clouds kneel like sultans over the peaks. Sagging shacks appear, flung about the hillside, half eaten by trees. Glimpses of Arcadian existence flicker in the green: chickens peeping around buckets and stumps of wood; then a man bent double, putting something on the ground – I can't see what – scattering the brood. Children trying hard to look at me through the glass. Parents trying hard not to. Small boys hunching around something with sticks. Remarkable unremarkable lives.

We stop to stretch our legs at a bakery of sorts. It is a small, dark shop, stacked high with old baskets – it looks more like an apothecary. We buy a box of a dozen doughnuts (I wasn't expecting to find these here). Adriane drops the box and half the contents end up in the jaws of a wolf-dog. While the others relieve themselves in the trees, I stand and gaze at the hills. Stacked paddy fields, as smooth and green as billiard tables, march up a blue forested wall, under a quilt of brilliant-edged cloud that sears my eyes.

We continue past a string of villages where sheds, planted cacti, palms, and people all jostle for position. Every now and again we cross a river – tributaries of the Chico, I think. Cliffs drop vertically to the water's edge, and even these are covered in an unbroken, dripping green mantle. Round and up, round and up we go, in a dizzy green blur. Prehistoric tree ferns unfurl like great fans of coral beneath the road; and above them on a steep bank fall reeds and fronds, outstretched like hands, greeting us like crowds cheering on runners in a race: reassuring us that we're almost there.

We make four wrong turns. To be more precise, we drive up and down the same track four times. Adriane (who undertook an expedition to the Balbalasang–Balbalan just a few weeks ago) can't quite remember the way; Pat hasn't been for a decade, and the rest of us are none the wiser. A line forms between Adriane's eyes as he tries to remember, but Pat is patient with him, like a father. Half an hour later, we park next to a broad stony stream overlooked by a concrete viewing tower, and this is the spot, I'm told: this is where we need to be. We've cut ties with the modern world now. Two days' drive and two centuries from the present.

So, Balbalasang–Balbalan: we've arrived.

***

Pat and Kuya Mande stand in duplicate, each with his right arm resting on the low wall, looking out over the trees, saying nothing. Until now I hadn't realized how similar they are in stature. Ana and Adriane crouch on the wall and take photographs on their phones. I know these people well now, I feel. We've trekked, bathed, and slept together; snapped at, cheered, and encouraged each other – cohabited a sliver of suspended life.

Adriane hops down a steep, rough path to meet the tribe.

Balbalasang–Balbalan is a protected area known as the 'green heart of the Cordillera'. The Cordillera, spanning 20,000 square kilometres, is the Philippines' least populous region, and the protected forests we are gazing over – its nucleus – are sparser still. Almost no one lives here.

It isn't quite as I expected, but is anything ever? Awkward pines scatter the land, giving it a dry, temperate feel quite distinct from the steamy lowland forests we've trekked thus far. An urgent stream spills out over pebbly banks, shelved like a shingle beach with strong tides. A makeshift bridge of five bamboo poles has been slung across it and leads to an overlapping series of huts with steeply pitched roofs, vaguely reminiscent of Japanese Minka houses. In front, a woman dressed in black, with intoed feet, stands staring at the water.

Presently Adriane returns with three men, each with crow-black hair. They help us unload our supplies from the rear of the van, carrying the boxes on their heads with well-muscled brown arms. We cross the rickety bridge (which on closer inspection has half-collapsed), the tribesmen with confidence, and the guests with spread-eagled arms. I watch them with interest; I've never stayed with a tribe before. The men carry the boxes into the hut and we pile our things in one corner. Here we're introduced to three women (one of whom I saw standing by the water), who are busy preparing lunch. They nod shyly as we introduce ourselves. Gentle people.

I wander outside where two men stand chopping wood. A smiling yellow dog regards me, then yawns and stretches, resuming nothing. Fresh, sharp pine-like smells and a silvery light fill the air. These, together with the stop-start drone of a bee, call forth a half-remembered spring – from my childhood, perhaps, I'm unsure. It feels calm and welcoming; that I do know.

Lunch is chicken with mango, with rice in a broth, which we eat with scooped hands from a big vat on a wooden table. As we eat, I'm told that if we leave soon, we may have time to visit the forest and return before sunset. There's a chance we may see *Rafflesia*.

After lunch we change into our field clothes. Adriane and I change silently and with care, like soldiers. I notice my figure looks even sparer, and a grey bruise is blooming across my thigh from my mis-adventure down a tree in the Sierra Madre. I sort through bottles of insect repellent, water, sample tubes, painkillers, and so on, pushing them all into the various pockets and compartments of my clothes and bag. I concentrate hard on these things, distracting myself from the vague foreknowledge that things are about to get tough. Safety in details.

As the others continue with the necessary preparations to leave the human realm, I clamber down to a wilder stretch of the stream we crossed earlier and wait. Reeds and over-sized ferns arch luxuriantly over a colossal boulder, bathing in the spray. A dove-like bird flicks between the fronds. The water at my feet is as clear as glass – surprisingly cool – and broken in places by little falls that frill around the chalky rocks. Its course curves around a reef of trees, pivots left, then tumbles furiously out of sight. I hop over the rocks and stand in the middle, watching it vanish.

As I stare at the wild water piercing the unknown, I ponder on how tired and wretched I've become here in this tropical wilderness, so far removed from my comfortable life in Oxford. How far we've drifted from safety. We're about to step off the map, into a phantom forest ruled by snakes, spiders, and tropical diseases. It'll all be worth it if we're successful. If we find it.

But *if* is a risky little word on which to gamble your life.

13.

Gambling, stealing, and murder – it all goes on in the forest. You'll see. Ecology is just another word for society: the complicated sum of life forging ahead, living by the law of nature. Following the rules.

Or breaking them.

Like a society, the forest has its scourges: deep-running rot, poverty, and disease. Recast by selection, we – the parts of that sum – fight to survive. Steadily we put down roots, invest in real estate – leaves, branches, and so on, and earn our place in the sun. Adapt and proliferate, in the face of ever-changing opposition. Let the stealthiest win.

Like people we have our personalities, too: ambitious, stop-at-nothing vines, snake-like tendrils, violent thorns, and hidden poisons. Flamboyant and plain, bitter and sweet – the lot. All co-existing sweetly with a smile. Frozen in time. *Your* time. But turn days into hours and you – plant-blind as you are – would see a savage garden unfold before you, struggling, lashing, and trampling to get by.

In every forest there is a snake. In every society there is a thief. (That's me, by the way.)

They say you get what you pay for in life, they who make the rules. But they're wrong because thieves don't pay a dime. Like all thieves I go under the radar, undetected. I don't make my own food. Hell no, I *steal* it. I'm not sorry. It's a redistribution of wealth around the forest, robbing the rich to feed the poor. I abandoned leaves and stems; no roots either – left all that behind me millions of years ago. Now I creep about inside the vines, down in the bowels of their pipework. The floor plan is hard-wired into my genetics, pre-determined, taking me up and down the plumbing.

Through the vines I pick up forest gossip, secrets from the underworld. Volatile organic chemicals, electrical signals – even the occasional gene, gone walkabouts. Vapours and traces. The forest whispers to me.

And I listen.

14.

We hear the forest's call and we follow it: four tribesmen, Adriane, Pat, Ana, and I, file into the hissing wilderness. Into the hands of fictional mapmakers.

With silent resolve we march into brilliant grasses and over a long bamboo bridge we cross with arms widespread and eyes fixed to the ground. The tribesmen are clad in khaki and gumboots. I am wearing high-street waterproofs and a white Adidas sweatband. I was aiming for intrepid but, seeing myself as they see me, I might be dressed for a game of tennis.

Stewed, leafy smells fill the heavy air. We clamber up whale-like boulders, and down into a ferny ditch dissecting a paddy field. We splash along this for half a mile. On a clayey bank, we pause to photograph an orchid with luminous pink flowers dancing along a dead-looking stem, and then another lycophyte – this one a min-iature Christmas tree with spore-giving cones for candles. I cannot name either species; nor can any of us.

'Probably new,' mutters Pat, regarding the lycophyte briefly.

We reach a fern prairie set about with enormous, rusty boulders devoid of moss. They look oddly sterile in this place where life co-exists in layers. The place calls to mind *The Lost World*, dinosaur territory. Like a human caterpillar, spacing apart then regrouping, we bore deeper into the quivering green, clocking several more probably new plants along the way. We cut across several streams that seem to run both backwards and forwards in this fathomless place without rules. Brown, silver, blue, green. Domes and prisms, all softly forested, and not a human mark in sight. Then I see it scrawled over the horizon in black: the forest, the line. Daring me to cross it.

At first it flickers in and out of view as we sink into a liminal, marshy place, then it looms immutably like a storm-drawn cloud. Humid light strikes a mossed-over branch, spotlighting another orchid, this one flowerless. It's clasping a pseudobulb – a wrinkled, pod-like structure it uses to store runoff rainwater that will pay off in later life. A pension. It clings defiantly, loyal to its branch; ignoring whatever the elements fling at it (which is a lot out here, I should think). Forest elder, a stalwart.

Adriane spots an orange-flowered mistletoe sparkling out of a tree. We squint at the branches, metres above our heads. Unannounced, one of the tribesmen, Kuya Missan, sprints barefoot up the canted trunk with ease, then monkeys along the branches. Like a tree frog he clamps his feet to the limb containing the mistletoe – now leaning with his weight – then reaches for the knife buckled to his waist. He slashes off a large bundle which falls with a short hiss and a thwack. As he clambers back down, we stand in a circle and peer at the curious fascicles of orange, dart-shaped flowers. No one can name it (later we dissect the flowers and christen it *Amyema acuta* – an endemic of Luzon), so we cart it off for the herbarium in Los Baños. Mistletoes, such as the one we're examining, are hemi-parasites; that is to say, they are *partially* parasitic. Like *Rafflesia*, they steal food from other plants, but in mistletoe's case, they do manufacture at least some of their own: they possess green leaves, chlorophyll. From the standpoint of an evolutionary biologist, they straddle the line between wholesome existence – earning a living through photosynthesis – and a life of crime: holo-parasitism (holo- meaning wholly). Some hemi-parasites do at least compensate for their profligacy. Yellow rattle, a plant that is common in European meadows, has been described as an ecosystem engineer: it steals food preferentially from the roots of grasses, suppressing their dominance, freeing space for many other wild flowers to prosper.[23] Robbing the rich to feed the poor.

The plants get out of control. A riot of enormous bamboo poles shoots up into the sky; I cannot see the tops. The prehistoric-looking grey pillars are thicker than a human thigh. We can't resist taking photographs of one another with the spectacle, like tourists smiling up at great monuments. The ferns, too, are oversized in this unruly green society, elbowing one another out of the way like thugs. The developing croziers rise from the ground like pythons, from stalks thicker than my arm. I pull an unfurled specimen towards me. It has black-peppered fronds and cat hair creeping along its stems; another behind it has arranged itself in parasols; all bear monstrous proportions.

We scramble up a steep rise and I look back over the ground we've covered, extracting every detail from the view: blue triangles of mountain, framed by reeds shooting up from the ground like knives, and the complicated silhouettes of tree ferns. Light glances over bundles of creepers piled high in the branches from which they hang like loose hair. I drink it all in. This is a place without seasons, where time isn't measured by calendars or clocks. No, time moves like entropy here; it's not the taut, linear form we inhabit. As I realize this, my heart beats louder.

Adriane catches up, pulling himself out of the undergrowth, wiping the sweat from his brow. His eyes shine bright like a child's.

'So beautiful,' he says, as we stand side by side, staring. He seems vaguely sad as he says this, which seems to make sense, though I can't explain why.

Wet through and covered in leafy detritus, we reach a sort of concealed opening writhing with ferns in the netted shade. The tribesmen slash through stalks and sedges to clear a path, unleashing sharp, sappy smells. We wade through storm-washed drifts of leafy debris, like seaweed spat out by the tide. And like the tide, quietly the forest draws us in deeper.

Snap, hiss, *plunk*. I fall through a false floor, sinking up to my waist in what looks like green minestrone. I was already sodden, so it makes little difference, I suppose. I haul myself out, then, disgorged, brush the debris from my clothes. A simple trick but I fell for it (or into it); the forest hasn't done with me yet. I must be vigilant, look out for myself. It'll swallow me whole if I don't.

We peer up into a globe of trees. The light changes; my shadow becomes uncertain. Emerald strobes of light touch the trunks at a diagonal, and I hear tropical birdsong above me, high and clear. The forest throbs and my heart pounds with it; I can feel it pulsing in my ears now.

We regroup under a pergola of rangy tree ferns, waiting for the stragglers. As my heart slackens I look at the party, and see how, once again, we have become different people in the forest, recast in the green light. For one thing, we hold ourselves differently, looking up, as well as ahead; but our expressions are changing too. We each have a new, fixed resolve; a sort of valour about our quest. But when we move on, all I see are snatches of clothing, a clenched jaw or a grasping hand, because once again we've become swallowed up by trees. Then my shadow disappears completely.

I've crossed the line.

★★★

I can't help thinking that, overall, the expedition hasn't gone quite as well as it should. Oh, there have been victories, I know – little *Rafflesia panchoana* on Mount Makiling, beautiful jade vines, rare orchids, and so on. I should be grateful. But the plants that really mattered – the rare species of *Rafflesia* on Mount Banahaw, and in the Sierra Madre – they hid from us, didn't they? Taunted us with tight-mouthed buds like guarded secrets. Their flirting only deepened my complicated love for them; like lovers everywhere, they've torn at my heart and made me sick. And now we're hunting one of the biggest and least understood: *Rafflesia banaoana*, in the wildest corner of the Philippines. The stakes are getting higher.

But perhaps, blinded by tiredness, I'm reading the signs all wrong. Were the buds taunting me, or could they have been something else entirely? Premonitions? I feel that stirring deep inside me again; the feeling I had on the drive to Kalinga yesterday. Only this time I let it flood through me warmly like a drug: hope.

Least understood, I said just now, but not by Pat or Adriane; they're well acquainted with *Rafflesia banaoana*. Pat discovered it, if discovery means bringing it to the attention of science. The Banao people have always known about it. Known about it, but avoided it according to Pat, who told me a couple of weeks ago about the evil spirit they believe to be possessed by the flower. In spite of this they've protected it, left it to fight its hidden battles, bloom undercover. While other species of *Rafflesia* were erased from the land (how many, we'll never know), the Banao people have been faithful custodians of *Rafflesia banaoana*; respectful of their forest's spirits.

Adriane was the second botanist to see it. Treading the untrodden track in the footsteps of his teacher, Pat, down into Kalinga's wild depths. I wonder what the tribe make of the curious botanists seeking to find the unfindable flower – Pat, Adriane, and now me, the foreigner. I wonder if they know why?

To answer this, allow me to return to *Rafflesia leonardi*, the ciphered flower, keeper of secrets. As I told you back in the Sierra Madre, some 300 kilometres south of where I am now, other botanists lumped *R. banaoana* with *R. leonardi* – erasing its status from science. But these authors never had access to *R. banaoana*; as I've already said, few people have seen it. Our work is revealing that *R. banaoana* and *R. leonardi* are indeed separate species, leading parallel lives. We've Adriane's penchant for detail to thank for that. Under Pat's careful supervision, and with a little input from me, Adriane has mapped the flowers' minute details, taken every measurement, and solved the equation. The answer lay hidden in their intricacies – little projections in the centre, and the hidden pollen and seed-bearing parts. *Rafflesia banaoana* and *R. leonardi* occur in different forests, among different communities of plants, and at different altitudes. The Cordillera Central – a crooked spine of mountains running along Luzon Island's back – probably acted as a barrier to genetic exchange, veering the species along separate evolutionary journeys in the respective plant societies in which they found themselves. The flowers are superficially similar, yes. But this obscured an important distinction, a plurality. And it *is* important. Species are units of evolution and conservation: without them, biology is a language without words.

We tend to think of species as fixed entities. But speciation – the patient evolution of new species, and their departure along separate paths – it's a *process*. What we are observing is just a snapshot. Take cats and dogs, for instance. Pretty different beasts, we'd agree? This is because they diverged from a common ancestor 40–50 million years ago; they've had plenty of time to hone their distinct personalities. Incidentally, the lineage in which *Rafflesia* evolved also diverged from its ancestors, tiny-flowered euphorbias, 46 million years ago, when strange beasts that were neither cat nor dog were roaming the land. But Charles Davis and colleagues have shown that most of the diversity we see in the genus *Rafflesia* today arose much more recently: most species evolved within the last 1–2 million years, some as recently as 600,000 years ago.[24] Others may even be on the beginning of their journey along separate paths – a process we call incipient speciation. Evolution in action.

Picture a living tree with intricate branches. Each branch is a lineage – a series of living things in a continuous line of descent. Generations. Now imagine that, rather than growing up through space, the tree is growing through *time*. The branches closest to the tips – those at the top – represent the most recently evolved lineages. The forks further down the tree represent former divergences, some of which I discussed earlier, back on Mount Banahaw (the branches that contained mosses, for example). Many of the lowermost branches fell long ago – these are extinctions; some we know about from fossils, but others have been lost to time. What we're left with at the top are living representatives: flowering plants, on a heavy branch crowded with life, then sparser branches that fork further down the tree. Conifers, ferns, lycophytes, mosses – and below all that, the branch containing the algae. In the forest in which I'm standing, where time is elastic, they all grow side by side, on top of or (in the case of *Rafflesia*) even inside one another: in other words, newly evolved plants didn't necessarily conquer the land by replacing their predecessors; many live on today in complex societies.

Returning for a moment to incipient speciation: by examining the processes taking place now, we can decipher patterns of evolution in the past. I once worked on another parasitic plant called broomrape (*Orobanche*). Like *Rafflesia*, broomrapes lack leaves and roots, and rob other plants of their food. Each species of broomrape has a preferred host, or collection of hosts – in other words it is only able to abstract nutrients from certain plants. The degree of choosiness is referred to as *host specificity*. An apparent exception to this rule of finickiness is common broomrape (*Orobanche minor*) – a species reputed to grow on just about any old thing. Except it doesn't. Years ago, I took seeds from populations of common broomrape growing on either red clovers or sea carrots. I cultivated the two populations of broomrapes in Petri dishes in the lab, both on clovers and on carrots. They didn't perform equally: broomrapes grown from seed collected on clovers fared better on that host, and vice versa. They were adapted to specific hosts.

Now let's consider the ecology of these hosts. Clovers are particularly fond of chalk grassland. Sea carrots, on the other hand, prefer south-facing, crumbling sea cliffs. The different environments of the two hosts may be acting as a barrier to genes flowing between populations of broomrape. Over time, the parasites are gradually becoming adapted to the hosts in different plant societies. They're changing personalities.

To verify my hypothesis of host-driven schizophrenia, I sequenced the DNA of clover- and carrot-specific broomrape populations. They were not just behaving differently: they were genetically distinct. Importantly this had been overlooked, because broomrapes are difficult to tell apart – after all, they have no leaves to examine. Their cryptic morphology was obscuring what was going on under our noses, but at a microscopic level. Just like *Rafflesia banaoana* and *R. leonardi*.

Leaping from one host to another may have been an important precursor to speciation in parasitic plants, driving their proliferation. I mentioned earlier that relatives of *Rafflesia* have been shown to contain genes they acquired from relatives of the cucumber and carrot – presumably former hosts.[25] Just like broomrapes, *Rafflesia* and its ancestors have probably switched hosts during their 46-million-year journey. Soft, fleshy *Rafflesia* left no trace in the fossil record laid down in the rock. But increasingly, DNA fossils[26] are beginning to disclose its secrets.

★★★

The forest is becoming denser now. We're having to duck under snaking vines and branches bearded in lichen and moss. I have the peculiar sensation of moving through a seabed: of venturing into wild, inscrutable depths that cannot be seen from above: maps without lines. This once *was* a seabed, in fact. As geology reorganized the continents, Australia collided with Asia, violently driving the Pacific seafloor into the sky. The resulting volcanoes gave rise to the Philippine archipelago. These 7,000 islands were never connected to another landmass, with the exception of Palawan, which bridged Borneo when sea levels dropped during the Pleistocene. It's this geological history that explains the exceptional biodiversity of the Philippines: life evolved here in isolation. For an evolutionary biologist, these islands are living laboratories.

Most species of *Rafflesia* are restricted to islands – both in the Philippines and across Southeast Asia. We're not entirely sure why. Among the many mysteries shrouding the biology of *Rafflesia* is how the plant is dispersed. Presumably it proliferated across Sundaland – a former landmass that connected the major present-day islands west of the Philippines, when sea levels were lower five million years ago; then as the land bridges fell around them, the lonely populations of *Rafflesia* became confined to their respective islands, divorced, and destined to lead separate lives.[27] Again, speciation.

Scientists have suggested ants may play a role in the dispersal of *Rafflesia* in the Philippines; this would explain why almost all species are restricted to individual islands:[28] they're unable to cross the straits that separate them.[29] Certainly, in the Sierra Madre we saw plenty of ants scuttling over the *Rafflesia* buds (and my legs); there's plenty of opportunity for these creatures to act as couriers. The dozen or so *Rafflesia* species in the Philippines are not just restricted to individual islands; some are restricted to a single mountain, as we saw on Mount Banahaw. This is largely attributable to the wholesale deforestation that's taken place all around them, rather than any natural process of isolation forged over millions of years. Perhaps we've simply lost too many of the pieces ever to reassemble what's been broken.

But as I look around me, I see that here at least the forest is intact.

Rafflesia leonardi in bud in the Sierra Madre, Luzon.

A rare species of jade vine (*Strongylodon elmeri*) in the Sierra Madre, Luzon.

A member of the Banao Indigenous Community with *Rafflesia banaoana* in Kalinga, Luzon.

Rafflesia banaoana in Kalinga, Luzon.

And while there are still functioning habitats left to protect, there must be hope. What other option is there?

★★★

We cross a weak stream leaking through jagged boulders. Storm-washed branches draped with leafy detritus have collected about its junctions – ghosts of former typhoons. Above the stream rises a slope: this is our destination, the tribesmen indicate, nodding solemnly up to the work in store.

The land slants up to our faces as we haul ourselves up the thickly forested slope, grabbing trees for poles. I lose my feet through an open weave of sticks and roots; it's like mountaineering a compost heap. A branch of *Osmoxylon* leans out of the gloom. Its succulent flowers and fruits are congested in a fat sprout like a cauliflower; the fruits are purple and the flowers are pure gold. Never before have I seen such a colour combination in nature. We pause on the steep bank to admire the spectacle lighting the forest like a Christmas decoration. Later we'll attempt to identify it; the most likely diagnosis is *Osmoxylon luzoniense*, but there are no photographs of this species with which to compare our specimen, either in books or online. Not that the internet exists here anyway. Like so many plants we've seen today, it will remain a mystery.

Steadily we comb the hill laced with roots and freighted with leafy debris. Filaments of light finger the thick, dark canopy as we scan the floor like a crime scene. Straying roots and branches get in our way, and vines arch out of the earth in circles, like serpents chasing their tails. Trip wires, whips, and lashes. Adriane tells me today's excursion is nothing compared with what awaits us tomorrow, where we will continue our search for *R. banaoana* – only a larger population; still, in my semi-delirious state, the plants seem to lean in oppressively and rear up out of the soil to grab me.

I know the signs now, and I can sense the trail is warm; even if I'd not been told to look here, I'd know. I've learned to pick out the battle scars on a vine, pocked from a former *Rafflesia* flower; to peer into a cat's cradle of roots to check for buds. I almost discern a flower nuzzling the trees a few metres ahead. Then it escapes me, like a half-remembered dream, or a ghost. Plants lurk in this dark hall of mirrors like will-o'-the-wisps.

A call from below. Has someone found something? I slip-slide back down the slope with the heels of my feet, pushing out leaves and avalanches of earthy rubble. My heart bangs. I know I mustn't get over-excited, because ten to one it'll be a marsh light.

Don't expect anything.

***

Buds. *Buds, buds, buds.* Glistening, in a line. Shining possibilities of what might have been. My mouth fills with brine.

You knew it could all amount to nothing. You knew.

Hope falls like a pack of cards.

We poke about the leaf litter disconsolately, as if a half-metre-wide flower might have escaped our notice. Two of the tribe vanish in the trees, and the rest of us crouch in a ring and turn our attention to the growing miracles. Some are small and creamy, rubbery-looking, like unripe conkers. Others are the size of fists, wrapped in overlapping papery bracts, like brown lettuces. They look poised for action, animated somehow; as if I'm watching them through a time-lapse, and someone just pressed pause. We take photographs while muttering observations, our voices strained with false cheer; pretending it doesn't matter, that it is enough to have found the plant at all.

We tramp back through the towering ferns and grasses, weary and lost in thought. Released from the dark forest, the colours shine brightly again: emeralds, coppers and golds; a living treasure trove. We cross the little bamboo bridge over the rapids, each carrying a drooping green bundle: the botanists with sprigs of mistletoe, fernery, and so on, and the tribesmen with taro leaves and other edibles (one, I notice, seems to have unearthed a lettuce from somewhere). We pass a gang of workmen repairing a road, who stare blankly at me when I say hello. Adriane asks why I always say hello to people I don't know; perhaps he's embarrassed by the foreigner. Over-sensitive from fatigue and disappointment, like a sullen teenager, I ignore him and retreat; then I realize it is I who am embarrassed.

By the time we reach the ranch, the sun is sighing over the mountains. I wrench off my wet shoes and socks under the yellow sky as the tribesmen prepare a tangled fire. After bathing with a bucket of cold water, I change into soft clothes and wander about with a bottle of beer given to me by Pat, in the haze of the wood smoke.

Adriane ushers me over to present a peace-offering: a Philippine eagle-owl. It's sitting in a large cage in a clearing; he tells me it is recuperating here (from what, it's unclear). It's a monstrously tall creature, approaching half a metre high, with cappuccino plumage. It stares hard at us through the grille with angry eyes that glow yellow in the half-light.

Leaning against a tree watching us watching the owl is a whip-thin man with a boyish face. Adriane recognizes him and we wander over to say hello.

'This is Kuya Willis,' Adriane says.

Kuya Willis steps forward and becomes silhouetted by the fire now blazing a few metres away. We shake hands. He moves with the laziness of a tall person, although he's average in height.

'Why you here?' he asks in broken English.

Aren't the simplest questions often the hardest to answer? I mutter something vague about plants although I'm unsure if he understands.

At night I close my eyes and watch the day dance before me, plant by plant, but there's one missing. Of course, such a flower could never be found so easily; on a half-day trek. How could it? Now I understand it must be earned. With the recklessness of ambition, and the authority of failure, I know it has to be *tough*. I'm cognizant of my irreconcilable need to find an open flower and for it to remain hidden from me.

The fight.

15.

Ready, aim, fire. I've pushed up a bud through the bark, like a missile. I did it when they – the vines – weren't paying attention.

Last time I did this, I misfired. Things didn't go to plan and I was detected: like a foreigner in the forest. Problem is, I got ahead of myself: tried to send a flower out into the world too soon. Elicited a bit of a reaction down here – of the cellular kind – among the vines. Tried to kick me out! Poison me, with their chemical weapons, and encircle me with a cellular blockade. Bit of an over-reaction, given how quietly I've been living here, minding my own business. Rent-free, I know, but still. Well, they've sent their shot across the bows, but this isn't over.

I took my time. Repositioned, and this time it's all systems go. Seven days it will take me. The time it takes to make a world.

Every day I watch my little bud swelling, proudly. The forest seethes and hisses above it, critters and leaves shift around it, the rain beats down on it, and I nourish it secretly from the grid. Out of the warm wetness my flower expands like rising dough. I smile as my beautiful plan comes to fruition at last.

Sometimes you just have to keep going: fight a battle more than once and lose occasionally.

To win.

16.

As I sleep, the vines creep deep into my subconscious. I seep back into the forest. It's a measureless place, so dark it could be night or day, I'm not sure. It smells of life and death. Rope-like creepers circle in the mist as I push deeper into the abyss. I'm wearing flip-flops – ridiculous – and it unsettles me because I can't see my feet through the leaves. They grasp my ankles like outstretched hands. Anything could be lurking down there. My feet slide out, propelling me backwards, making me feel like I'm falling. I can sense an unquietness; it's insubstantial as the cloud in the trees, and I don't know what it is. But my sole focus is to find that flower, whatever it takes; that I do know. Anyway, there is no way out.

So I fight.

17.

I reorganize my things in the half-light. I do this carefully, listing and repeating the items in my head in an organized trance, estranged from myself. Creeping behind a twilit wall to bathe, I plunge my arm into a bucket of cold water to reach for the yellow plastic dipper, then pour it all over myself in a shudder. My lips are pursed to keep out the water-borne agents of illness; it might be safer to remain unclean. I do it anyway, then blot myself dry using my precious grey towel. Next, I baste myself in greasy repellent to outwit the airborne agents of illness.

Now that I'm slightly mad, I can see things clearly; see the threats that are steadily weaving themselves around me like self-sewing lace. *But I'm ready*, I chant quietly to myself, like a mantra. *I'm ready.* I vowed to be with the plant in sickness or in health, and I will.

Adriane and I wait for the others in the grey light of dawn. It still smells of night. We stand shoulder to shoulder, watching a fingered mist creep over the continents of forest like a spirit. The silence is so absolute, I can hear him draw breath. Suspense hangs about us thickly, like the moments before an exam.

Apropos nothing, Adriane hitches up his trouser leg and points to a vengeful black scar running down his calf, then looks at me, as if he's presenting me meaningful evidence of something.

'What is it?'

'Sand fly. Bit me last time we trekked this forest.'

He watches my face carefully as I peer at the sprawling ink stain.

I wonder how I've not noticed this before. Perhaps he's wondering that too.

'It was red, then it hurt, then it was infected, and then it turned black.'

I nod, as rapidly he counts off symptoms and makes the sounds that seem appropriate for a sand-fly bite.

We stand in silence for a while, watching the hills as morning creeps up to their tree-clad shoulders, while their feet hold on to night. Kuya Willis, Pat, Ana, and two other tribesmen wander over to join us in the spreading brightness. The tribesmen are wearing mud-spattered gumboots, and an assortment of floppy hats. Kuya Missan (who climbed a tree yesterday to fetch our mistletoe) is thickset and a little older and sterner than the others; I sense authority now. The other two men, Kuya Bullman and Kuya Dito, whom I've not yet had the chance to examine closely, are in their forties, I guess, but wiry, like teenagers; both are hollow about the cheeks and have the same uncertain look, as if everything surprises them mildly. Perhaps they're brothers. A secret, mischievous smile flickers across Kuya Willis's features as he watches me study their faces. Something is hiding behind his eyes.

We make the last few clicks and adjustments, keyed up for the trek, and then we strike out: first Kuya Willis and Kuya Missan, then the rest of us, one after the other, wide-eyed as the Children of the Damned. Adventure clings to us like an invisible light. In the distance, two of the women who cooked for us last night stand watching us leave; I wave vaguely at them, but they just stare as we file off into the sun.

★★★

The silhouetted forest is guarded by a thick curtain of giant reeds. Their rotting mass beneath my feet unleashes yellow smells like unsmoked tobacco. We bore into them, pushing through dripping trees and glistening-wet ginger leaves, pausing to help one another clamber over the antlers of a fallen tree, down to the river. A mythical stump bears reflexed ears and a snout; flat-faced and spiteful like a hissing cat, warning.

The river is white with intent, crashing about the rocks in broken rapids under a low-slung bridge of tree-poles. A cool breeze wafts up from the water, carrying with it mineral smells. The tribesmen have already reached the opposite bank by the time I stoop and flail a crossing, resorting to hands and feet two-thirds of the way. I don't want to fall in so close to the start line; I still have much to prove here.

As I pause to look up at the other side, for the first time I appreciate the immensity of the rising forest, spilling through boulders, tumbling down the bank, unable to contain itself. The great black walls of the prism of my infatuation.

We clamber awkwardly along the bank, pulling ourselves along using hanging tree branches for balance, then regroup under the broken canopy, breathing deeply. The sky above us is a pristine dome of blue, but where we're heading we won't see that again for hours. More people have stepped on the moon than the place we're about to chart. We're about to enter the abyss.

That orchid, smiling sweetly? Beguiling, sweet-as-sugar pink? It's a game. Like a person's, an orchid's smile belies a darker nature. Lying, cheating, fraud, kidnap – even sex games (especially sex games).

Orchids?

Yes, orchids, *and* I'll tell you this: in the Plant Kingdom – our Confucius-jilted society, where natural selection is the letter of the law and evolution is our judge – orchids ride herd. Thirty thousand strong, they possess the greatest power of life to move forward in this forest, to expand and branch; to conquer.

Life is a dirty game. Whoever makes the fewest mistakes wins.

We push into the trees. There's a strong, wet smell of moss. I feel the forest breathing, drawing me into its dark embrace. The damp heat is intensifying: my senses are heightened and the voices inside my head seem louder now – the commands and, beneath them, whispers of the forest.

Impossibly large, unopened fern croziers rise like sentinels either side of me in the gloom. These are common miracles to me now, and I ignore them. I have bigger fish to fry here: a singular purpose drawing me forward. Something like excitement, only bigger.

See how I've forgotten to pretend not to care? To feign indifference? Well, I'm beyond that now. I've swallowed it down long and hard enough, don't you think?

But you know as well as I do by now that it may all come to nothing. The slightest twist of fate – a week too soon or too late, the replenishing rainstorm that never came, or the monsoon that flooded our path – it could all be our undoing. Destiny shaped by the sly workings of a flower conspiring with fate. Man against nature. Who will win?

***

We huddle around a bubble-gum pink orchid suspended in a mossy tangle, admiring its features. I don't know which species it is. I don't even know to which genus it belongs. Of all the flowering plant families, the orchid family (Orchidaceae) contains the most species – an unknowable number running into about 30,000. These tropical forests in Kalinga are a cornucopia of them.

I ply back the sepals and rummage about for the hidden pollinia – these are the yellow bundles of pollen produced by all orchid flowers: just one of the secrets of their success. Memories from another time and place crowd in on me again. Friendly memories. For now.

'What you must understand is that everything about an orchid's biology is economical,' Simon told our audience of second-year undergraduate students. They stood in a natural amphitheatre under the hot Portuguese sun, peering at the pencil Simon was waving about before them, like a wand.

'And their pollen is no exception.'

The studious among the group at the front nodded slowly while writing urgently. I noticed a lad at the back discreetly rolling his cigarette paper.

Minutes before, I had probed the flower of a bee orchid with the nib of the pencil – our proxy for an insect – and teased it into ejaculating its wad of pollen (the pollinium). The sex life of an orchid was to be their biology lesson that day.

'Pollination is one of nature's ancient bartering systems: insects couriering plants' pollen in return for sugar-rich nectar.'

The students nodded harder, pens poised (lad licking the paper). They knew that already: pollination is one of the fundamentals of plant biology. But what they didn't know was that during the steady evolution of this plant–insect quid pro quo, a corruption had taken place. The corruption of orchids.

'Now watch.' Simon held the pencil forward, and the spell was cast. The students stared rapt in anticipation of the forthcoming incantation.

We waited, fidgeting. A million bees hummed contentedly in the background and the sun smarted the backs of our necks. Goats' bells tinkled faintly somewhere in the hills. A warm breeze brought warm smells of fennel, French lavender, camphor thyme, and cigarette smoke.

'*Look.*'

We returned our attention to the nib of Simon's pencil where something minutely significant had taken place; an event. The pollinium had undergone a *tropism*: autonomously, after being divorced from its flower, it had curved 90 degrees over the tip of the pencil, all by itself. Like a pointing finger.

They looked at one another astonished, as if they had witnessed something magical, not of the biological world.

'As you can see, just minutes after being removed from the flower, the pollinium has become primed. Now it is optimally positioned to hit the stigma – the receptive part – of the next flower the insect visits. You see, it is quite unlike the diffuse, sometimes even wind-dispersed pollen in most flowers. Why is the orchid flower's pollen picked up and delivered in one hit this way? Well, this ensures minimal wastage.'

A disturbance in the bushes nearby distracted us.

'It is highly efficient. Now. Your turn.' I handed out pencils and the students dispersed themselves across the pasture, talking excitedly among themselves. They crouched among the fennel canes, their sun-scorched faces eye-to-eye with the orchids. Then, moments later they held their own pencils to the sun, and waited for the miracle.

Back to corruption. The insect who visits this orchid in Portugal and across the Mediterranean is offered no reward for his service to the plant. No, he is its sex slave. Driven into a frenzy of blind lust, the male insect thrusts himself against the flower in a misguided attempt to mate with it; in so doing, he becomes saddled with its pollinia. Off he buzzes, bewildered, and the pollinia jammed on his head repositions itself, ready for touchdown on the next flower he has the urge to call on. This is called pseudo-copulation, in the jargon.

Why would he behave in this way? Bee orchids' flowers look curiously like insects: blackish, with waspish markings, furry, and large-eyed; some even have a pair of glassy wings. More than that, each type of bee orchid *smells* exactly like a female insect of a particular species. Scientists have isolated the volatile chemicals that have perfected this molecular-grade fraud. Their forensic analysis has revealed that a series of minor tweaks and adjustments to the chemistry of cuticular waxes – substances produced by all plants to protect their leaves from sun damage – have led to a peculiar accuracy in the mimicry of female insect sex pheromones.[30] The orchids have interrupted the insects' reproductive cycle and hardwired it into their own. They've made a mockery of the sex-crazed male insects: outwitted by millions of years of evolutionary alchemy, they didn't stand a chance.

Ten thousand miles away, another scandal unfolds. Our hustler is *Caleana major*, an orchid native to Australia; better known as the 'flying duck orchid' (careful how you say it). Picture this: a peculiar flower unfurls, and a hovering sawfly has it in his line of sight. In profile, the flower possesses the *exact* shape of a duck in flight: it has Donald Duck's head and bill, a craned neck, and upswept wings, poised for take-off. You may think I'm exaggerating but I'm not.

There is no biological reason that the flower should resemble Donald Duck: fun, yes, as a *trompe-l'œil* of nature. However, the flower *is* a mimic. As the flying duck orchids' flowers unfurl, male sawflies emerge from dormancy with singular focus. With a weather eye, one tests the air for the sex pheromone of a wingless female, whom he has plans to carry off and mate with in flight. Only something's not right: our male sawfly is mounting a hoax. Yes, like the bee orchids we saw in Portugal just now, flying duck orchids have mastered the chemistry of sex pheromone forgery, only here things are more complex. The sawfly clings to the duck's head: this, he believes, is his prized female. But as tries to extricate the bogus insect from her stalk, the duck's flexuous neck swings him like a paddle ball. The harder he tries, the more vigorously he is thrust headlong into flower's inner mechanism. Driven by the force of his own urges, he is hammered violently, repeatedly, faster into the climax and then: there. *Release.* The pollinia are dispatched.

He zooms off dizzily to the next expectant orchid.

North European orchids are not without their victims. I used to live near a nature reserve in Oxfordshire called Warburg: rolling hills of chalk, cuckoos, beech trees through which the light shines luminous green – a gentle sort of place. There in the Chilterns' leafy heart grows an innocuous-looking orchid called a helleborine (*Epipactis*). Unlike most other orchids in this part of the world, which bloom in early summer, the helleborine sends up its purplish spires in August: a time when the bees are calming down, but the wasps are gearing up. Apple orchards up and down the land are crawling with them. They're crawling all over the helleborines too – a whole scrum of them; but let's pause here for a moment – because there's something curious about the wasps' behaviour. Falling about, disoriented, tripping over one another and themselves . . .

They're blind drunk.

How? Let's step back into the apple orchard. Here the wasps pick up microorganisms (bacteria, fungi, and so on) from the festering fruit. Alighting on the helleborine, they inadvertently transfer these microorganisms to the nectar-producing part of the flowers. Micro-organisms produce ethanol (alcohol) in the presence of sugar, which, as I mentioned earlier, nectar is replete with. The flowers the wasps paw become veritable Petri dishes, teeming with microorganisms.

And then they become a brewery.

So the wasps are the agents of their own intoxication. Sex slaves – OK, that made sense – pollinia got from A to B after a little head-banging pseudo-copulation. Pollinator grooming, if you will. But who needs a drunk wasp in the plant kingdom? Well, wasps are abundant in late summer and they are strong long-distance fliers: perfect pollinators for an orchid with a patchy distribution in August. Unfortunately for the orchid, though, wasps are also effi-cient groomers: no good for pollinia (all your pollen in one basket). But like elsewhere in life, too much alcohol makes a wasp stupid. And the helleborine didn't select its pollinator for its wits. No, no: a punch-drunk wasp will linger for longer over the orchid's flowers, staggering from flower to flower, clinging to each one like a drunk to a lamp-post. Behaving this way, it's more likely to pick up and deliver its pollinia. What's more, the uncoordinated creature has been robbed of its grooming abilities.[31] In other words, it's racked up a tab of pollinia after a few too many orchids, and now it's stuck with them. And keeps going back: the helleborine has become its enabler.

Yes, some flowers are all sweetness and nectar. And then there are orchids.

I look again at the flower dangling innocently above me. A beau-tiful sham. I'll add this to the other tricks this forest has up its sleeve, then: the layers of deceit. Evolution is a ruthless mother.

I am perceiving the world around me with a new kind of purity –
threatening, unforgiving. I'm in a place I can admire from a distance
and rebuild later with words, with paint, with science; but it's a
place to which I'll never belong. Worn out senseless, and tormented
by nature, I can see things differently now.

I've probably already told you that.

***

The air is close and the canopy weighs down on us like storm clouds.
The forest is choked with ferns, vines, and creepers, and Kuya
Missan slashes them down in a flourish. Like a herd we drift apart,
intent on our blind path, reconvening occasionally to check that no
one has disappeared, or to admire an unusual plant someone has
spotted. After an hour of green shade, impenetrable vegetation, and
nothing else, we reach a clearing full of white noise and light. I close
my eyes and when I reopen them, nothing is the right colour. We're
back at the river; only here the broken falls are wilder, some fifteen
metres across. And there's no bridge.

Reflections quiver like dragonflies cast in light; they scintillate as
we wade in. Beyond the protruding rocks, the water looks polished,
barely troubled at all. The tribe crosses first, scouting, testing the
depth and shouting back instructions I can't understand. The others
follow, crawling through the boulder-strewn bed like crabs. I go last.

I'd underestimated its power. The current is deep and swift – it's
like boarding a moving train. Clouds of gravel dislodge beneath my
feet. Cool water pounds with motive, pushing heavily through my
splayed fingers, pulling me, drawing me in deeper. It wavers in
depth between waist and knee, and we each have to pause regularly
to rest as the foam rages around us. Every so often we look back at
one another and laugh – mocking the danger, proving we're
unfazed. But it's impossible not to slip. Halfway across, I'm over-
whelmed by rapids.

Grey blur, white noise, flooded sinuses. I steady myself on the
rocks, dragging myself forward through the pounding water.
Beyond the roar, we reach a calmer maze of rivulets and frothy
pools; and after that, an isthmus of shingle, where we rest on silver

boulders that blacken wet beneath us. I shake my hair, squeeze my clothes, and empty the sodden contents of my pockets and bag. Water dribbles out of my mobile phone which, unsurprisingly, has frozen. Time is absent here.

Now there's nothing to measure it.

Excitement strikes: a lipstick plant (*Aeschynanthus*)! Adriane spots it hanging above our heads in a web of creepers. The plants are named after their lurid pink, cylindrical buds, which emerge like fingers of lipstick out of the vinework. Ana asks Adriane which species it is; they ponder over the plant above our heads in Tagalog; it's clear neither of them knows its name. We call Kuya Willis, who returns from hacking a path twenty metres ahead. He has tied a green towel around his head, and a loop of pliable, cable-like vine around his waist. Stretching on tiptoes, he draws his machete: a flash of silver at the end of a brown arm, shaking leaves, and then a bundle of creepers falls apart, catching the branches on the way down. We pull at the snagged mass and carefully disentangle our prize.

Kuya Willis wanders off, and Ana, Adriane, and I peer at the fantastic flower with absorbed attention, our sweaty faces bowing close. Like a foxglove, it's tubular, white, and spattered intricately with pink. Its stigma and stamens – the business parts of the flower – hang crookedly from their tube, like the legs of a hermit crab from its shell. Adriane drops the flower into a vial of spirit (this will preserve the three-dimensional arrangement of flower parts, which pressing would destroy).

'New,' says Pat when we show him the specimen later, as he regards it briefly. He's correct. The plant is unchristened, a mystery to science; later, we will describe the species officially.

Again and again the river returns, and each time we wade in its personality changes. Now it has become constrained angrily as it slices the forest's shadow like a knife. Looking-glass-clear broken rapids lunge and explode over the rocks. I'm soaking anyway, so it's liberating to confront it. I laugh hysterically as the cool water presses the clothes to my skin, washing away the dark heat. I grope at the sparse slimy boulders, whipping the air with my arms across the voids, as we push diagonally upstream. On the opposite bank, fern-splashed overhanging rocks barricade the forest, and we have to hunt for an intersection where we can ladder up the river-washed weft of roots. Again and again, shaking ourselves like dogs, we re-enter the dark halls of the forest in a bath of heat. I've lost count of the crossings. And now I'm losing my place in the land of mapmakers' fiction as well.

Disorientation is setting in.

It's not just space that's troubling me. Linear time has lost its meaning here too. Around me, ferns, mosses, conifers, and flowering plants – living relics of the abyss of ages – are all fighting for a place: deep time intersecting the present. Two weeks ago, on Mount Makiling, I wrote about the work of Linnaeus, of taxonomy assigning everything to a hierarchy of names – and didn't we sort things neatly? I'll leave those sentences there but they're less true to me now. Oh, it makes sense logically, but doesn't it give a limited picture of living existence? Aside from the fluidity of speciation I discussed a couple of days ago, taxonomy says nothing of the molecular connectedness and processes that transcend time and space. Traded genes, new birth: composition and decomposition, living on the dead – atoms traded back and forth through time and space. *Rafflesia*'s threads of entity, interwoven with my own.

Yes, the forest ecosystem is four-dimensional. As a scientist seeking to make sense of this, to bring order to the chaos, I am bereft of the symbols I need to solve the equation. Taxonomy concedes evolution: it's blissfully clear! Just a fortnight ago the world felt so much more straightforward, something I was confidently qualified to make sense of. I believed in the currency of Publication Records, Impact Factors, and the Research Excellence Framework; traded tacit boasts over the table at college dinners, then after the gowns were hung up, washed the dinners down with rather expensive port by the fire. (A different kind of fraud?)

But all that was before I heard voices in the plants and got dragged halfway to oblivion.

★★★

More weaponry. Whip-like roots are rising out of the earth like lassoes again to trip me. I feel a spike of adrenaline as I stumble into one. I sense eyes on me as I trip, mocking; but no one's there. Only the same hostilely beautiful forest pulling me ever further along its warm, wet arteries, down to its beating heart. Trees, trees, trees. A self-referential paradox of them.

I touch the phone in my pocket in a panic, checking my lifeline to the real world. It would be useless here even if it did work. Another spider of sweat crawls down my spine. All lines are broken.

Pathless forest. Hah! I've said it aloud. I call out for my audience, but it's useless above the hiss; the others are somewhere ahead of me, I think. Or behind me. The birds and insects accept my words.

I push through an intricacy of heavily lichened vines rushing out of the earth. Ferns rise like a stag's antlers from the arms of a tree. Rattan palms snag my skin like barbed wire. Strange white fungi march up a tree like frosting. Occasional swords of light fall through the green clouds, cutting menacing stripes and gashes. I grasp at a slippery vine, steadying myself to admire the lacework of a threadbare leaf under the weak lamp of the sun. Wiping the sweat from my brow, I detect the distant rage of water somewhere to my left. At least the water is something to mark the land by in this hall of mirrors. A hundred channels through the trees snake out from where I'm standing: there are no units of scale or differentiation. Perhaps I will get lost and die here. The back of my mind draws uncertain outlines of blame, of absolution.

Why am I here?

I wait in the vault of trees with no direction. It was the right thing to do, because several long minutes later, Kuya Willis appears, nodding. I follow him as he weaves between the poles. Every so often he gashes a tree with his knife, cutting a ragged scar through its flesh. Reddish sap oozes thickly. Navigational purposes, I guess. So that we can get out.

Threads and vines, creeping together for millennia, have traded secrets here. An inestimably complicated web of plants, insects, fungi – a plenitude of microscopic life, holding conversations we can't understand. As I pause to rest the left side of my chest, my mind is drawn down to it, through the subsurface of hidden roots and connections; into the hidden cosmos beneath my feet. Soil communities in a single ecosystem like this contain countless millions of species – and billions of individuals: a universe of life. Evidence is mounting that this inestimable belowground microbiota helps shape the biodiversity and the functioning of whole ecosystems aboveground. But how these communities are distributed in space and time, how they respond to global change, the consequences for plant communities – whole biogeochemical cycles, even? Much of this remains a mystery.[32] Our understanding is biased by what we know to exist above ground: what we can see.

The humid earth angles up to our chins and fists as we labour through the darkness. Our pace slows with the steepness, and over my shoulder I see through the trees beneath us that the others are catching up. Kuya Willis and I pause, saying nothing. A few metres apart, we recline in parallel against identical great grey columns bearded in moss. The brine-stiffened folds of my T-shirt tremble and pause as my heart slackens, and sweat dribbles down my temples.

Reunited, the party busy themselves with bags and bottled water. We compare notes on what we've seen: wild mango relatives, unidentified *Hoya* vines (Ana is particularly fond of these), and Philippine ground orchids (*Spathoglottis plicata*) on the river bank. Adriane presents a gift he has plucked further down the wooded slope. I can see the forest in his eyes as he hands it to me. The translucent white flower is smaller than a fingernail and held aloft a wire-thin stalk. It has a pleasing geometry, like origami, or those napkins you see folded into swans. Pat and Ana lean in, and the four of us bow over the specimen. *Burmannia*, we decide to name it, nodding and smiling, like new parents.

Burmannia is a parasite, but not of the roots of other plants; this plant is parasitic on a fungus. Called mycoheterotrophs, such plants are scarce and poorly known. On an expedition to the Ryukyu Islands of Japan a few years ago, I searched high and low for a similar plant called *Oxygyne* without success. A tiny, polyp-like creature, shocking sapphire-blue – dearly I wanted to see it. But I never did; few people have. Mycoheterotrophs are elusive, like transparencies, questing up from the underworld to the shifting forest floor. Sometimes they don't even make it to the surface.

Fairy lanterns (*Thismia*) are another example. These botanical sprites lurk unseen in the depths; most species have only been discovered recently. Silently they push their way up through the dark air, illuminating the forest floor with their yellow, orange, or whitish clawed chalices. They're like deep-sea coral. In 2020 a botanist from Malaysia called Siti Munirah shared with me some photographs of a flower that a rainforest explorer called Dome Nikong had found. He discovered it on Gunung Sarut, a mountain in the Malaysian state of Terengganu. Siti and I studied the photos. To our astonishment, what we were examining was a species of *Thismia* new to science. The orange, lantern-like flower had three pillars holding a warted parasol, the function of which remains a mystery.

Siti and a team of Malaysian botanists searched for the plant repeatedly; to their dismay, the only known population had been destroyed by wild boars. The plant has only been seen twice and may never be seen again – all attempts to relocate it have failed. Dead on Arrival, it shot straight to the top of the peril ratings, with a conservation status of Critically Endangered (possibly extinct). Around the world, new species of plant are still being named and described every year, while others are losing the battle against the threats they face: discovery in close combat with extinction. Here in the Philippines, countless species were lost before we even knew they existed.

At our desks, 6,500 miles apart, Siti and I set to work describing our new species, illustrating the plant, documenting its features, conjuring it back to life with words and pictures, so that other botanists may identify it reliably in the future, should it choose to reappear (which I doubt). We named it *Thismia sitimeriamiae*, after Dome's mother Siti Meriam; he asked us to name the plant in honour of his mother's support for his lifelong effort to conserve the plants of the Malaysian rainforest.[33]

★★★

The forest falls, and I feel the strain around the tops of my legs and backside. As the slope levels out, we pass a colossal fallen tree. Light filters through the canopy, illuminating the great scar running along the abyssal plane like a shipwreck. The caved remains of the toppled column have acquired a mantle of green velvet, from which other, intricate growth is rising like coral. Instinctively, we stand gazing over the fallen city, mesmerized by its scale. Using remote-sensing technology, scientists have estimated that a mature sycamore tree's branches equate to 10.8 kilometres. 'Weighing' trees in this way has enabled scientists to estimate their size and volume from precise 3D data. In other words, they scan the forest's architecture. This technology will allow us to monitor carbon stocks and fluxes, and quantify the vague promise of greenhouse gas reduction linked to forests.[34] Truth in data, queries and recommendations; dealing with the powers of nature using symbols. Science and technology: stabilizers on humanity's freewheeling future.

Near the fallen tree's beach of torn earth, we discover another act of nature glinting at us from the leafy chaos: a ghost orchid (*Epipogium roseum*). Ghost orchids are widespread but, true to their name, they are rare and unpredictable; to find one anywhere is special. It has a translucent, slender stem to which two whitish flowers are clinging like nascent moths, their flexed wings poised for flight. Ephemeral. Like seeds of a dandelion clock, to be marvelled at once and lost in a trice.

We regroup in a bowl of light hewn by a weak, pebbled stream; I see a red negative of it when I blink, after the dark damp heat. Like a river of blood. We pause, wiping the sweat from our faces and pulling the wet tendrils of hair from our eyes. Above us, a great cirque of boulders looms into focus. Arching feathers of tree ferns and reeds lean out of the crevices extravagantly, and their spent leaves and branches snag the jagged edges of the magnificent rock. Kuya Willis has scrambled to the top of the shallowest face – about six metres up – and tethered his reel of vine there around the base of a small tree; now he's crouched like an athlete, looking down at us with his clever face. The kinked green rope follows the contours of the boulders; it looks precarious.

Kuya Missan stands at the base of the scarp on a pitched rock, legs apart, frozen in march. A large *Colocasia* leaf flops over his head, presumably to keep out the sun. He holds the rope for me, encouraging me with raised eyebrows. I grasp it with both hands and my body sways with its weight. The rock is green and slippery, unforgiving. I'm conscious of being watched from above and below, and I take care as I clamber heavily up the clefted rock; still, twice I topple sideways. I shimmy up the last two metres and Kuya Willis and I slap hands. The audience cheers. I wish this was being documented on film so that I can show people at home; flaunt our contempt for danger. Showing off, I suppose. Adriane arrives next with a fixed, determined expression, followed by Ana (tired), Pat (tired), finally Kuya Missan (invigorated) and the other two men. I can't quite believe what we've just done.

We've reached a sort of platform. The twisted cliff continues to rise in a great fang, curved and potent. Scaling this would be impossible so we must continue around it; but first we pause to crouch under its great mass, drawing strength. Fibrous ropes of root drape just shy of the ground, where the source of the stream below sluices indifferently under a pool of shadows. The jungle screen looks prehistoric. Tremendous rocks and ferns tower into the sky, conspiring to blot out the sun. Light of a particular greenness seems to emanate from within, illuminating our faces from underneath. We sit quietly, each staring at nothing, lost in our thoughts.

You'd think you could escape yourself out here in the wilderness, in the absence of time and technology. You can't. Words you said or didn't; friends you made and lost; memories you tried to forget, or never knew you ever had. Without life's daily distractions, forgotten knowledge bubbles up and swarms like the tide. I am ten years old. In my hands, an open book . . .

'Are you tired, Dr Chris?'

'Yes, Adriane, a little.'

'Me too.'

My thoughts refracted, we hoist up our bags and continue. The forest falls and rises, opening between the thickets then closing in on us again, breaking its promise. Bars of light flit across my arms as I trudge through sun-splashed ferns and reeds, and jam my feet between the hidden rocks. Drifts of silver lichen sway in an invisible current like seaweed, and half-rotten trees rise, lush with moss. The group disbands, regrouping occasionally, silently, before pressing on again determinedly.

I find Kuya Willis and Kuya Missan waiting for me among the spear-straight trees, with outstretched hands. They present me with a fruit they have dissected lengthways. I fondle the greenish-orange knobbly half-spheres and piece them back together like a puzzle. It smells of pine, only faintly rotten, like a pumpkin. They look at me expectantly, but I fail them. I think it's a pandan (*Pandanus*: a genus of tropical plants also known as screwpines), only it's much smaller than any I've seen, so I'm uncertain. We shrug and the fruit is cast aside. A few metres on, I see the answer in the spoked roots of a pandan tree, only it's too late – the tribe has vanished and so has my opportunity to sun in the glory of their respect. I feel disproportionately distressed by this, because I'm losing sight of what matters.

I pause for breath under a mass of vines, python-thick. Lesser creepers have begun clinging to my clothes as if rooting there, taking possession. I touch one; it feels charged. Pictures flash about my mind like silver. I see tendrils creep down my arms and curl about my wrists.

And then the forest tightens its grip.

★★★

If you can listen to the bright water from a distance, if you can see natural beauty on all sides, if you can forget the sharp smell of fear; you might also forget the forest's enmity; forget that you're condemned. You might even feel happy to be in the lost world, paradise.

Grateful.

Paranoid.

Another thing you feel here. I haven't seen or heard the others for half an hour now. The earth around me rises and falls in mighty waves. I've lost the damn trail: no ribbon of smashed-up stems, or sap-spattered earth to follow; no rope to cling to. A helicopter couldn't spot me here if it tried: enveloped by trees, numberless trees, I'm invisible in the hallucinatory green.

In the lost world you can't be found.

142

Panic sparkles. I rock to and fro on the earth, trying to take stock – desperate to see a way through this funk. I could stay put. I could go back, or forward. These are what my choices have narrowed to. I trawl an empty well for rational thought. But my sanity is a fast-sinking ship. The forest's hiss drowns out everything else and amplifies my wild solitude.

And then my thoughts are unmoored completely, lost to deeper waters.

Yes, I am ten years old and in my hands is an open book. A black and white picture of a forest draped in vines and creepers. Exotic-looking. A fascinating place – one that I want to step into, so badly it hurts. I am not at home. Nor am I at school, although I *am* standing in a classroom of sorts: some sort of field station I think – a place with wildlife posters on the walls, and rows of empty ice-cream tubs for pond-dipping – that sort of thing. A teacher wanders over from across the room. She seems put out, tells me that's enough reading thank-you-very-much and that I need to go and play with the other children outside now, please.

Playing with the other children is the last thing I want to do because they make fun of me – the kid who likes books and nature and can't play football. I don't tell the teacher that. I put the book back on the shelf and I do as I'm told. But I was happy, lost in that book. And now I feel rebuked for misbehaving – ashamed even.

Of course when I was ten I didn't know a thing about life; didn't know the teacher was trying to help.

A rush of leaves behind me. Kuya Willis appears, which is odd because I could have sworn he was in front. I'm not lost after all. As I said, paranoid.

***

Shiny-wet rocks glisten out of the moving foam like mountain peaks. Reunited, we send up showers as we plunge into the shallows, laughing – now reckless with ambition. Boulders knock my feet as we drag ourselves deeper upstream. Water blossoms around us, then the floor falls away as we enter a new kind of stillness, like calm between the tides. The emptiness beneath me feels inviting.

We monkey up a vine straddling the opposite bank, and heave ourselves onto the slope, helping one another with slippery hands. We're faced with unfriendly vegetation again – this time, a writhing mass of stems. The tribe tears it down and we stoop and follow them into the darkness. I look up and there is no sky, only close-set leaves. I look down and I can't see my feet. I am suspended in green chaos, a dimension that belongs to neither earth nor sky.

The close-knit thicket concedes to a looser gallery of trees. But it's louder here, febrile: an unwelcoming, rhythmic scream throbs and hisses. A deranged formation of vines loops down out of nothingness and I snatch at them, pulling myself on course. They rear up to trip me again. I stumble and bash the side of my hand as I break my fall. The pain throbs to the beat of my heart, like a living, breathing extension of my being. I lick away the blood and realize there's more than there should be. It's sliding down my arms and temples, dripping to form cartoon sun-shaped splashes on the upturned leaves. Where the hell is it coming from?

Leeches. Little neat rows of them have sprouted along my arms, like hanging black socks; downloading my blood, my energy, and the dregs of my self-preservation. I've come across these plenty of times before in the tropics, but now I'm covered in them – they're even in my hair. I can feel them beneath my fingertips, yielding and unwholesomely smooth, like slugs. I smack them off but they won't budge. So I rip them out one by one in a panic, undamming fresh tributaries of blood.

I notice Kuya Willis standing behind me again, measuring me with interest. 'Leave. Fill, then? Fall off, all by self,' he says, making little flicking gestures along his left arm to rid himself of invisible leeches, holding my gaze insouciantly. My need to believe him, and evade them, divides my loyalties. I stand motionless, staring at my arms.

I think the ship has sunk.

***

A bundle of ribbons – black and white – presents itself, like an exotic gift. I pick it up, open it. A peculiar lichen has fallen from the canopy. It resembles a seaweed (a form known as foliose, in lichenology).

I've never seen such a specimen; nor might anyone else, given where I am standing. Lichens are not plants; rather they are strange composite organisms in which algae live among the filaments of fungi. Each of the algal and fungal partners can, in turn, interact with myriad other microorganisms: what I am observing is a self-contained society in the palm of my hand. A bizarre urge to nibble it steals me as I recall the passage from *Alice in Wonderland* in which the talking caterpillar hands out mushrooms; perhaps because, like Alice, I'm losing my grip on reality.

My musings on Alice and misguided instincts are severed by a burning sensation spreading along my left arm in a panic. Five hundred fathoms into the abyss, bitten and bloody, now I've been stung.

And badly.

I see the source, leaning mockingly out of the tangle: *Dendrocnide*, a stinging tree. Already a mess of fresh and dried blood, my skin is now blooming angrily, and all the hairs standing on end. It looks and feels as though hot acid has been poured over my arm. My heart thuds as I consider this latest affliction. When a stinging tree is touched, the tips of minute tiny glassy needles penetrate the skin, where they break to release toxins. The skin often grows over the needles, making them impossible to remove. The results are intense pain and local sweating, reaching a peak after twenty minutes, and sometimes lasting for days or even months (my own burns will persist long after I leave the Philippines). Related trees in Australia and elsewhere in Southeast Asia have been recorded to induce unconsciousness and, in one case, even death.[35]

Miserably I hold up my limp arm to Kuya Willis, who recognizes the symptoms instantly and nods with a slight smile, though not unkindly. He scans the screen of knotted vegetation, pulls out his knife and severs a stalk; then he strips back the bark, as if peeling a banana. He hands me the pale stick to use as a balm which I rub over my weeping skin. It eases the worst of the pain instantly. Paradoxically, the antidote is the sap from the stem of the same bush that stung me: an obscure connectedness the Banao people understand, which I never will.

Kuya Missan appears, followed by the others. We reach an impenetrable wall woven in leaf and rock under which Kuya Missan crouches like a sprinter, peering up uneasily. Fathoming the work in store, he inhales deeply through his nose, as if breathing in the necessary information. Slowly he stands, raises his right arm, and hacks the nest of frond and tendril violently. Leaves the size of people fall to our feet. Then he disappears.

I pause in front of our uncertain path, then start to worm my way into the tunnel behind him. The air is dark and close. I thread through cables of vine, picking twigs and leaves out of my hair and clothes. Plants spring back into position behind me, like a self-erasing aisle. The vegetation is three-dimensional – so thick in fact, that deceased branches cradled in a precinct of vines are rotting in mid-air. The broken floor of rock and slashed stems angles up to my chin, and draws blood – more of it. I fight shy of the leafy barbed wire, shielding my withered arm from the onslaught. But my sole focus is not to die here now.

I'm on all fours. Begging for mercy. Aware of every painful second: a hundred strikes of lightning, a million tons of matter spat into space by the sun, and the earth turning, as eight fight in a line, driven by blind desire.

Do anything, you said. Take any path, you said. Didn't you dare this?

Yes, didn't I? Didn't a small part of me *want* to get stung, risk everything for you? That feverish part of me that makes me more wild-eyed and skinnier by the day and will stop at nothing to reach the unreachable? And wasn't I warned? Words from the wise, risk assessments, contingency; diphtheria, rabies and typhoid – with hubris I laughed it all away, but now here I am, unreachable, delirious, and leech-stricken.

But a ticket to something so remarkable could never come without its price.

I'll pay for you in blood.

★★★

Crawled through a tunnel of sticks and came out clean the other side.

We're spat out in the river. It's a relief to stand, to see my feet again. Kuya Missan waits for the others by the water and I follow Kuya Willis through the rapids, now urgent. He pauses in the wreck-run of white flowering water. The jungle glows green behind him. He raises his right arm and points to the rising hinterland, looks at me with bright eyes, then smiles. He says nothing and nothing needs to be said. Seeing without looking. I already know.

Vaguely aware of the others on our tail, we scramble heavily up the bank.

I hear the siren-song above the forest's wild music and my heart beats in time.

I feel the delicious pain of a thousand bites and stings.

I'm half-sick with desire.

'I see it!' he shouts.

And three words are many enough to change a life.

★★★

Everyone has an apogee, a moment which all others lead towards and flow from. The thread that connected my childhood dreams to my calling as a botanist drew me to the forest like a magnet; the thread that took me over cliffs, upriver, pulled me ever deeper into oblivion. This is where it has led me: to a place where no one goes. A place less trodden than the moon?

As if in space, we walk slowly to the flower. As if we rehearsed it, we each take our place beside it. Then in the leafy light we sit and stare at it.

I see us in freeze-frame in the green lamp of the forest: Adriane cocking his head, intently, as if the flower's telling him something that requires immense concentration; Pat breathing deeply, muttering, and fiddling with his camera in a panic, as if it might disappear in a puff of smoke; Ana smiling patiently a few metres from the others. The tribe watching; Kuya Willis smiling, knowing.

Gently I brush the flower's surface as we whisper commentary about it. A tear rolls down my cheek and I wipe it away, hoping it went unnoticed. More gather, so I turn away from the group. All this for a flower. *Pull yourself together!* But I cannot. I sit there sobbing soundless, stupid tears and I can't make them stop.

***

For half an hour we creep under the thick, dark canopy, stalking flowers. A quiet field of excitement surrounds us. The slope is steep and thickly forested so it's difficult to discern how many there are, but we're all fluent enough to read the land: the scars of former flowers carved into the vines like graffiti, the buds thrusting from the earth like extrusions of the underworld – toothsome, hungry-looking, and closed to the light. There must be thirty specimens, and half a dozen in full bloom.

We approach another mature flower reclining arrogantly, watching us from an elbow of vine. We weave and duck, forcing through the hanging maze, our faces slick with effort. Holding ourselves in suspended animation among the vines, we let our excitement earth through them, back to the forest. And then we stare.

It's certain of itself, and red as blood. A statement. In fact it's vaguely obscene. I have the strangest perception of needing to look away. As if witnessing the flower has awakened some primal instinct in me; something almost sexual, corrupt. Perhaps we're all feeling the disquieting effects of the flower-creature in our midst: Pat smiles at it obscurely, his eyebrows circumflexed; Adriane is fixed on it intently – his eyes level with the flower, as dark as the forest; Ana waits patiently a few metres away for her turn, her face serene. The tribesmen are still regarding it reflectively, their heads cocked slightly, as if listening to it.

The spirit of Banao: it's cast its spell on us.

A shard of light casts an unearthly glow over the red eruption, spotlighting its otherness, the violent contravention of realism. I can sense sap rising through the vines beneath my fingers, like arteries: life blood to the forest, threads of entity, powering a flower, nurturing a monster. I force my face further into the morass to observe it more closely: the red, muscular flower gaping in its locus of vines. Measuring it with my eyes, I can see it spans half a metre. Its petals frame an open mouth filled with fangs; frozen mid-scream. As the others shift around me and take photographs, I stare at the white stars sprinkling its surface, blinking them back into focus.

High on the slope we find a fresh one unfurling an earthy dais. It's the colour of fire. A half-accomplished wonder, frozen in time; it's almost audible in its assembly. The petals are pristine, heavy-looking, flicked all over in white paint; I see them in high definition. Its surroundings are blackened, burnt out, as if lightning struck and pulled the plant right out of the earth. We position ourselves among the moss-wrapped creepers, dividing them like divers parting sea-weed to peer at a giant octopus. And I do feel afloat. Our faces are fragmented by leafy shadows and lichen trusses; and we watch the flower become gilded by an unearthly light, set apart from the other plants in the weave of its throne.

Phoenix among swans.

Like Alice, I wondered which way to go; grew curiouser, then saw my world blow up. Impossible flowers unfolded around me in wonderland: an orgy of them.

Kuya Willis with Rafflesia banaoana *in Kalinga, Luzon.*

Sensing our ecstasy, the insects have hushed now, and a miasma has crept into the mist-filled forest like a spell. Yes, I've entered another world. Their world.

And for a trice in the incomprehensible history of existence, an intersection in the chaos: the flower and I co-exist, and one sits looking at the other.

Frogs murmur softly as we leave the pantheon of root and vine. We cannot speak about what we saw. To do so would rob it of its wonder. But the flower exists deep in our souls now, of that I'm certain. Often and often I will summon it, retrace my steps to it: relive a moment untroubled by past wrongs, anxieties. Pure, like a beautiful dream, but not half-remembered as dreams are; no, this will be a moment forever lucid, diamond-sharp.

I'm so happy I feel like I've died.

★★★

A wild black sky rolls in. Pat shepherds us to a table where we inaugurate the evening's proceedings with gifts by firelight. We present the bottle of whisky we bought in Los Baños to Kuya Willis. He looks at the bottle and nods, looks up at us, then smiles mischievously. Unequal measures are sloshed out all over the place as the bottle is passed around the circle. The air smells charged, energized by the findings of the day. Pat is larger than life tonight. He speaks passionately about his past adventures in the Balbalasang–Balbalan.

'Imagine my excitement,' he says with a voice as bright as brass, looking around the group, wide-eyed. 'We trekked for days through the forest, up rivers – so, so tough – and suddenly, *there*! *There* was my *Rafflesia*!' he beams proudly.

We understand how much it means to him, each of us. As I look from face to face under the starry sky, I realize that we have all been touched by the flower in our own way. It's what brought us together – pulled my orbit into theirs.

And, as I look from face to face, I see something else too: the whisky is kicking in. Rather more violently than I had anticipated. Kuya Willis seems to be the worst affected. He snatches the bottle and pours out a long stream of it, to form a puddle several inches to the left of his glass.

'Whisky,' he murmurs, staring into his glass and blinking slowly, then he knocks back another.

After two failed attempts, he manages to stand, steadying himself with one hand on the shoulder of another tribesman. Then he staggers three metres, turns his back to us, and relieves himself loudly in the bushes. I hear a great sigh of satisfaction over the tinkle. Twenty minutes later, he slumps forward and sprawls across the floor like a starfish.

Soon everyone is slurring their words and falling about. As I watch them stumbling into the bushes and into one another, I arrive at the appalling realization that I have somehow managed to get the tribe drunk.

On the unsteady wings of this misadventure, we make our way to bed. As the others settle down, I look north. Out of the blur of crazed tiredness a new plurality is coming into focus: a part of me longs for warm water, cereal for breakfast, wine by the fire, and clean comfort. Routine. But something else is crystallizing. In shutter-clicks I see trees fall and burn – a nightmare that cannot be woken from – then a tunnel of ferns; in the dark, miracles unfolding. A fight. Cryptic pleas for help from a faraway land: text messages from a forester, and the voice of a flower.

Like dominoes in reverse, the pictures file and align in a crescendo of clicks and then stop.

Rafflesia needs saving.

The Banao indigenous community with Rafflesia banaoana *in Kalinga, Luzon.*

18.

I shouldn't tell you what happened in Turkey, but I will.

Every two years, the International Parasitic Plant Society (IPPS) runs a 'World Congress' with the aim of 'advancing scientific research on parasitic plants'. In 2009 I was invited to speak about my work on broomrape evolution in Kusadasi, on the Turkish coast. This was my third international conference and I was keen to make a good impression.

I queued at the reception desk, doubting the registration instructions in my hands, which were shadowed by a middle-aged couple in matching red swimming costumes. Sure enough, as the bronzed pair waddled off, a poster came into view: blue and corporate, like something from a bank. It was inviting me to 'help make Kusadasi a platform to discuss scientific topics'. And for the avoidance of doubt, it had on it a collage of parasitic plants.

Bar music wafted into the lobby from somewhere on the breeze as I stepped to the front of the queue.

'Welcome to Pine Bay holiday resort,' said the lady, smiling.

A snatch of nasal consonants – Russian, I think; coconut sun cream, and a mess of tubular water slides, like complicated plumbing blown up in the air. I scanned the poolside apartment numbers over the rim of my sunglasses, and recognized the wide gait of a tall man with silver hair; he was conspicuous for being fully clothed in this place where people went about their business almost naked. Chris Parker: grandfather of parasitic plant research.

Chris started working on parasitic plants in the 1950s when he was employed by a chemical company in South Africa to evaluate herbicides on field crops. This, he once told me, was where he first encountered witchweed (*Striga*). Witchweed is a parasitic plant that made an evolutionary leap from its ancestral host plant to cultivated crops, for example maize, millet, and sorghum. It can have devastating effects on crop productivity, especially in tropical Africa. Chris returned to the UK, where he dedicated years of trial-based research to controlling witchweed and became a global expert. Controlling witchweed was a hot topic. It is still.

'*Good* to see you,' he said in aristocratic vowels from another age.

I had once visited Chris and his wife in their Georgian townhouse in Bristol; baby grand, heaped books, dust. He seemed incongruous here in Pine Bay, I thought, as I heard a father and child screaming down a water slide into a splash.

'They say we're not far from Ephesus,' he whispered, nodding, as we went into our respective rooms; as if this explained something.

Two days into the conference I got bored. I know I shouldn't say that but I did. I'd delivered my talk in the Evolution and Phylogeny session early in the programme; then I paid close attention to genomes decoding before my eyes and new species blossoming on the screen. But when parasitic weeds cropped up, I began to fidget. My interests were in evolutionary enigmas, in beautiful science. *Rafflesia*. Yet witchweeds marched through the agenda unchecked, a thicket of them, rioting for attention. So I fled.

Navigation to the pool through the potentially bewildering labyrinth of bars and loungers was easy, because all the parasitic plant biologists were fully clothed and congregating purposefully around the conference hall; I simply had to avoid them. Along the way, a man in turquoise shorts listed popular beer brands to me. I thought he was inviting me to a round of drinks. Then I realized I was dressed in white shirt and black trousers similar to the Pine Bay bar staff. Plus I have Mediterranean features. Good, a disguise.

In a lazy Mexican wave, I turned in the sun with the other holidaymakers. I lathered up my face in a high SPF to avert future evidence of my escape, as children hurtled down the flumes around me, and the Pine Bay-branded photographer slunk between the loungers, snapping family portraits under the spidery shadows of a palm. A Russian lady and her daughter, both impeccably turned out, angled for his attention.

'Here is. Waitink. Waitink,' they called, as an insect buzzed indifferently.

Cicadas, chlorine, palms under the sun. Like a vital drink after a long day, I let it all wash through me. I planned to return to the conference hall, nod politely, and contribute. I planned to *help make Kusadasi a platform to discuss scientific topics*, I really did.

But I fell asleep.

On the last evening of the conference, Chris Parker called me over and introduced me to somebody important to discuss recent advances in witchweed control. I was keen to seem keen; he was keen that I listen. But as I shaped up for a fork in the conversation, something caught my eye at the back of the conference hall. A sequence of photographs, blown up like billboards, began to appear on the wall. For ambience, I suppose; or perhaps the holidaymakers were expected to buy prints, as souvenirs. Anyway, a vaguely familiar scene started to form from the projected images, like memories revisited in freezeframe: sunset through fingered palms, loungers by the pool; elements, orange, blue, and brochure-bright; the crazed smiles of a heavily made-up Russian lady and her daughter.

People in the congregation started to look up at the magnified procession coming into focus. Inflatable pool toys; red bikinis; a boy's raised arms emerging from a slide, out of focus in the spray. A man sprawled on a lounger, one arm hanging off, sunglasses askew. Vicissitudes of Pine Bay life.

What an unusual place to host a research congress, I thought, as a murmur rose across the room, like a hum.

My colleague paused and I took the cue, reached for something intellectual, impressive. But my rehearsed entry fell hard on a distracted look. I noticed heads turning; people dividing their attention between us and the man in swim shorts now stretched languorously across the wall. He, too, seemed painfully familiar.

Because he was me.

***

In my defence, my interests always tended towards *growing* parasitic plants, understanding their nature; not eradicating them. I should be clear: it's difficult to overstate (or quantify) the devastation caused by the parasitic plants that have vaulted through evolution from forest to field. Witchweeds alone infest millions of hectares of crops, costing billions of US dollars per year, and smallholders pay the price.[36] Cereal killers. Broomrapes aren't guilt-free either; they, too, mob pea and bean fields across the Mediterranean and North Africa. It's understandable that significant effort is directed towards their control: parasitic weeds declared war on agriculture and now they're winning.

But witchweeds and broomrapes are the minority. Most species of parasitic plant are the casualties of a counter-attack; our own assault on nature. Rare, vulnerable, or threatened with extinction; ripped from the earth and shoved into the pyre along with everything else. These are the plants that had been banished from the conference agenda. Ignored. In a recent paper I estimated that 76 per cent of parasitic plant species are absent from cultivation and conservation strategies; most have never been grown at all.[37] This number is only as good as the databases that informed it; I suspect it's a gross underestimate. Curators of botanic gardens – caretakers of our world's flora – often perceive parasitic plants to be intractable to cultivation. Impossible.

But they're not. As with all problem children, there are rules:

1. Build the relationship
2. Be consistent
3. Don't give up

I should know. I've parented enough of them: much of my early research was spent coaxing the stubborn sprouts out of pots and Petri dishes, hydrating the seeds and willing them to split. I discovered old protocols; pored over German and Latin prose and diagrams. Like trying complicated recipes, I set out to resurrect the forgotten techniques, conjuring life from dead books. I sprinkled seeds like fairy dust then clapped my hands and waited.

Down the microscope lens, alien forms unfolded. Like fleshy babies' fists wrestling adult fingers, I watched them curl around their hosts' roots. Fingered, orange polyps, snatching. Steadily they drew strength, and I monitored them, charted their microscopic lives like a helicopter parent. Magnified, my brood grew unplant-like and predatory, like miniature octopuses clamped to a rope. Then success: they blossomed; fled their pots and Petri dishes in an armful of flowers.

My first experiments were on broomrapes. They taught me the rules. Early on, I learnt the importance of host specificity. Each parasite is brand-loyal; you'll recall those I told you about earlier that performed better on either clovers or carrots? Each species of broomrape (sometimes even a population *within* a species) evolved alongside a particular host (or range of hosts) cheek by jowl; they've led parallel lives.

But what enables a parasitic plant to grow on one host and not another? What are the measures of success?

First things first: germination. The seeds of parasitic plants are typically minute – sometimes light as dust – and sent out in abundance. A classic trade-off exists concerning reproductive biology: invest in fewer energy-rich offspring, each likely to survive if the conditions are right; or if things are unpredictable, many energy-poor offspring of which few might survive. Think frogspawn. The odds are stacked against you if you're a parasite with exacting requirements. Better to produce copious seeds in the hope some might find the correct host on a fair wind. Hedge your bets.

The seeds of broomrapes, and indeed many parasitic plants, are wind-dispersed. Flung into cliffs, churned with the sand, washed into the soil: they get everywhere. And where they end up, they can survive for decades, centuries, or even longer. This is why witchweed is so hard to eradicate: its seed bank is vast and persistent. To sit and wait for the right host is baked into its life cycle.

But how does a parasitic plant's seed 'know' it has found the right host? While most seeds gamble their existence on warmth, water, and light, those of parasitic plants respond to signals secreted by their hosts: molecules called strigolactones. In 2005 Kohki Akiyama and colleagues shook things up when they demonstrated that strigolactones trigger the branching of arbuscular mycorrhizal (AM) fungi – organisms that form symbiotic associations with most land plants.[38] In other words, plants communicate with root-colonizing fungi through strigolactones, coaxing them into the fold. Cooperation.

But parasitic plants were eavesdropping: they hijacked the molecular dialogue of plant–fungal life cycles and hardwired it into their own. Witchweed-hunting scientists, in turn, joined the conversation. They developed an arsenal of artificial strigolactone ('analogs') to drench infested fields, inducing a mass 'suicidal germination' event, eliminating the witchweed seed bank.[39] Chemical warfare.

So, germination, I said. On detecting the right combination of strigolactones, our seedling sends out a questing radicle. It finds a root. Like ET's fingertip it reaches out, touches it. In the bond of this molecular caress, intrusive cells begin to form. The band of cells pushes into the host root, divining water-conducting vessels at its core; the plumbing behind the wall. And then it's in. The dam is breached; the bridge is built: a living cellular connection called a haustorium is formed, and a molecular stream from host to parasite marks the end of the beginning. A transfusion of sap, molecules, viruses, proteins, even the occasional accidental gene, begins to flow. The host's fate is unsealed, gases to gases, duct to duct.

All being well, the parasite will prosper, illegally plugged into the grid. But returning to my question, why does it perform well on one host but not another? Back to the Petri dish: cosmos of molecular possibilities. My IVF broomrapes showed me that developing parasites and their hosts behaved differently, even under the same conditions. In my *in vitro* society, all hosts were equal but some were more equal than others.

Fault lines began to appear in the development of my brood: blackening tissue, necrotic lesions, and festering tubers. Down the lens, a massacre was afoot. I dissected and scrutinized the aborted hopes under epifluorescence microscopy, illuminating the problem. It became clear that some of the host roots had detected the intrusion and were shutting off their reserves. A cellular blockade had dropped before the parasites. The dam was rebuilt and fate resealed.

Scientists call this process *host resistance*. Plants have evolved an artillery of defence strategies against pathogens and parasites. My own observations showed that along various checkpoints in a broomrape seedling's development, an occupied host root can detect its squatter and kick it out. The sum of compatible or incompatible interactions defines how well a parasite performs on a particular host.[40] Like all parasites, broomrapes exist in an arms race with their hosts: the battle between competing sets of co-evolving genes. An escalation of adaptations and counter-adaptations. Again, war.

Host specificity simply measures the number of winners.

***

Growing broomrapes made me bold. I set out to cultivate other, harder things at Oxford Botanic Garden. Ignored by conservation strategies everywhere, parasitic plants were crying out for a living collection – the first of its kind – to safeguard their precarious existence. However humble my efforts, I needed to do *something*. So I made a plea to my fellow botanists and botanic gardens across the world. Steadily, wax-paper seed packets rose on my desk in a rattling stack. Next to it, a pile of signed permission slips offered words of consent and good luck.

One by one they surfaced, like deep truths. First, broomrapes – foreign forms – species never before grown in the UK. Conjured from their pots, they rose like exotic asparaguses; amethysts, pinks and browns – a kaleidoscope of them glinted through the cold-frame glass like candy sticks in a jar. Then *Cytinus* shook out of the sand like a small red Psammead. Meanwhile, in the heated nursery house, *Balanophora* forced its brown, lumpen fist through the earth. Daily, the gardeners and I peered at the potted marvels, whispered questions about their needs. And in my own back garden, one spring, purple toothwort announced itself under the weeping willow. I was surrounded.

But one beast has always proved harder to tame than the rest: *Rafflesia*. The plant has a reputation for being ungrowable. Absent from conservation collections and seed banks everywhere, it is defenceless in the face of habitat destruction. It is exceptionally difficult to grow and its seeds are recalcitrant, meaning they do not

survive storage. The only botanic garden in the world to have propagated the plant and seen it bloom repeatedly is in Bogor, Indonesia.
Bogor's propagation wizards managed to tempt it onto a vine: spent
years peering intently and breathing on the latent marvel; then
stood back one day and gasped. One small step for mankind, one
giant leap for plant conservation.

Still, much of the life cycle of *Rafflesia* remains a mystery. After
all, for most of the time it's as visible as a tapeworm. Its earliest
stages of development are uncharted. It can't be persuaded to grow
in a Petri dish; goodness knows, people have tried. Its seeds stub-
bornly ignore strigolactones, even though the seeds of most parasitic
plants find strigolactones irresistible. Over and over again, the seeds
refused to germinate in the lab. *Rafflesia* will not be a supplicant to
science.

But we do know from looking down the microscope that once
Rafflesia launches its invasion, it begins to reconfigure the world
around it. As I tap these words into my laptop, cell division is taking
place in a vine somewhere deep in the forest. Under the direction of
an imposter – a thief – a reservoir is being constructed, expanding
steadily. Hydraulic infrastructure, engineered with military pre-
cision, diverted to a growing artillery. Plans. Threads of entity:
molecular processes, brought to bear by evolution. Like human
thoughts.

***

Finding *Rafflesia banaoana* in Kalinga created a fork in my path. Two
fates converged in that place beyond the reach of the real, away
from the world's kept promises of trade winds and tides, life
and fire, babies born and species lost. It was an event around which
my future was to pivot.

Yes, something became fixed there and my life is beginning to
unfold differently. *Rafflesia* grows daily in my thoughts now, living
off them, ballooning. How couldn't it? When I went off the map
and down into the abyss to reach my uncharted summit?

Yet still the seeds of childhood dreams creep forward through my
consciousness like mycelial threads. Images flash before me like

pages in a falling book I can't quite catch: the burning pyre, the for-ester, the fight, yes. But now new things besides: witchweeds and magic; instructions and dust; wonderful flowers brought forth from human endeavour. All of them stealing towards a compass point: saving *Rafflesia*. But how?

I need a plan.

19.

Pray for us to be safe, Mr Chris.

Every day I am checking, Mr Chris, checking, but *Rafflesia* isn't home. And a rodent has been in the forest today – yes – I know because I saw him.

But the track is a dangerous track. Rainy season does mean rain.

Pray for us to be safe.

20.

'This one?' he says, not looking up. 'No work. No enough the root.'

Mr Ngatari runs a careworn hand over an invisible shelf a metre above the earth and we listen to him intently. We can't afford to miss a word.

'This one new . . .' He drifts off as if that wasn't all he planned to say. He nods at it once – bows almost – then makes to leave the cage-like contraption in which we're standing.

Mr Ngatari is a wizard. He is the only man in the world who has managed to successfully propagate *Rafflesia* repeatedly, and we're here to learn from him. We're introduced by Joko, who is a botanist based here in Bogor. Fifty-ish, thick wire thatch over a gentle face. I've worked with Joko on various things over the years, including parasitic plant conservation and tropical fruits. He has a calm sincerity, an air of Obama about him. I doubt he's raised his voice once in his life. I see him as a friend.

Minding the snaking vines breaching the soil, we hopscotch onto the mossed brick platforms. Each is just large enough for a person, and spaced out, so the six of us are scattered across the enclosure. No one is quite sure who will use which platform next, so we shuffle about in a contemplative way, like human chess pieces.

'This one my best,' Mr Ngatari says, pointing to a triple knot of vines, green with age. He may have said 'beast'.

He looks up to check we're still paying attention. I nod and lean in to peer at the complicated mess. Rope-like creepers have absorbed one of the bricks in an embrace and dispossessed their metal label; pushed it back defiantly. Plants in charge.

'Yes.'

Did he read my mind?

Crouching to run a finger along the vine, I read the markings like runes. Every scar in life denotes a significant historic event, and these are no exception. One is round, with drawn features, like a sloth's face; this tells me *Rafflesia* bloomed here. Another is a circular constriction, indenting the wood, like a strung-up ham. The binding ring. This speaks of wizardry.

We step out of the cage into the dappled light. The air is green and rich, and insects drift through it like plankton. I smack at a mosquito but not in time. A lichened vine has escaped its lair; it's pouring out of the breached wire mesh onto the ground alongside a crooked brick path. A row of *Rafflesia* buds are popping up along its surface like balls of rising dough. The largest is the size of a cantaloupe, flesh-coloured and heavily deformed by blackened spots. Mr Ngatari sees me clock the disfigurement. 'Too many sun.' His eyes follow an invisible balloon rising slowly into the canopy at which he squints, then shakes his head. 'Many, many sun.'

With his camera, Pat drops to eye-level next to the cabbage-like bud. Adriane photographs him taking photographs. I reach for my notebook, a green leather-bound one I bought especially for the expedition. *Bogor Botanic Garden*, I write at the top of the page, in a crisp, orderly font. Always so neat at the start. Won't last. Not when things get tough.

7H pencil, not pen: hard, enduring; well, it needs to be on a trip like this. Invulnerable to rain, blood, and tears, I've learned. Still, the book will disintegrate; they always do. I chew the end of the pencil and feel a frisson of excitement as I hear my lead rasp the paper.

Lesson one: vampire hates sun.

★★★

Since the 1850s, *Rafflesia* has been lured out of the warm wet earth here at Bogor. As I've mentioned, this is the only botanic garden in the world to have managed it. The nineteenth-century Dutch plant

165

collector Johannes Elias Teijsmann – once *hortulanus* (director) of Bogor – reports digging up *Rafflesia*-infected vines wholesale from the wilds of Java, then establishing them here at the garden. It flowered repeatedly for him. I can imagine his broad, whiskered face peering at it over his spectacles. Later that century, letters traded back and forth by collectors and botanists indicate three species of *Rafflesia* blossomed in the garden. Quite how the early botanists achieved it is unclear from the addled reports: some allude doubtfully to seed, others mention transplants; one even cites seed from a self-pollinating flower, which is impossible.[41] But achieve it they did. The renowned Italian botanist Odoardo Beccari reported in the 1870s that *Rafflesia* bloomed here every year. It must have been a sensation when it did; but, like the plant, people's reactions were lost to time, and we're left speculating, because in the 1920s the flowers began to retreat, and by the 1930s they'd disappeared altogether. By then there were none left within easy reach in the wild to replenish the stocks: they'd all been plundered.[42] *Rafflesia* vanished from Bogor. Until now.

'Meet Sofi,' says Joko. 'She is Curator of *Rafflesia* here at Bogor Botanic Garden since 2004. Working with Mr Ngatari many, many years.'

We shake hands. I have co-authored a paper on parasitic-plant propagation with Sofi, but this is the first time we've met. She's immaculately turned out, with a sky-blue headscarf pinned by an elegant brooch. Fire to Joko's earth, she has a mild urgency, a single-minded quality about her. Just as well, given her subject.

A few metres away, Mr Ngatari is wielding a whip-like root he's severed. From where, I'm not sure; I need to pay closer attention. We huddle in a ring surrounding the little old man. Mystery creeps about the group and binds us. In conspiratorial silence we watch him pinch the root between a weathered forefinger and thumb, then raise it to the air for inspection. In its centre we see a corruption in the bark's flow – a swelling no larger than a walnut. Easily missed, but to us it's unmistakable: *Rafflesia* is in residence.

'*Rafflesia patma*,' he says.

This species is one of three that occur here on the island of Java, and one we hope to locate later during the trip. Its first documented collection was made in 1818 by Karl Ludwig von Blume, then a twenty-two-year-old surgeon and naturalist, posted from Holland as 'inspector of vaccines'. He carried out extensive surveys of the Indonesian flora and was based at this very botanic garden.[43] Today, few wild populations of *R. patma* remain; no one seems sure how many, from the conversations I've had. It means the specimens propagated here at Bogor are precious.

Mr Ngatari ushers us to a python of vine at the end of the little brick path. He crouches awkwardly beneath it and extracts from his pocket a small tin case. He sets this upon the ground with a clink, beside his trailing line of *Rafflesia*-infected root. Then he flicks open the case to reveal a set of small kitchen knives and a folded square of polythene.

'Must be big,' he says, acknowledging the vine looming above us. 'Must be morning.'

I scribble this down without question as he begins to unfold the polythene, revealing a cartoon bunch of vegetables.

'Must be *bawang*.'

I look to Joko enquiringly.

'Means garlic wrapper,' he says.

I have my doubts but write this down too – leave nothing to chance – as Mr Ngatari begins stretching the polythene into a taut strip. He puts this to one side like a tangle of floss, then with a small kitchen knife begins slicing a tributary of vine with his brown, crab-like hands. Then he makes an identical incision in the *scion* – the possessed root.

'Must be this.' He indicates the optimal length of the scion with spaced arms. He holds this posture crookedly for a moment to allow Adriane to take a photograph. I judge the distance and make a quick annotated sketch. 'Must be this.' He demonstrates the necessary width with an invisible vine between his finger and thumb. Then he unites the half-lives with a ring of spiralled garlic wrapper. Locked. If our graft is successful, *Rafflesia* will be teased out of the infected scion into the roots of the stock plant, hidden beneath a scarred ring. And the risk of extinction of *R. patma* falls again.

'Must be this.' He covers the betrothed vines with leaf mould to complete proceedings, flicking the leaves with the back of his hand, like a chicken. 'Must be this,' he mutters one last time at nothing in particular, and painfully he hoists himself up, using the vine for support. He hands over to an authoritative Sofi.

'Gardeners know when to water. Every day they check. If there is trouble, we examine the colour,' she explains. Sofi squats beside the vine and makes a small nick using her nail, then points to a vital streak of apple flesh. I assume this is the colour it should be. 'Then we wait two years,' she says, waving away some thread-like roots hanging over her face. 'Sixty per cent chance of success but only when the technique has been mastered, in the correct site, if the weather is right.'

I feel like a patient learning variables around a diagnosis. Fate by numbers.

'And never bend it. Mr Ngatari has mastered the technique,' she adds, smiling, then pauses. 'He knows everything.'

Our vine doctor nods sagely, then folds his crab-like hands, signalling the end of class. We pick our way out over the bricks, leaving our chimera in the hands of nature. As I look back at where we were standing, I feel something quietly powerful wash through me. Secret knowledge: an invisible power, potent as magic.

Next we're shown the rootstock nursery. A dozen hopeful vines are fleeing their black polythene pots in pursuit of the light. They've been collected from rainforests across Indonesia to establish a bank of *Tetrastigma* to infect with *Rafflesia*, we're told. Their young, nettle-soft leaves resemble those of a grapevine. No coincidence: they're cousins. *Tetrastigma* and grapes belong to the same family (the Vitaceae). In a large plastic washing-up tub, a grapefruit-sized *Rafflesia* bud has announced itself in the angle of a heavyset vine. 'That won't live,' Sofi says as she sees me sketch it. She chuckles gently. 'Too advanced when the gardener cut it. Better smaller.' *Lesson two.*

Behind us, Mr Ngatari is busy spooling loops of thread-like root around his left arm in a sort of wreath.

'Trellis,' says Sofi. She senses our confusion. 'We tie it to the vines with a stone, then we throw it to the trees. It takes them to the sun.'

Mr Ngatari grafting Rafflesia *at Bogor, Java.*

It's agreed that none of the vines here are ready to launch; anyway there are no stones. So we leave the nursery, blessing the plants on the way out. We have an appointment in Bogor with Dr Andes, Head of the Research Centre for Plant Conservation, Botanic Gardens, and Forestry, to discuss plans for future collaborative research. But there's one more thing to see here in the botanic garden, we're told. Something special.

***

We stoop under the hazard tape, rigged up like a crime scene, and huddle in the shaded clearing. Vines rear up before us like cobras. A green metal label with hand-painted white writing has been banged to one of them.

'*Rafflesia arnoldii*,' Sofi says. 'Last year it flowered for the first time.'

We peer at the empty stage of earth where the plant made its big performance. Often confused with other *Rafflesia* species, the flowers of *Rafflesia arnoldii* span a metre across: of the forty known species, this one rules them all. None of us has seen it before apart from in books and childhood dreams. This is the species I magicked out of the ground with papier mâché all those years ago.

Cages and wire-mesh cylinders have been dropped over the reptilian vines as if there's a concern that the plants might creep off. Inside their enclosures, buds like footballs wrapped in brown paper are peeping through the leaf litter. The largest, the size of a small pumpkin, is blackening. I suspect it has aborted; a high proportion of *Rafflesia* flowers miscarry for reasons we don't know. Like most things concerning their biology. Hardly surprising: I'm looking at the sole specimen of *R. arnoldii* in cultivation. A living enigma.

'Ten years ago, we planted it . . .' Sofi pauses. 'From seed.'

This cannot be. Every rafflesiologist knows *Rafflesia* will not be summoned from seed. Multiple attempts over the last two decades suggest it's nigh-on impossible. The only reliable reports of successful propagation are by grafting – the technique we've just been shown by Mr Ngatari. Even that's a leap of faith.

'From *seed*?' says Pat.

Sofi smiles at our visible disbelief.

'Yes, it's true. At first we gave up hope,' she says. 'Every day we checked the seeds for more than a year. They did nothing for us. Then, one day, a member of the public spotted it from the path. And – well. There it was.'

She gives a modest shrug, then adds, 'How do you think the seeds are dispersed in nature?'

'We saw ants crawling over the fruits in the Philippines,' Adriane ventures, eager to be first.

Ants are one of the more convincing options that scientists have put forward for *Rafflesia* seed dispersal. Birds, squirrels, tree shrews, and the soles of elephants' feet are others. Nobody knows for sure. Sofi looks to the trees, as if the answer is written there, before turning to face us.

'I think they're taken underground by termites. I've seen them,' she says.

We watch this new truth rise before us. So much of Rafflesia's cryptic biology exists unwritten: in observation and local wisdom; in our thoughts. Our sacred class in Bogor is drawing to a close and I feel an urgency to absorb facts, as if memorizing the floorplan of a burning house. I step back through the morning's lesson, make a mental list.

'What is the *most* important thing?' I ask. 'Of all the things we've learned, what *must* we do right?'

'There is one more thing you should know,' Sofi replies, then pauses. 'One thing more important than the rest, when grafting *Rafflesia*.' Her voice drops to a confidential whisper.

(But I can't disclose this here. It's not my secret to tell.)

I encrypt the sine qua non on the first page of my new notebook: opening chapter to an unknowable future. Fraught with risk and endurance, no doubt, but that's a contract I'm bound to now. Love recast as duty. That's why we're all standing in this shaded corner of Southeast Asia's oldest botanic garden: impelled to save a plant in peril, something for which we care deeply.

Once again *Rafflesia* has played chess with our lives: dragged us from across the corners of the board, this time with a keen motive. Time is running out, but a plan is afoot. We must learn, and fast.

We need to grow the ungrowable.

21.

Well, Mr Chris, Bengkulu is sick again. Fruit season from rain. Heavy rain from fruit. And the floods, Chris, the floods. But I wanted to let you know that the rodent is eating the seeds again. That I do want you to know.

22.

'We're so delighted to be here!' My words sound flat after the silence, but everyone nods cordially. These meetings can be awkward at first. I scratch a nagging insect bite on my forearm. A family smiles at me from a framed photograph on a side table. Through the office window I see the tops of trees. Steady rain. A canyon of cloud, lit peculiarly, as if from beneath.

An assistant enters with a tray of coffees – black, with sugar – always served this way. Our host, Dr Andes, keeps vigil as the cups are handed about. A serious man; someone who likes a process. He leans forward to address the group. 'You are welcome here in Bogor. I hope our institutions will work well together.' Polite smiles.

'In the Philippines, Professor Pat and his associate Adriane showed me several species of *Rafflesia*,' I say, nodding at Pat and Adriane over the table. 'I am deeply grateful to them. Now we would like to extend this work, here in Indonesia, with Bogor Botanic Garden. Together, we hope to establish a new global network for the conservation of *Rafflesia*.'

I'm pleased with how that sounded.

'Yes, yes. Joko is ideally placed to work with you on this. He is an excellent taxonomic botanist with significant experience.' Dr Andes half-waves in Joko's direction.

'Indeed. We're delighted . . .'

'Listen!'

Our host cocks his head as if the tiles are telling him something urgent and confidential. I notice a poster on the wall depicting masked cartoon people socially distancing. It has on it an orange bubble shouting '3H!' For the life of me I can't think what this could mean besides the eighth position of the 22-point scale of pencil hardness. H for hard. I prefer a softer pencil myself. Gunmetal grey. Even black.

Stapler, muddled pens; lady in mauve headscarf walking briskly down the corridor – running in fact; rain-stippled glass to dreary sky. An unbidden recollection of a spell spent in hospital staring at the wall. Dalí's floppy clock. An electric whine. Dr Andes is now resting his left hand on the table as if recharging. We stare at him expectantly.

Then the cups begin to shake.

***

The earthquake lasted for half a minute; quite long, they said. A pinprick in earth's geology; a million consequences rippling out. I didn't know it was an earthquake at first. Stupid really, because what else could it have been? The building rocked from side to side with a loud creaking noise, like a wobbly bed. I recall wondering why the rain continued to beat against the glass unstirred. I can't think now why I would question that.

This isn't my first natural disaster. A few years ago I was carrying out botanical survey work on a volcano in Japan when a violent eruption occurred. Thunder, smoke and ash, then the earth was a blown-out candle. Of course we fled – when a volcano erupts, you run for your life, and that's that. But volcano and earthquake evac-uation procedures aren't necessarily transferable skills.

'What do we do?' I asked the air, as the world began to sway like a ship.

'Hide under the table or leave. But we are the first floor. So we should leave,' said Dr Andes.

By then people were sprinting down the shaking corridor, so this was obvious. We jumped up and followed them. *This is exciting*, I'm ashamed to recall thinking now; I wish I hadn't thought that.

The violent heaving petered out by the time we reached the lobby, and so did the sprinting. A cat appeared from nowhere and began to scream, which was strange, but nobody seemed to care or notice. Then everyone reached for their phones in near-synchrony; it was almost funny. At the time I thought they were posting feverishly on social media (a common compulsion), but now I realize they were checking the location of the epicentre. Wondering how bad it was. Whether they might know someone who was killed.

'Thirty-seven miles,' someone said. 'That's close.'

'I left my phone upstairs!' said Adriane. He looked genuinely concerned. 'Do you think I can go back and get it?'

'No,' I said.

Ten minutes later we went back up anyway. By then, no one seemed of a mind to continue with the meeting, so it was abandoned. As we left the office I smelled vomit.

We re-examine the event over lunch: *bebek kampung muda* (duck), which we eat with greasy hands in a café with three solid walls and a sheet of hissing rain. Five point six on the Richter scale, according to our phones; bad but could've been worse, Joko says. We talk about how we felt when the floor began to move, rehearsing our experience for the outside world. I tell the group this was my first earthquake, to which no one says anything, because it's obvious. Repeating ourselves, we moor our excitement with a weak anchor of words such as 'scared', 'strange', and 'weird'. Tamed from a safe distance, the drama starts to take a shape. I leave the table to wash my hands at an outside basin, something you find in all these cafés. By the time I return, Google has started a death toll, but still our feelings aren't real. Yet, anyway. In time they'll come.

I resume my real life for a few hours through the prism of Microsoft Outlook. In the evening Pat and Adriane buy beer from a market which we cart to a restaurant called Betawi – a place with photographs of the food and everything numbered. I have concerns about bringing alcohol into a Halal restaurant, but no one seems bothered. The beer softens the day's edge.

Later, on the hotel bed, I watch the horrors unfold on television. Over a hundred dead in Cianjur – a number that will eventually multiply sixfold, although many of the deaths will go unreported. The earthquake will earn itself an official intensity rating, but no

175

one needs this now – it's obvious, even with the sanitized reporting: 'Despite its moderate size, the shallow depth caused strong shaking'. Blue flashing lights weaving around smashed-up homes and lives flicker across the hotel room screen like a nightmare. People around the world are watching. Grief reduced by thousands of miles to sympathetic curiosity. Then forgotten. Like all the natural disasters dealt out across Southeast Asia over the years.

People send me text messages from home; I don't admit fully to myself that a small part of me savours their concern. An international drama and me in the thick of it. I'm wary of my feelings. As I summon sleep I hold the hardest thoughts away from me. It's a brave mind that can sink beneath the tangled shards to visit the last few moments of a life: the roar, the crush, the entrapment. Desperate to surface. Desperate to breathe.

Ringing silence.

★★★

'Saving plants' we decide to call it. The webinar at the National Research and Innovation Agency (BRIN) has been cobbled together at the last minute, but Joko is confident we'll get an audience. None of us is feeling particularly well-prepared. It will be held in Cibinong, on the outskirts of Jakarta; a city within a city. On the drive we talk about a recent sighting of *Rafflesia rochussenii* that Adriane has spotted online. He's like a radar for these sightings. *Rafflesia rochussenii* is an exceptionally rare species, first documented about thirty miles away by an unknown collector at Bogor Botanic Garden in 1850.[44] It was apparently declared extinct until it was rediscovered in 1990 in the forested hills we can see from the car. We take it in turns to admire the defiant red flower on Adriane's phone.

'I think it's nearby,' says Adriane, fiddling about with Google Maps.

'Oh-really?' says Joko. He answers every question this way. 'Too far. Two-day trek,' he says, inspecting the map.

So that's that. He hands the phone back to Adriane and we resume staring out of the window in opposite directions. I fidget as I gaze over the hills of Hambalang and Mount Salak where *Rafflesia* hides. Beneath the heaped grey peaks, gangs of motorcycles weave between the cars, intent as wasps. Men in matching black kopiah hats sit in a line along the side of the road staring at their phones; I wonder if they're looking at yesterday's earthquake. None of us in the car has mentioned it today out of a presumed respectful politeness. 'Last Christmas' by Wham! blares from the radio as the driver circles out of the main road towards a sky-blue metal gate with three bored-looking security guards. 'Because of this,' Joko says, pointing to the red and white sticker on the windscreen as we sail past them, but I doubt they'd have stopped us anyway.

Pat, Adriane, and I give our lectures in a clinical white office with small windows to ragged banana leaves under a bleached sky. Pat's lecture focuses on tree extinction. Pat is a Red List Assessor, meaning he monitors the relative risk of species extinction over time. 'The Philippines is one of the most threatened countries, with only little of the original forest remaining. Many tree species there are known from a single location and have not been seen since they were first documented. Although more trees are threatened than animals, there is a greater conservation effort for animals.' Nobody looks surprised. 'Moreover,' he says, looking up from his notes, 'areas protected on paper aren't on the ground.' Wordless agreement. 'Taxonomy gives plants names. Red List Assessment gives them a voice,' he says in closing. Then Adriane presents photographs of his *Rafflesia* dissections, like sliced mushrooms. He points out anatomical discrepancies like a forensic scientist leading a postmortem. '*Rafflesia* is like humans: sometimes mysterious, sometimes confused,' he concludes.

In the last presentation, Sofi expands on the *Rafflesia* cultivation protocol she demonstrated yesterday in the botanic garden. 'Operation *Rafflesia*,' she calls it, in her high, staccato voice. She describes a litany of failed attempts dating back to 2004. 'Day 628, still no sign,' she says referring to an abortive seed inoculation. 'Our first bud was in 2009.' Grafts tied up, she moves on to the next impasse: pollination. *Rafflesia* flowers are rare and unisexual, their pollen is viable for just seventy-two hours, and most populations are dominated by one gender. No pollination means no seed. All things considered, probability is against them. 'They're lonely and they need a mate. So I call the forest rangers and I ask them: do you have a male for my flower in the garden?' She concludes the session with uneasy sentiments about retirement and lost knowledge. Her words are unvarnished but behind them stretches a lifelong passion. No one knows *Rafflesia* better than Sofi. We have so much to learn from her in a short time. I can't tell if the urgency is hers or mine.

We have lunch in a canteen open to the elements on both sides, but not quite; a perforated wall has been erected as if to keep something out. Behind a steaming cauldron of rice, a thin woman in a yellow headscarf shouts orders to the kitchen staff. Joko asks what I'd like, but I don't know what anything is.

'Yes, I like chicken, and noodles, yes, eggs too,' I say, which is just as well because all these things come together in a yellow confection called *soto ayam*.

In the afternoon we're given a tour of the Herbarium Bogoriense. Established in 1841 in the colonial era, this is the largest herbarium in Southeast Asia, home to a million specimens of plants and fungi. We're led by a lady in a matching pink smock and headscarf who forgets to draw breath between sentences. The building is new. Electric light bounces down the corridors of the vinyl flooring and grey cabinets. I can't help but think of mortuaries as we pad about in special shoes looking at dead specimens.

We're taken into a room containing the spirit collection. Here, plants with fleshy fruits and flowers unsuitable for pressing and mounting on herbarium sheets are stowed in enormous jars of liquid. It smells of hospitals. Wild banana specimens thrust out of their stained ponds like cadaverous hands; a miscellany of gingers and bromeliads press their faces to the glass; and among all this: pickled *Rafflesia*, like deep-sea creatures, staring. The labels tell us they were collected from forests all over Borneo, Java, and Sumatra in the early twentieth century. Long before the wholesale destruction. I wonder if any of those forests still exist.

At the end of the tour we're shown dried specimens of *Rafflesia*. We fossick through the spidery black remains taped to old-smelling pages. Among them are life-sized black and white drawings, shaded in charcoal – unconventional for botanical illustration. Competing lines resolve anatomical features that Leonardo might have produced. Faded words gallop beneath them. One is labelled *Rafflesia gibbosa*, a name none of us recognize. Later, I discover it was proposed by the Dutch botanist Sijfert Hendrik Koorders, curator of this herbarium in 1892. At the time he had insufficient material to describe the species, and he died before he could publish his manuscript. It was christened *Rafflesia micropylora* by another Dutch botanist, Willem Meijer. He too worked at this herbarium, and dedicated his life to *Rafflesia*. His papers of the 1980s betray an urgency: 'I have been able to obtain extensive first-hand knowledge of the genus, which I hope to present soon in a full-fledged revision . . . it seemed therefore necessary to publish the 5 (or 6) new taxa before that time.' Perhaps because, like all of us, he was troubled by a vanishing world; felt he needed to describe them, before they'd gone: 'A few years ago *Rafflesia* was seen by a local entomologist . . . When he brought me in 1983 to the site it was destroyed by logging. Nearby splendidly virginal montane forest was logged in 1983.'[45] A black and white photograph of Meijer taken after his expedition to Sumatra captures bright eyes and a knowing look I can't forget.

On the way back to Bogor, I feel sad as I reflect on all the failed attempts and bottled hopes. History repeating itself. Conservation defeated by extinction. I watch an old man wander by the roadside with a sack of greenery slung across his back. He's in tune with the land but looks lost somehow. I wonder if he too is worrying about the world. My thoughts land on Mount Salak nosing the horizon, the place where *Rafflesia rochussenii* was lost for over a century. A quilt of cloud has crept over its peaks at a jaunty angle, like a badly made bed. *Too far.* Still, I wish we'd tried. To see *Rafflesia* in a forest, rather than through pixels and jars. How couldn't I, when we're this close? While it's still there?

But I must be patient. You'd think I'd have learned that by now.

23.

We clamber into the vehicle by streetlight. Today we're driving to Pangandaran – home of *Rafflesia patma* – the rare species we saw in bud a few days ago at Bogor. We must travel 230 miles to see the flower in the wild. There's no guarantee we will see it; in fact, we probably won't. Still, it's blooming in our minds' eyes. Like reality without perception.

Our driver is called Mas Bamba. He has a serious demeanour and eyebrows fixed in a question at the road ahead, which is infiltrating a chaos of accidental-looking buildings. It's early and there are no people about, just cats slinking; all shoulders, no tails. At the rear of the vehicle, Adriane's face glows blue from the light of his phone. At the front, Joko, Pat, and I share stories about fieldwork to Mas Bamba's Nintendo-style backing music. We hurtle thus, east into the rising sun.

I ask Joko how much time he spends in the field. 'Before Covid, many, many time. But now the government has, how-to-say, restricted funding.' Pat spends more time in the field, but still laments a lack of funding. I throw bureaucracy into a ring of violent agreement. We've strayed into the paradoxical borderland where ecology meets economics: progress slaying biodiversity, but funding for conservation depending on progress. As I watch the onward rush to progress outside my window, I consider words I've put into the world over the years; the froth: 'urgent conservation action required' and 'data informing conservation priorities'. Saying is believing. I catch Mas Bamba's eye in the mirror as we swim with a shoal of bikes. I wonder how much of our conversation he under-stands; what he thinks of the changing world outside? And me, its guest.

Having shrunk our nation's funds in a race to the bottom, we agree Japan supports conservation research generously. This matter resolved, we opt to tackle less abstruse hardships, such as the cost of petrol.

'One US dollar per litre in the Philippines,' says Pat.

'Oh really, I see. Less than that here,' Joko replies.

I can't recall the price of petrol in the UK, so I reach for a number that sounds appropriately expensive. Perversely satisfied by our troubles, we turn our attention to Karst Padalarang: the knife of rock thrown up from the hazed, crowded plain. Beneath it, open trucks packed with men in baseball caps zoom past raggedy bananas, lopsided shacks, and golden pirouettes piercing the mist. Little, tile-topped huts scatter the cartoon-green paddy fields. Along their margins, workmen in yellow helmets crouch watching the traffic, laughing at something. They look happy.

'Joko, is it the policy here to use native species for landscaping?' asks Pat, watching a stereoscope of roadside trees.

'You know that, commonly, it is to use the exotic ones,' he replies.

'I see. In the Philippines people are now appreciating the native trees for ornament,' says Pat.

All field botanists read the land through the bifocal lens of native and invasive. Native species pose no threat to the natural environ-ment. By contrast, those introduced to new places by humans have the potential to become *invasive*. This inconsistently defined term generally refers to a species that thrives in its new environment free from natural predators, and outcompetes native populations. In-vasive species include plants, animals, fungi, and microbes. Dogs and cats, rabbits and rats, cane toads – they all left the ark where they had no business being, wreaking havoc on the local biota. Mean-while invasive plants including various cacti, grasses, trees, and vines have choked deserts, forests, and grasslands everywhere. Most countries have legislation in place to protect against them. The IUCN has established a 'most wanted' list of offenders. On Mount

Banahaw in the Philippines we saw drifts of tropical invasive plants that, to an untrained eye, might resemble a lush haven for wildlife. Deforestation and habitat destruction are a visible, violent assault on the land. Invasive plants pose a more insidious threat. But it's just as real.

The hours pass. As we approach Bandung, the capital of West Java Province, we watch an enormous stratovolcano bearing up through the mist. Mount Tangkuban Perahu, Joko tells me; its name refers to the upturned boat in the legend of its creation.

'I understand,' I say, thinking perhaps I do as we circle the capsized kingdom climbing out of the cluttered ocean of human enterprise. Glistening palms; domestic fire smoke; great columns of a viaduct; under these, a woman in a purple headscarf directing an audience of small children with raised hands. Cars, trucks, and bikes all drone into file.

'Now, how-you-say expressway.'

By and by, the expressway yields to a lesser road wrapped with numberless stalls from which no one is buying anything. Corrugated-iron roofs strung up with clear plastic bags containing pink crackers; hills of sweet potatoes; family washing; crouched men with bare feet fiddling with bikes and engine parts. Pat points to a line of planted Moluccan albizzia trees (*Falcataria falcata*). They have meandering grey branches with tiered leafy clouds that temper the light. Near them we see a great log pile with attendant workers in tattered trousers.

'In Mindanao, in the south of the Philippines, this is an important source of plywood.'

Joko turns his head slightly. 'Oh-really, here in Java it is used to make boxes,' he says.

As the merits of albizzia wood are traded east to west, I see two small boys in matching clothes and black kopiah hats running, holding hands. Near them, a girl sits on a step holding a cat by its neck with one hand – sagging like water in a bag – and stroking it with the other. They all look content (except the cat). Behind them extends a Toblerone of grey-faded peaks, its crest squared off by a reef of cloud. The road parts an ocean of paddy fields. Farmers in conical sedge hats wade slowly about the green, like stalking herons.

After about seven hours, we stop for lunch at a town called Ciamis (pronounced Chah-mis) which has a small park named *Rafflesia*. Hah! Islamic noon prayers drown the traffic as we file into a café. Assorted chicken platters heaped on banana leaves glisten under a helicopter fan. Mas Bamba sits on a separate table, which he considers carefully, smoking, while the rest of us identify plants in the salad. *Solanum* is the only one we can name with certainty. After lunch, Adriane tracks our progress on his phone as Joko orders coffee. We still have another sixty miles to drive south to Pangandaran. As I compliment the owner on his strong black coffee – first of the day – Pat asks Joko whether or not he drinks beer. I think he's testing the water for tonight.

'Just sometimes.'

'Yes, sometimes. Like me. Some times a day!' says Pat.

As we leave, Joko hands our surplus box of this morning's breakfast rice to the first man he sees. The man bows deeply thrice. 'Better than no one has it,' Joko says.

Back in the car, I revisit my notes from the grafting workshop with Mr Ngatari and Sofi a few days ago. Vines creep impetuously over the paper through crowded annotations of runes and numbers, like complex incantations.

It's not the first time I've crossed paths with plant magic. Enter mandrake (*Mandragora officinarum*). As Stephen Harris, the Curator of the Oxford University Herbaria, puts it, few plants in Western botany are surrounded by as much folklore, mythology, and nonsense.[46] For millennia the plant has been ritualized, revered, plucked, swallowed, and swooned over. At low doses, it induces drowsiness, a little more might trigger a violent dream; at high doses, a nightmare. But the margins between medicinal and lethal doses were tight. Administering it was dicey.

Squint at a mandrake's root and it bears a faint resemblance to the human form. Under the Doctrine of Signatures – in which plants' physical characteristics denoted therapeutic significance – this bred superstition. 'Old wives' and 'runagate surgeons' cautioned that the shriek of an uprooted mandrake would drive its harvester insane; better to tie one to a dog and have him rip it out. Knock-offs were whittled out of root vegetables and sold on the black market. Genuine mandrakes with a strong human resemblance became sought after. The likeness of a hanged man was said to manifest in a mandrake that grew from his 'dripping juices'. Hence they would spring up under gallows.[47]

Our own mandrakes spring from the southwest corner of Oxford Botanic Garden, in the medicinal beds. As received wisdom surrendered to practical observation in mid-seventeenth-century plant lore, mandrakes were among the first plants to be grown in the University's botanic garden.[48] Today their location is marked by a bald patch of grass where the Harry Potter fans hang out. Each November, under the long shadows of a magnolia tree, the mandrakes sprout like cabbages. One spring at the Botanic Garden, we decided to harvest one.

According to doctrine, incantations with sword-drawn magic circles protect a harvester from harm. Better still, a dog. Leaving nothing to chance, we followed all the pre-Renaissance herbalists' rules. I pored over their ancient tomes depicting leaf-crowned earthen limbs, rooty penises, and mad dogs. Then in the cool shade of the old stone walls, we began our séance with the mandrakes.

Things got off to a bad start when our dog Beau (on loan from a lady in the admin team) tried to eat one. But we pushed him aside, undeterred. With our backs to the moon, we drew the magic circles. I ran through my rehearsed lines. Stooping over my spade with the shaft against my knee, I plunged into the twilit ground as many had before me. The sods smelled cold as I went deeper. I dug hard into four centuries of 'muck and dunge', and I drank in time.

'Would curses kill, as doth the mandrake's groan!'[49] I cried.

Then the spade screeched as the root snapped under its metal.

I think it was the spade.

***

A five-metre-long marlin diving into the sky marks our arrival. The metal monument is hoisted from a large paddling pool serving as a roundabout. Beyond it are swathes of clipped grass, ambitious palms, and billboards shouting 'GRAND PANGANDARAN' and

'YOUR FUTURE PANGANDARAN' and 'INTIMATE WED-DING PANGANDARAN'. Along the beachfront we pass Hotel Sunset (three of them) and stands of sunglasses and cartoon seahorses.

'Tourist place,' Joko says, still looking ahead.

We park near the sea beside a green skip belching plastic, in which a large grey macaque is foraging. He clings to the lip with all four paws, his long tail draped over the edge, like a rat. He seems indifferent to me taking his photograph. Then he turns, parts his legs in what looks an uncomfortable posture, to expose a large pair of twisted testicles, and stares at me.

We lean against the car to change our shoes and prepare for the trek that we're told will be gentle. Joko, straightening his baseball cap, says he's found us a guide called Iwan who knows where *Rafflesia* grows; he also told Joko that people have fled Pangandaran for fear of a tsunami, following the earthquake two days ago.

'Big tsunami here in 2006, Chris,' explains Joko. 'Waves many, many metres. Dead, many, many dead.' I vaguely recollect flashes of toppled palms and houses, splintered wood, a woman with both hands clamped to her face and a lost look. But now these images seem conflated with those from Monday.

The outdoor versions of ourselves file towards the sea, like refugees in reverse. Iwan is waiting for us by the coastal path leading to the forest. Late forties, eager, facial features small for their frame; he introduces himself by asking each of us our nationalities, then declares himself Javanese. Mistakenly I think he said Japanese, so my surprised reaction is over the top.

'You know where *Rafflesia* grows?' I ask him.

'Yes but rainy season. Twenty-three of Novembers. Wrong time. Flower a barrel and rots.'

Seeing our crestfallen faces he adds quickly, 'But OK, OK, I seen a bud, I seen a bud.'

We're paying him a tourists' rate, so I'm unsure if his change of heart is to avert a lost deal, or if he's just willing the flower into existence. Like the rest of us: we all have skin in the game here.

The Penanjung Pangandaran nature reserve is the point of

an exclamation mark on the mainland. Seen from above, the 10-mile-long island is a mirror image of Ireland on a map, and a dense emerald green. It might be the only place in the world where *Rafflesia patma* grows wild; it's difficult to tell from the literature. The few localities within easy reach of Bogor were all mined for specimens to transplant to the botanic garden long ago; and those forests have probably all gone now anyway. Sofi's stocks at Bogor were harvested from the reserve we're visiting today. Local ecologists surveyed the island a couple of years ago and identified four populations of *Rafflesia patma*. They reported 'fifty-four dead buds, twenty-eight living buds, thirty-two rotten blooms, and no flowers blooming', plus a steady decline over the last decade due to illegal logging and wild-animal hunting. People and *Rafflesia* rarely mix well. Or, as the authors put it bluntly: 'Human influence tends to be negative and leads to their extinction.'[50] I'm not optimistic about us finding a flower today.

Iwan escorts us up a block of concrete steps into the dark, dripping forest. Pat and I keep pace with him, while Adriane busies himself with a portable tripod at the rear with Joko. Adriane's planning to film the excursion. I feel a pressing desire to pee after the long drive but to do so would seem disrespectful here so I do my best to ignore it. Macaques crawl about the path, dragging their tails, while the insects scream at one another. Humming to himself, Iwan halts abruptly and points to a disturbance in the trees. 'Black leaf monkey. He rare one.' Pat fiddles with his camera and I take out my notebook. There's a hiatus in the canopy as the monkey pauses to look down. Then he showers us in piss.

Iwan asks Pat and me to remind him of our names. 'Yes, Mr Kiss and Mr Fat,' Iwan says nodding, 'there is seven monkey here.' He holds up six fingers; I notice a stump where the seventh should be. As we clamber over a root-webbed hillock, he asks if we have children. Then he points to his paunch and says 'I am pregnant, Mr Fat.' He laughs and points to Pat's belly for emphasis, 'Like you, boss!' Pat takes this well.

The fringe of the reserve betrays a heavy footfall – flecks of foil, faded bottles, divorced flip-flops, and so on; the plastic sewage of crowded life. But a mile in and the forest is unbothered by that.

Damp, hissing heat; green dappled light. Nature in full possession. We cross a milky brown stream and ascend the steep bare ramp of its source, ducking under the taut creepers pitched like guide-ropes. Joko points to a Salak palm (*Salacca zalacca*). The fruit of this palm is a polished brown snakeskin that peels to reveal cloves of hard, white flesh. I sampled one a couple of days ago in Bogor; the strong flavour bore a strange resemblance to bubble gum.

The forest climbs into the sky. At the top of the ramp, we watch a small green snake vanish in the chaos. 'Venom snek,' Iwan says. 'But most dangerous snek is in bed. Mek baby.' He laughs, almost uncontrollably this time, then holds up his hand and says 'Give me four.'

A few metres from 'venom snek' we happen across a sprig of orange, berry-like fruits I don't recognize. No one seems eager to name the fruit, but Iwan knows it. 'Monkey eat when pregnant.' He nods slowly, grinning. 'Vitamin.' He seems hooked on pregnancy.

We're presented with a mighty strangler fig. Interlaced roots writhe along the ground and pour into the sky. It's a feat of engineering. Iwan considers the ground with an air of preoccupation. I realize he's looking for *Rafflesia*. Pat sees it too. 'But you know, this is a strangler fig, Iwan. Not *Tetrastigma*. *Rafflesia* will not grow here.' Iwan has misfired. Joko and Adriane appear and we bring them up to speed on the situation. We take off our bags and convene under the colossal trunk. 'Oh,' says Joko, peeling a banana. Pat looks disappointed. Iwan looks distracted. I cast about for a tree to avail myself of, and Adriane begins filming.

'But you know,' says Iwan, unintentionally imitating Pat, 'there is another place.' He's lost credibility now. We pause to take stock as Iwan trudges through the papery leaves. I decide to relieve myself behind the fig, informing the others over my shoulder. Iwan calls after me:

'Monkey grab your dick. Think it banana.'

24.

I wait here. In my own habitat there are some that will bloom. I didn't have time to make a video for you Mr Chris, but I heard it erupt. Yes I did, Sir.

Because plants have quite a lot of mystery, don't they? But they can't talk like animals, can they?

Or if they do, it rarely happens.

25.

'Blocked drains'.

'Sewage'.

'Pigs' shit'.

It's strong, we can agree on that. *Rafflesia patma* is the worst-smelling *Rafflesia* any of us has encountered, and that's saying something. Its miasma hangs over the forest floor like a death. Iwan stands a little way from the group with a half-smile, his hands clasped around his paunch; he's pleased with himself for delivering on his promise. The rest of us kneel before the toxic flower, batting off bluebottles, trying not to gag.

It spans an arm. The five peeled lobes frame a cupola pointed at the trees. Tilted on its axis; poised. I stroke the beast, tentatively, as you might a fickle cat. It's rubbery, like silicone bakeware, but brittle, and frosted all over. Small white accretions fall in an intentional-looking pattern, like the shell of a sea urchin. I run my finger around the arched interior wall, lifting flies. Beneath my skin runs an unexpected coarseness, like close-cropped hair; somehow less plant than animal. I swallow a compulsion to stroke my own beard, to compare. Odd. All *Rafflesia* possess a microscopic forest of stalked outgrowths called 'ramenta'. Up close, they resemble sprigs of coral. Taxonomists have obsessed over these, although no one knows why they're there; how they serve the flower. I step away to see the work whole again: a thing of pure wonder.

Unfortunately it's damaged goods. Something has attacked one face of the flower. It looks as though it was grazed by a dinosaur. Or kicked by one. Shattered fragments of the plant litter the floor like a dropped plate. Sabotage is a regular obstruction to *Rafflesia*'s plans – one that in a thriving population might be shaken off. Curious ecologists once set up camera traps here to identify the cause.[51] Their video footage revealed large, rat-like creatures with cats' eyes scrabbling and gnawing at the flowers: Sunda porcupines and Java mouse deer. Our cracked wonder is probably the work of one of these vandals. Still, it's *Rafflesia* and it's in flower. No one could ask for more. So we creep about contentedly looking for the best angle to capture the flower intact, looking as though we might pounce on it.

It has a dark allure that's hard to look away from, like a beautiful corpse. The flies agree. Black bands of them lift and settle as one. I see a pair zoom haltingly into the central orifice: the target. Beneath it, an arched chamber concentrates the bouquet of noxious volatiles, guiding the flies towards the flower's reproductive parts where it needs them. The complicated architecture and markings in the dark hall of a *Rafflesia* flower collude to process the flies blindly in the right direction, like airport passengers. Deep within the flower's mechanism, scientists have observed flies crawling into hidden grooves tucked under a disc.[52] Bristles force them into position, where they sit quietly in a ring, as if recharging. In a male flower, the flies become saddled with pollen dispensed from liquid stalactites. In the rare event a fly then locates a female flower, once more it is conducted towards a tight spot. Waggled into position, it pauses to think (insofar as a fly might) and the liquid pollen is transmitted to the flower's receptive area – the stigma. Fertilization precedes a chain of molecular events ending in a seed. Little things making big things happen.

But it's a stinking great sham. In they go, buzzing, twitching, and vomiting. Seduced stupid. Female flies are targeted specifically, their maternal instincts exploited: the bigger the corpse, the better the resource for their offspring. *Revolutions are effected in two ways: by force and by fraud*, said Aristotle. He knew. Having stolen every fibre of its being and forced its way into the world, *Rafflesia*'s criminal thinking turned to fraud. I peer into the cavity to catch a glimpse of deception in action. I'm met with a raised disc armed with waxen thorns. Called 'processes', no one knows the function of these; presumably they *are* functional, because most *Rafflesia* species possess them. My research, undertaken with mathematicians, on vaguely similar structures in a wholly different mechanism, the *Nepenthes* pitcher, suggests such things are expensive to produce, energetically speaking. You wouldn't make them for nothing. The only suggested function I'm aware of in *Rafflesia* is that the structures act as 'radiator fins', directing thermals to facilitate odour dispersal.[53] But now we're guessing.

Bigger is better, I said. Does size matter in Rafflesia's sex life? Logic tells us a trade-off must exist between the energetic cost of flower construction and pollination efficiency. A value equation. Across the plant kingdom, flowers range from the size of a pinhead to the great carcass sprawled before me. Charles Davis and his colleagues examined flower size across the evolutionary scale.[54] A striking pattern emerged: gigantism tends to be associated with *sapromyiophily* (flowers mimicking dead meat to seduce flies). They suggest gigantic flowers are appealing to flies because the insects are typically drawn to larger dead things; their larvae are more likely to survive on an abundant food source.

So size *does* matter. But how was this brought to bear by evolution? Let's clamber a few branches down the plant family tree to consider an orchid. Charles Darwin famously predicted the existence of a long-tongued moth after observing the drawn-out spur of a Madagascan comet orchid (*Androecium sesquipedale* – the specific epithet meaning 'a foot and a half long'). His prediction was the existence of a moth in possession of a proboscis some 40 centimetres in length – sufficiently long to reach the nectar sequestered in the spur's tip – but such a thing was unheard of in the insect kingdom; it was considered, quite frankly, ridiculous. Whoever saw such a thing?

Twenty years after Darwin's death they did. The flower and its pollinator must have evolved in an arms race, each having to respond to an incremental bolt-on in length to keep up. Returning to *Rafflesia*, it costs an egg-laying fly its offspring to pollinate it; the flower's mimicry needs to be good for evolution to sustain it. Perhaps gigant-ism evolved as a response to a steadily climbing threshold in size required for the deceived flies to bother visiting.[55]

Now let's consider the stench (I can hardly ignore it). *Rafflesia* is not alone in this respect either. One hot day in June in the 1990s, I remember returning from school to find the rubbish bins inverted, hosed down on a darkening patch of the parched-blond lawn. The air was laced with disinfectant, but not enough to mask a high note of bad meat. I smiled, and a curled spathe – like a dog's mouth and panting tongue – smiled back. My dragon arum (*Dracunculus vulgaris*) had unfurled, fooling the flies and my mother. Here is another of evolution's masters of chemical deception. Deceit blossomed across the arum family. Many – dragon arums included – not only plagiarize the chemical equations of decompo-sition; they're also thermogenic (heat-producing), which gives their reek a greater reach.

It was in a flower-spangled nose of rock jutting out into the Aegean Sea that I detected my first wild dragon. The gut-wrenching aroma reached me on a warm breeze and I followed it, nose to the ground like a truffle hound. The trail grew hot as I pushed my feet through the sun-dazzled sand and gorse. An unmistakable smell, I thought, armed with the certainty of experience. I heard the hum of a thousand flies as I stumbled through the thicket to receive my prize from nature.

Maggots spilling out of an open carcass.

A real one: unmistakably dead goat. My instincts had run smack against me: this time I'd been duped.

A whole herd of dragon arums graces Oxford Botanic Garden's Mediterranean display in early summer. Each year I pluck one and spirit it off to the lecture theatre in the Department of Plant Sci-ences where I watch the students retch as they pass it round and inhale. 'Mark me well,' I tell them, 'this is *Sapromyiophily* and you'll not forget it.'

The dead horse arum (*Helicodiceros muscivorus*) is a distant rel-ation of the dragon arum once removed by geography, which stalks gull colonies along the cliffs of the central Mediterranean islands. It sends up a rod-shaped bud, aimed at the sky like a gun. Under a big blue sky one unwraps itself, casting its red flag over the white-spattered rock, announcing itself open for business. A fly, rubbing its front legs like sharpening knives, pauses for a moment; diverts its attention from the dead gull it's occupied with, to the dead horse arum. Its spathe is deliciously thick with fur, like an animal's. The way to heaven is on horseback, they say, and this fly seems to have found paradise on our dead horse arum. Possessed, it crawls into a funnel, through a ring of forward-swept spines, to emerge in a dark, foetid chamber crammed with flies. And nothing else: no gore, or entrails to dream over; nothing. Dimly aware that something's amiss, our confused fly tries to make its escape; trouble is, it can't get a purchase on the slippery walls of its cell, and there's that barricade of spines to contend with. It's stuck.

The hours pass. There's no light down here, but a falling temperature hints at nightfall. Our fly might be asleep, or deep in contemplation – without eyelids, it's hard to say – either way, the trance is broken by a heavy discharge from above. During the course of the night, there's been a gender switch: the dead horse arum's female flowers have deactivated their receptivity, and now the male flowers are detonated. Pollen, dumped like snow, forms drifts around the base of the chamber and clings to everything like static. The following morning: all change again. The barricade shrivels, freeing the escape route. Our pollen-dipped fly crawls back up the funnel, out onto the withered spathe. Under the assaulting light, it rubs its legs, pauses, thinks for a bit. Then diverts its attention to the next dead horse arum.

Rafflesia doesn't kidnap its pollinators like a dead horse arum. But the dome-like cupule I'm looking at does bear a resemblance to its spathe: both structures concentrate stinking gases to direct their subservient pollinators' behaviour. Each dead horse arum contains both male and female flowers, their activation decoupled by a day. The herd blooms synchronously – certain clifftops in May become a dead horse massacre. Flies are drawn confusedly from one plant to another, slaves to nature's cruel masters. I once dissected a specimen on a clifftop in Mallorca in which some of the flies had died – presumably from sheer exhaustion. *Rafflesia*'s sex life is less predictable than a dead horse arum's: its flowers are unisexual and they appear erratically over space and time. But on their separate continents, both plants' mechanisms evolved to ensure cross-pollination – the transfer of pollen from one individual to another. This tends to benefit the fitness of populations in the long term. Both, too, are crooks: their supplicant flies are flim-flammed out of a nursery for their brood. Evolution, like economics, hasn't banished fraud. But how did it manage to span the eons? Why don't the flies learn?

I've discussed this question with my friend Jeff Ollerton, a professor of biodiversity. Jeff says, 'Flies aren't stupid. Like bees, they can learn to zero in on food quickly. But these flowers are tapping into a deeply ingrained urge: to lay eggs where their maggots can find food, and fast. Any fly that didn't take advantage of a rapidly perishing food resource would forfeit the chance to pass its genes on to the next generation.' Jeff also points out that if counterfeit flowers like *Rafflesia* and dead horse arums were to outnumber the object of their mimicry (corpses), they might negatively affect the abundance of insects that suffer a reproductive loss by laying eggs on them.[56] This balancing process is called negative frequency-dependent selection: an organism's reproductive success decreases as it becomes more common. Dead horse arums bloom for just a few weeks; then, and then alone, a veritable orgy of flowers ensures reproductive success. But as we saw in the Philippines, to find *Rafflesia* in bloom is an uncertain miracle. Perhaps *Rafflesia* outwits its pollinators with unpredictability. It's hard to know for sure, but it seems intuitive that the flowers' scarcity, like their size, is hardwired into their pollination strategy.

Jeff works on *stapeliads*, sometimes referred to as starfish flowers. These succulents form low thickets in the dappled shade of the semi-arid deserts of Africa and Asia. They also grow in pots along my windowsill. Once in a while, a finger-thick stem sends into the world a fleshy star. The stars come in a motley assortment of colours, patterns, and textures. And scents. I often notice the smell before I see the flower. They're mostly unpleasant and discernibly unique. These strange stars are a shining example of the intricacy of pollination by deceit. Scientists have analysed the volatile compounds produced by various stapeliads and identified a pattern of mimicry associated with specific sources of putrefaction. Let me explain. The various combinations of chemical volatiles mirror those that waft from specific sources, including stale urine, rotting meat, carnivore dung, and herbivore dung (*that which we call a rose by any other name . . .*). The different chemical cocktails may be linked to specific pollinators; and this in turn may have ushered the species along separate evolutionary paths, blossoming in the diversity of flower forms we see among the stapeliads today.[57] Adaptive radiation, in the jargon. Might such a phenomenon exist for *Rafflesia*? Might the different species each have different pollinators? A divergency of colours, shapes, and sizes of *Rafflesia* can be found erupting on the various islands sprinkled across Southeast Asia. What's more, I'm convinced they all smell different. Like a sommelier at a wine pairing, I know what goes with what: *Rafflesia patma* I saw on Mount Makiling smelled like my potted stapeliad, *Orbea variegata*; *R. banaoana* resembled the dragon arums of the Aegean; and the vengeful flower of *R. patma* in front of me smells vaguely reminiscent of a stinkhorn (*Phallus impudicus*) – a fungus that erects itself on the floor of European woodlands after autumn rain. Only worse.

Plants speak. We fill the world with words. They communicate through the language of volatile organic compounds (VOCs). A stream of molecular vocab drifts from the mouths of flowers everywhere; leaves and roots too. VOCS are used for plant-to-plant dialogue, to attract – and at times deceive – insects. We saw this earlier in bee orchids, and now in the massacre that's sprung up over the last few pages. Corpse flowers. These strange accidents of evolution have run riot across the plant family tree. Once again: convergent evolution.

I take a last look at *Rafflesia* as we prepare to leave the forest: a design, seemingly beyond invention, in the evolutionary cosmos of possibilities. Around it, a small audience of buds is surfacing steadily from the silken threads of an earthen womb. Expanding, cell by

Joko with Rafflesia patma *in Pangandaran, Java.*

cell, at the speed of thought. They, too, will bring pollen into the world, long after I've left this jungle. Pollen with an uncertain future borne on the wings of flies. It's unlikely to fulfil its ambition: to hand down a story that began forty million years ago; one with no ending. More likely it will perish in the municipal bin guarding the entrance to this forest. My thoughts creep into the mental space of their world and ours. VOCs and vines. Entanglement: everything connected to everything else through space and time. And the feeble words we use to make sense of it.

***

The forest tumbles into a tropical beach. We take off our shoes to slap our feet along the hard, wet sand. On the horizon, the melting sky glints gold along the rusted roof of a capsized ship. I'm reminded of the fabled kingdom we saw yesterday from the road. But I can't remember its name so I just stare at it blankly. 'Illegal fishing,' says Joko. We circle an anvil of rock thickly crested with greenery, to enter a brown tide curving into the bay. Monkeys rattle and swing from the trees as we wade through, ankle-deep. We haven't booked accommodation but Iwan knows a place, so we follow him on his bike to a small hotel set about with mango trees and coconut palms.

We drink beer and peanuts outside our rooms in the gnat-slapping heat. Mas Bamba breaks his Halal and cracks open a bottle, which we agree is reasonable given we found *Rafflesia* today. We have dinner in a satay restaurant made of rattan. A blue, grilled-meat fog hangs thickly and clings to our clothes. Joko dispenses green tea as Pat bootlegs beer from a black plastic bag under the table. The restaurant owner's son watches agape, but his father whisks him away, so I think we're acquitted.

We wake to grey dimpled pools and steadfast rain. Back on the road to Bogor, we pass a written-off car that's nosedived off the verge, carving a void in the trees. It looks serious. There's no sign of a driver, but an unsophisticated stop sign of heaped sticks has been constructed by someone, as if they were minded to start a bonfire on the road. Mas Bamba steers us carefully around the disaster. 'Crash,' says Joko.

We pass a deceased palm devoured by ferns, and top-heavy bananas festooned with trumpeting morning glory. A young woman shakes a pan of dried rice; behind, her mother sculpts flowers out of mangoes. Beyond them, a pair of men in bare feet stare intently at the wheel of a bike, with cigarettes clamped between their teeth (every bike in Indonesia comes with an attendant mechanic).

We stop for lunch in a café in the lee of a paddy field near a village called Loji. Blue moon butterflies flit aimlessly about the custard apple trees, papyrus, and hung washing. Our bowls of *soto ayam* (chicken, *lontong*, and noodles) contain a parsley-like member of the carrot family (Apiaceae). We pass around and scrutinize the sprigs, but none of us can put a name to it. I wonder if Mas Bamba finds it curious how botanists diagnose their food this way.

Back in the vehicle, we hold a conference on local nomenclature. In Indonesia, *Rafflesia* is known as *Bunga bangkai*, Joko tells us. This name is also applied to the titan arum (*Amorphophallus titanum*), which causes confusion.

'Sofi told me that visitors have travelled to Bogor expecting to see a titan arum when *Rafflesia* was in bloom,' I say, pleased to be able to contribute. 'They were disappointed, she said.'

How anyone could be disappointed by *Rafflesia* is beyond our comprehension. In the Philippines, the various species of *Rafflesia* are named differently. On Mount Makiling, *R. panchoana* is called *Malaboo*, while on the island of Panay *R. speciosa* is known as *Karagay*, Adriane tells me, leaning forward to show me the spelling on his phone. In Mindanao, *Rafflesia schadenbergiana* goes by various names including *Bó-o*, *Kolon busaw*, and *Bulak ta busaw*, he says, depending on the tribe. It means 'bad spirit'.

'But you know,' says Pat, 'bad things will happen to anyone who destroys *Rafflesia banaoana*. That is why the plant is so well protected in Kalinga.' Adriane looks at him anxiously. 'But Sir, on Mount Banahaw, they *cut* the flower.' We all turn to look at him.

'Why?' I ask.

'To play with it.'

My thoughts turn from the toyed-with existence of *Rafflesia* on Mount Banahaw, to *Rafflesia patma* perched on its little island in a changing sea. Petals like torn hopes. I consider the lost populations from the wilds around nineteenth-century Bogor; the ten-hour drive to Pangandaran, now the nearest within reach for Sofi's grafting experiments. Surely something out of this world should never be thus; should be unassailable in the face of extinction. We couldn't let it die out? Could we?

Contemplative, I scroll through my phone's daily stream of consciousness. I've received another message from my friend Deki, in Sumatra. There is no text, just a photograph. Mindful of the flower wreckage brought to me by former messages, I'm apprehensive as it comes into focus.

The photograph depicts a written note. A ponderous hand has listed each of our names (minus some consonants), and the words WELCOME IN SUMATERA.

Underneath the spidery list, the note says, 'Bloom Prediction 25 November.'

And underneath that is a waking dream.

26.

Twelve thousand metres below my feet, it stirs. Down under the fathomless halls of air; down further, under the eternal shade of trees, far from the split-white sky. There in the dark, my thoughts creep into the leaves, along a ledge of root and fern, and up a step. Neurons coalesce towards a point, and earth there, holding a picture before my eyes; holding it still.

Freed from the bonds of crowded Java, I watch with interest as a new place emerges through my little plastic oval windowpane. Humans have left a lighter tread on this land; left nature's course unturned. Below the sunlit quiet, I see Sumatra unroll before me as a cartographer might: flung out into the ocean, with a broken fringe and spine. A sprawling dark ocean of microscopic trees. Brown capillaries creeping through green tissue, feeding hungrier arteries that empty themselves into the sea.

Look closely and nicks appear: rectangles here and there of leaves the wrong shade of green, singed brown, or too symmetrical; the green snowflakes of palms; the beige cast of a rubber-tree farm. Human progress. But I can read between these lines and I know it's a place of wonder still.

Forest beasts prowl the depths – tigers, rhinoceroses, elephants, and orangutan – sneaking and crashing about the trees. I can't see them, but they're there.

And steadily, imperceptibly, from a nest of vines: plants rise out of the mist.

Plants as big as you and me.

Deki escorts us from the Arrivals Lounge like an attentive nurse, ushering us into the car and directing the driver to arrange our luggage. I look at him covertly; it's strange to meet someone for the first time after communicating through text messages for so long. He's a little shorter than I'd guessed, stockier, and has an earnestness about him; he's eager to please. But his serious face rearranges all its lines when he laughs – something that happens often and forcibly, I discover. Deki is accompanied by Regi Sunandar, a lad of about twenty who is, I'm told, Deki's assistant. Regi has bony arms, and a mop of black hair over an elven face with protruding ears. In the rear of the car, Deki and Regi exchange volleys of machine-gun Indonesian and high-pitched laughter. From the front, Joko converses with Mas ('older brother') Deki over our heads, sending back the occasional translated word.

On the drive to Kota Bengkulu, we follow a coastal road flanked with straw-topped huts and fishing boats scattered among the furzy-grey casuarina trees. Shards of sea glint between their limbs. An unmanned wooden shack peddles dried fish stacked on large plates; above them hang bundles of wrinkled, shark-like creatures with thorny spines and eyes fixed to the sky.

'This, Bengkulu,' Deki says to no one in particular. 'First, to University Bengkulu. Later, Kemumu. Outsiders never been.'

I'm making a habit of that.

We clamber out of the car, into the warm wet air, in the shadow of a large building striped like the Union Jack. Here we're met by Professor Susatya, a small man with a wise face and kindly eyes. I like him instantly. He regards Deki as he might a son he's not seen in months, then guides our party through a polished lobby, along open-sided corridors around courtyards of clipped trees, and into a boxy office. There he sits, clasping his hands, and carefully considers the table as the rest of us arrange ourselves, books and pens. Regi photographs preliminaries under Deki's close supervision.

'There are five *Rafflesia* species in Bengkulu,' the professor says. 'But all are rare and unpredictable. To see *Rafflesia* is a gift.' Spirited agreement. 'And today you are lucky. You will see flowering in Kemumu: *Rafflesia kemumu*. Deki has said one will bloom there today. Deki knows this.'

Upon hearing his name, Deki nods soberly, then looks at Regi. Regi takes another photograph of us doing nothing. Pat smiles at Adriane. And I look out of the window at the tropical wet foliage, and think about what's waiting for us out in this new world.

'Toadstools and broccoli.'

I've lost him.

'Both simple and compound.'

Ah yes, ramenta. '*Rafflesia kemumu* has distinct ramenta,' the professor says, nodding.

Rafflesia kemumu was named and described by Professor Susatya, together with Deki who grew up close to where the plant is found in northern Bengkulu. It was first documented in a pathless place near a gold mine in 1934. The plant was observed repeatedly in the twentieth century, but identified inconsistently. In 2015, Professor Susatya held a conference called the 'International Symposium on Indonesian Giant Flowers' in which a group of scientists sought to become acquainted with the flower. They mapped it like an atlas, scrutinized its lines and joined the dots, then concluded it was sufficiently distinct to earn a new title.[58] Few scientists have seen it bloom besides them; fewer still from a foreign land. As Deki said: 'outsiders never been'.

We turn to the importance of local communities in the conservation of *Rafflesia*. Most people live in privately owned forests, meaning conservation relies not on law but on a common understanding of the harmony between people and land; that once *Rafflesia* is lost from the land it can never be found. Everyone needs to care deeply, we agree.

As if summoned by thought, a *Rafflesia* god appears in the doorway. 'This is Dean Jansen,' says Professor Susatya. The dean is dressed in a long red gown with cartoon *Rafflesia* flowers dancing along the seams; an extraordinary garment on which we congratulate him heartily. I wonder if he wore it specially. Sitting at the head of the table, he reaches for a bottle of green tea as the professor introduces us. The dean has bright eyes in a round face, and an ebullience about him that sparkles like static. Breathlessly, he tells us about his research in ecophysiology: how organisms' physiologies interact with the environment. He is particularly interested in the plumbing necessary to sustain Rafflesia's enormous flowers.

'I have been trying to measure the flow of sap in a vine above and below the point of a *Rafflesia* flower's attachment,' he says.

Most plants are producers: they manufacture their own food using raw materials from the world around them. In ecophysiology, a plant organ that absorbs resources from the environment (carbon from photosynthesis, for example) is known as a 'source'; an organ that uses or stores these resources is known as a 'sink'. Water and dissolved nutrients are transported around the plant through sap; but the pipes from source to sink are manifold and complex; fine-tuned. Throw an 11-kilogram parasite into the equation and you'd expect a host to notice. The hydraulics necessary to sustain such a beast are poorly understood, but a reconfiguration of the host vine's water-conducting tissues seems to be key.[59] Perhaps slow-growing vines syphoning water over long, meandering paths to the light were a crucible for the evolution of gigantism. As we saw earlier, fly pollination most likely explains why *Rafflesia* evolved the world's largest flowers; perhaps ecophysiology explains *how*.

As the dean talks excitedly about sap, I let my mind creep through the window and up, out into the forest again: that living, breathing temple and, growing to its heartbeat, the fabled flower. Each of us sitting around this table is connected to it now. Like neurons in a brain.

★★★

We have lunch in Kota Bengkulu. The small café has three orange walls and an open front where rain lashes a square of trodden earth. Women in black headscarves sit in the corner watching it. Deki orders a selection of dishes including *soto padang* (noodle soup with beef, onion, potatoes) and *rempeyek* (battered peanut crackers), which we hand out with jugs of warm green tea. Back-of-house, I part a small army of chickens and kittens as I hunt for the facilities. When I return to the table, Pat is raising the possibility of having beer this evening, to which Deki laughs, but it's not clear if he's understood.

On the drive to Kemumu, Deki sits in the front to navigate. Along the way he practises his English on me, asking questions over his shoulder such as 'Do you eat pork?' or 'Did you see that cow?' We pass strange boats with helms carved into scowling dragons. Palms spew out ferns, and jackfruits balloon in the trees. The narrow road weaves gently in and out of palm-oil and rubber-tree plantations. Cups have been strapped to the rubber trees to collect their latex; it's gathered at night when the temperature cools, Joko tells me. In the midst of the rubber trees we pass a house on stilts where a family is preparing for a wedding. Plastic chairs have been arranged around a red throne and women are replicating food, smiling; away from the throng, two girls stand braiding a younger one's hair. Families sit by the road beneath the trees, watching us pass; once in a while they see me – the outsider – and do a double take. Then the children shout and run after us.

We pass a tree that Deki calls *melinjo* and I know as *Gnetum gnemon*. I see it every day in the glasshouses at Oxford Botanic Garden, but I've never seen one in the wild before. It looks like all the other broad-leaved tropical trees here, but it's an unlikely member of the gymnosperms: cycads, and conifers such as pine trees, Christmas trees, and so on. It even has red, fruit-like structures enclosing its seeds (gymnosperms do not bear true fruit). Joko tells me the seeds are used here to make soups and crackers.

The grey-dappled rubber plantations give way to rice. Terraces of stiff red clay and square pools hold a mirror to the sky. Distant figures crouch under large cone hats. The view swoops over them and across a gulf of trees, up over soaring hills, up again, to a coned peak.

'Bukit Daun,' Deki says, pointing to the mountain bullied by clouds.

'I see,' I say.

'Lake,' he adds, suggesting perhaps I don't. Then he asks me if I'll sing 'Hey Jude' for him, and laughs when I look politely puzzled.

Ragged banana leaves, eddying cloud; blue hut, pink hut; football, chickens; staring faces. We park outside a small building neatly underlined by potted plants: Deki's parents' house, Joko tells me. We take off our shoes and pad into a white-washed sitting room where his parents stand to greet us. They're gentle people who want me to feel welcome – they say this clearly without words. His mother, a small lady dressed traditionally in emerald green, takes us to a sink at the back of the house to wash our hands; I notice a rice hat hooked to the wall. Before we return to the sitting room to have coffee, Deki proudly shows me his collection of durian tree saplings, and a potted tetrastigma vine outside the back door. He speaks to me in Indonesian. We both pretend I can understand him, which I suppose in all the ways that matter most I do.

Back in the sitting room, coffee, biscuits, and a home-grown stalk of bananas have appeared. Joko, Pat, Adriane, and our driver sit on wicker chairs and chat, as I'm shown a shrine of framed photographs at the back of the room: Deki on his wedding day, smiling relatives, children dressed for an occasion – things like that – and in the centre, like a matriarch: *Rafflesia*, staring defiantly.

As we leave, Deki's father shows us his wild water lemon (*Passiflora foetida*) sprawling up the side of the house. He plucks a handful of bristly fruits that look like sea urchins, which we shell and nibble as we return to the car. They taste of bicarbonate of soda. He and his wife wave us off and I feel a pang of sadness, which seems ridiculous considering I first met them just half an hour ago.

The mud road peters out so we abandon the car, leaning against it to adapt ourselves for the jungle. Insects make a layered, electric shriek. We march towards the green horizon along a sylvan path, where a family has gathered beneath a durian tree. They watch us covertly. The track becomes a steep ramp of forest, half planted with palm oil, half wild with ferns. The forest tumbles into a course of white rapids gushing out of hidden peaks and cloud, seething about the rocks. Here, boastful ferns and grasses clamber up the bank and over one another, snatching the light; above them, white-trunked trees as straight as arrows shoot into the sky. There's a low-slung bridge of planks and rope leading into the forest – and we follow it, swinging towards our bliss. For a moment – and just a moment, on that bridge between worlds – fixed thought is replaced by a sort of purity I can't make sense of. Too pure to be real. As perishable as time, then lost like a dream.

We file into the shrill forest. Deki – still in chinos – is easy in his movements; he was born to this. Pat and Adriane are kitted out for professional adventure (although earlier, Adriane told me he considers the terrain easy compared to the Philippines – I'm minded to agree); Regi – short-sleeved T-shirt – and Joko has gone for eco-tourist: ball cap and yellow boots.

Beyond the bridge, we follow a mud path along a ditch packed with ferns. Soon we reach a lad of about Regi's age waiting with his bike. Above him rises a wall of root and frond to which he's rigged a taut yellow hose that pivots around the thicket and vanishes. Deki scrambles up the vertical terrain and crouches on a ledge in the green shade. Then he beckons each of us up the slope, starting with Pat.

'OK? One step. OK? One step,' he says over and over again, as we heave ourselves into file, up the hose pipe. The air is full of whispers. Deki spirits us up the embankment with ushering movements and murmurs of encouragement. I pause to look over my shoulder and see Adriane a little way below me, face glistening, eyes shining. Below him, Joko squints up at me, as if through a mist. We're leaving the real world behind us now – each of us knows this. We're sixty heartbeats away from our summit.

Sixty beats from bliss.

***

Under a fast-moving continent of cloud, seven men sit on the sill of the forest. Awkwardly they hold on to the slope, each with one leg lower than the other; one crouched like a cricket batsman; another holding a loop of vine like a straphanger on the Metro. The cant of the slope has aligned them, the thing that called has engrossed them. And they're content – no, happy; but unsure of their own emotions, as men are prone to be. In their midst: the watchful red flower, a stride across, roars silently.

'Wow,' says Adriane quietly. He looks to the flower for his next thought, but nothing we say could ever fit. We mutter observations over it – obvious things about size, colour and so on – as we creep about the high green wall; but none of us is really listening. Regi has lowered his camera and stares vacantly at the trees; Deki, beside him, looks at me with a proud smile that distorts his features. Then we all turn to face the flower again, to stare at its soul.

★★★

The five great orbs are gently arched and fiery, like the expanding wings of a seraph intent on the sky, held to the earth by vines. Their white spots fall deceptively over the contours like a work by Escher; they make the flower seem larger than it is. Yes, the commanding plant is an obscene caricature of itself, of its size. I peer into the eye of the flower. A glossy pedestal of thorns thrusts from a red ocean flecked with lifted grey hyphens, like plankton. At the ocean's shore, a forest of cauliflower-like ramenta is pustulating. Up close, they look unwholesomely healthy – like fresh acne. The smell is faintly rotten, like a pumpkin's – nothing like the high, putrid note of *R. patma*. I stand back to look at the work whole again. Rigged up to the forest's feed lines it looks keen; hungry.

'Kiss it,' says Deki.

I do, and they watch.

After a half-hour's dreaming over the flower, Deki leads us further up the steep wilderness, squinting and ducking under the knocking vines. We reach a drift of rotting sticks and leaves falling out of the sky. There isn't room for us to congregate in the enclave of trees, so we're processed by Deki one at a time up the scarp. After a short scramble through the loose thatch, we reach a nursery of budding seraphim. The waxing globes are half-buried in the forest's tissue, their wings clamped shut to the light. I place my palm on one. It feels warm-blooded – everything emanates warmth in this invincible heat – and gently ribbed with veins, like my own hand. I feel my pulse throb beneath my palm.

'This is,' says Deki, holding my hand, leading me to another swollen bud pushing out of the twigs, beaded with dew. Wrapped in black papery bracts, it's like a half-opened gift, and red as the moon. 'This is,' he repeats, pointing to it, then he looks at me and says: 'One. Two. Three. Four.' Adriane is also whispering numbers as he

Deki (left), Regi (centre), and their friend with Rafflesia kemumu
in Kemumu, Sumatra.

creeps about the trees; he's counted thirty-two buds, he tells us. One the size of a tennis ball has swivelled on its wandering vine to present itself in profile. The three of us crouch to examine it and take photographs. It's held at the base by a wooden chalice, like the cup of an acorn, called a cupule. This chimeric structure is produced in part by the parasite and also by the host as a wound response caused by the rupturing bud.[60] We venture further up the steep shelf of forest, where questing roots snake out of the leaves; some bear the battle wounds of former *Rafflesia* flowers.

Snapping through leaf and twig, we stumble across a bud the size of a football, blackened with rot. As I mentioned in Bogor last week, no one knows the cause of these miscarriages. Perhaps an obstruction to the flow of sap plays a part? A loser among battle-proud flowers. Vine and *Rafflesia* co-evolving, keeping apace in their age-old race. A race with no end; at least no natural one. War, under the rules of nature, and chaos will be the judge. My thoughts swim off into an uncertain future as we clamber down the wall of roots, leaving a trail of sighs in our wake.

'Deki told me this is private land,' Joko says as we leave the forest. 'It's not protected, Chris.'

'It's a beautiful place,' I reply, because there's nothing else to say.

27.

I dreamed of the forest again. The others were there and I expect we were looking for *Rafflesia*, although it didn't feature. We gathered around a great tree with a naked brown trunk, which Deki called *Buah Pala*, and he wrote the words for me in my book. He added them to a long list of plant names that had already filled the page; I was concerned he'd written the names in pen, not pencil; the words would leech off the page, I said; and although he seemed to understand me perfectly, I felt he *wanted* the ink to run. Time lapsed and I felt late for something. I was worried we were lost, but then Adriane appeared and said this forest was a *kitten* compared to Kalinga's – and look, there was a path! As we stood on the newly found path, Deki drew me a map, and handed back my book, smiling. Now the names had arrows beside them, showing where each plant grew on the map.

Deeper and darker we went until an overhanging limestone crag sprang out of the trees; suddenly the others had gone, and Deki was sitting on the rocky pillar, looking down at me, calling for me to come up. As if on a sunbeam, I journeyed up the cliff. Little black beasts fluttered around me like moths, only faster. We stood on the crest of rock, watching them vanish into the sun. I turned to ask Deki to write the names of the creatures in my book, but I saw he was weeping. Then a cold tingle crept down my spine and the hairs on my arm stood on end: the moths had turned to cinders and I realized a great lake of fire was raging towards the cliff. When I looked back over my shoulder, Deki had vanished; I was alone on

my island under the rolling smoke. I remembered the map annotated with plants.

But when I looked down at the open book in my hands, it was
wet, and all the ink had bled.

***

Often I dream of the former forests of Southeast Asia. Intact, they
must have been a botanical paradise for the early explorers. Empty
spaces on the map; rolling waves of trees so green they must have
appeared black. Between the seventeenth and nineteenth centuries, voyages from Europe sought exotic curiosities from these
unspoilt wildernesses. They amassed vast collections of plants for
botanic gardens and herbaria. As we saw earlier, dried specimens in
herbaria are an important repository of information about which
plants grew in a given time and place. Herbarium curators are
the heirs of a rich botanical legacy from an era of prodigious
discovery.

***

But discovery by whom? Many of the plants described were already
known and had been used by people for millennia. This imbalanced
endowment of discovery is reflected in the names we use today.
New species found by colonial botanists were often given names in
honour of the people who brought them to Western attention.
Rafflesia arnoldii was one.

Looking at the letters about the various *Rafflesia* encounters
exchanged among the colonial governors, botanists, and naturalists,
it's hard not to feel a certain romanticism for the time. Their excitement leaps from the page: the intrigue, the astonishment; the race
to be first. This was the world of meaning I was born into – books
on wonders of the natural world; black and white engravings of
intrepid Western explorers in the jungle, pointing aghast at impossible flowers. Claiming them. I suppose these were the people I
imitated as a child when I pretended to discover *Rafflesia* in the
cemetery behind my family's back garden. But colonial exploitation
was carefully airbrushed out of my books; the first inhabitants of

Southeast Asia, and users of the plants, were unrecognized, uncompensated. Invisible.

Rivalry among the British, Dutch, and French was rife in the great 'Age of Reason' – a period of intense scientific discourse in Europe. Europeans first encountered *Rafflesia* when a French surgeon and naturalist, Louis Auguste Deschamps, journeyed through Java from 1791 to 1794 amid a backdrop of upheaval in the French Revolution. But Deschamps's notes and diagrams were seized by the British in 1803, and lost to Western science for decades, before reappearing in a public sale in 1861.[61] The first British people to see *Rafflesia* were Stamford Raffles, a British colonial official who served as Lieutenant-Governor of the Dutch East Indies; his wife Sophia Raffles, a botanist; and Joseph Arnold, a naval surgeon and naturalist. They found the plant here in Bengkulu, in 1818. Arnold died of malaria, but not before writing an animated letter to an unknown friend, in which he describes his encounter:[62]

> One of the Malay servants came running to me with wonder in his eyes, and said, 'Come with me Sir, Come! A flower, very large, beautiful, wonderful!' I immediately went with the man about a hundred yards in the jungle, and he pointed to a flower growing close to the ground under the bushes, which was truly astonishing . . . To tell you the truth, had I been alone, and had there been no witnesses, I should have been fearful of mentioning the dimensions of this flower, so much does it exceed every flower I have ever seen or heard of; but I had Sir Stamford and Lady Raffles with me . . . who, though equally astonished with myself, are able to testify as the truth.

He goes on to describe how he and the others pinned four large sheets of paper together, then cut a precise template of the flower:

> It measured a full yard across . . . and the weight of this prodigy we calculated to be fifteen pounds.

According to Arnold's letter, the people of Sumatra called *Rafflesia* 'krubut'. When I asked Deki if this word is used here now, in his lyrical way he told me: 'Wrinkled is the name for *Amorphophallus*. If

Rafflesia is *cawan skedei*, then *cawan* is the cup.' *Rafflesia* and *Amor-phophallus* are often conflated by local vernacular across their range; perhaps this was true even then.

Raffles wrote to Sir Joseph Banks, a renowned botanist who sent other botanists around the world to collect plants and established Kew as a world-leading botanic garden. Raffles informed Banks of the flower, and Banks delegated the scientific description to Robert Brown, another eminent eighteenth-century botanist. Brown read his paper on *Rafflesia arnoldii* at a meeting of the Linnean Society of London on 30 June 1820,[63] thirty-eight years before Charles Darwin and Alfred Russel Wallace outlined the theory of evolution by natural selection from the same lectern:

> *This gigantic flower . . . was discovered in 1818 on Sir Stamford's first journey from Bencoolen into the interior. In that journey he was accompanied by a naturalist of great zeal and acquirements, the late Dr Joseph Arnold . . . It is proposed, in honour of Sir Stamford Raffles, to call this genus* Rafflesia, *the name I am persuaded that Dr Arnold himself would have chosen had he lived to publish an account of it.*

A second paper on *Rafflesia* by Brown, read in 1834, included plates by the leading Austrian botanical illustrators of the day, Franz and Ferdinand Bauer. The Bauer brothers' paintings were the closest most Europeans could get to visualizing the sensation. Though not entirely accurate, nor beautiful, Franz's depiction of a whole specimen of *R. arnoldii* certainly captures something of the plant's mystique. It must have staggered the natural historians of the time.

Although vast collections of exotic curiosities were amassed from faraway lands, not all were pressed and dried. Tropical plants were transported in sealed containers called Wardian cases, which protected them from exposure during the long voyages. Presumably botanists attempted to propagate *Rafflesia* in Europe, although there are scant accounts to suggest they did. Willem Meijer, who dedicated much of his life to *Rafflesia*, reported that in 1853 the Dutch botanist Willem Hendrik de Vriese illustrated *R. rochussenii* from a specimen grown in Leiden Botanical Garden in the nineteenth century; he presumed it was transported with its vine in a Wardian case from Java.[64] Curious to know if the plant had indeed flowered there I asked a friend, the Director of Leiden Botanical Garden, Paul Kessler. Paul and his collection manager Roderick Bouman explored the archives and spirit collections. Based on the accounts they unearthed, De Vriese did refer somewhat vaguely to such an event:

> I submit to the judgement of botanists, the following observations on the two known species of the island of Java, of which we have had the living Rafflesia rochussenii *on* Cissus *in the greenhouses of the Garden of Leiden, in 1851.* [translated from the French][65]

Paul and Roderick also managed to locate several bottled specimens of *Rafflesia*, preserved in alcohol, dating back to this period. One of the labels pointed to a provenance in the wilds of Java; the other labels were either too damaged or unclear to decipher. We may never know if *Rafflesia* flowered in Europe.

Back to Sumatra; island of dreams. The year 1818 was the dawn of an adventure and wonders were afoot: it was a time of planetary occultations, and other remarkable things; things that would change the face of science. A flower not born of this earth bore up out of the crumbling ground one day; a truly wondrous flower, larger than any other. Raffles and Arnold could never have guessed what lay in wait for them as they left Kota Bengkulu to head deep into Sumatra's wild interior.

Precisely where we're heading today.

***

I wake on a mattress on the floor with Deki conducting his Fajr prayer on a mat beside me, and the smell of woodsmoke seeping in through the warm air outside. My palms are clammy and I have slept fitfully; I rarely achieve REM here. After finishing his prayer, Deki kneels beside me quietly and asks if I would like to shower. 'So soon!' he whispers when I say I would. Then he shepherds me into the little shower room at the back of the house containing a bucket of cold water and plastic dipper, and waits attentively, barefoot, outside the door.

***

Deki's mother-in-law, Masita, whose house I'm staying in this week, has arranged for me to be paraded along the street so that the neighbours can observe their unusual guest. She ushers me out of the house with Deki and watches furtively through a hanging birdcage from the porchway.

First, I'm presented to the neighbour opposite, a small elderly lady who peers up at me like a nun. 'This is single mother,' says Deki. He might mean widow. Single Mother and I exchange halting pleasantries in our respective languages while Deki takes a photograph of us outside her front door. Next, aware of Mother-in-Law's and Single Mother's watchful eyes on us, I'm escorted down a small, pleasantly ramshackle passageway. It leads to a square of trodden earth and unenthusiastic trees, where we meet a group of small boys with a football. 'Bruno Fernandes, Bruno Fernandes!' chant the boys excitedly, pointing to me and laughing (this is the name of a Portuguese footballer, I learn later). 'Photo,' announces Deki, arranging us in a line with me in the middle. I'm given the ball to hold.

Next we perambulate through the neighbourhood to observe the tropical fruit trees. 'This is . . .' Deki repeats, waving away the missing words with a batting gesture; most of his sentences die this way. I notice Mother-in-Law has sent out one of her daughters on a moped for surveillance under the pretence of an errand. She appears three times during our circuit; I suspect she's returning to the house at intervals to report back.

Once I've had my photograph taken with every neighbour, we return to the house an hour later to find a selection of breakfast items arranged on a small table in the porchway. Mother-in-Law, Father-in-Law, four daughters (one of whom is Deki's wife), and an elderly man (who has appeared for the first time) settle down to watch me eat. I reach for a grey, gelatinous creation encased in a square of banana leaf.

'Delicacy West Sumatra,' Mother-in-Law says, beaming, as I hold it to my mouth; only, everyone gasps and rushes over to stop me. I'm not supposed to eat the leafy wrapper, I learn quickly. Next (with caution), I sample a ball of rice.

'You should love it. Delicacy West Sumatra,' Mother-in-Law says. It contains a rich, sugary filling.

'I like it very much – no I do,' I say.

Father-in-Law wanders off and returns with a brown crystalline brick for me to examine. 'Palm sugar,' he says, nodding. 'Delicacy West Sumatra.' After breakfast, we drink strong black coffee (another delicacy), and play with Deki's baby daughter Momoy – who looks at me with serious eyes – while we wait for the others, who are staying at a nearby hotel. Then we head east into the hills of Bengkulu under a half-cloudy sky, hoping for a miracle.

We pass a string of villages consisting of wood and tin huts braided through the trees. The largest is Taba Penanjung, a village flung about the hills beneath the softly forested peaks of Bukit Sanggul. The road is solid but winding; I suspect nauseating, if you're prone to such things. Along the way we stop beside the road to stretch our legs and enjoy the view. As the others relieve themselves in the bushes, I photograph a pair of bloated jackfruits leaning heavily against their trunk, looking out over still misted pleats that seem to belong to a Marianne North painting. I wonder if *Rafflesia arnoldii* is lurking down in those hills; place of legend and discovery, still obscured beneath the cloak of time. The flower that rules them all: the freak of evolution. The plant I created models of and obsessed over as a child. Question is, will we find it? Has the ground obeyed? Rare is the union of chance and success in this game.

I know how things stand now and so do you.

We have lunch in a gaff called Rumah Makan Saiyo on a street containing more motorcycles than people. Small men wander into the room carrying great sacks of rice over their shoulders as an Islamic prayer wails from a screen rigged high on the wall. We share small dishes of *telur dadar* (omelette), *perkedel* (fritters), and *bakwan jagung* (more fritters) with wilted heaps of cassava leaves. As I return from the facilities, a girl of about twenty presents me with paper and pencil. I suspect a complication with the bill, but Deki wanders over to explain with ushering gestures that she'd like me to write my name in English for her. Then he orchestrates a photograph of us in the doorway and scribbles down the girl's number, so that he can send it to her later. Sucking in the drowsy heat and fried smells, we clamber back into the van and continue east for the hills under the eddying cloud.

As I gaze over the still trees, my thoughts return to the centre of my obsession. Those fateful days in Kalinga a few months ago seem like a story only the deliriousness of exhaustion could devise; but the photographs tell me those flowers were real. I wonder if the early explorers also mistrusted their own judgements? They had only sketches and their recollections to guide them. My journey in Indonesia has a new texture to it. The terrain here is gentler than the wilds of Kalinga – as Adriane likes to remind me. I've not endured the full onslaught of the forest's gift of leeches, stings, and lunacy – not yet, anyway. But still I have things on my mind: fragile miracles born from a silken web, one easily frayed; Deki's devotion to the forest; the smell of woodsmoke, and a flower in peril. Uneasily, I watch the trucks piled high with palm-oil fruits as they trundle down the hills in the opposite direction. In the Philippines the lowland forests had mostly gone – had been smashed and burnt before I was even born. But here the future has yet to arrive.

We reach the green heart of Bengkulu Province. Giant ferns splash over the vertical banks; their arched feathers crown the narrow road, meeting in the middle in places; above these, sublimely high grey trees meander up into tangling leaf and vine. We abandon the vehicle in the green shade and wander along the verge where we find two middle-aged men crouching under a pergola of branches. Al, and Min Juanda, Deki tells us; his friends. Al has dark skin, a scraggy beard, and a ready-to-laugh expression; Min Juanda has a mournful face. They've rigged up a long, white sheet on which they've painted the words 'Bunga *Rafflesia arnoldii*'. Promising.

Al says something to Deki, who responds with uncontrollable laughter. 'His beard like your,' Deki whimpers, pointing to my face; bent double in a fit of giggles, he turns to Joko to translate the rest, who says: 'But less hair on his head as he has been thinking too much.' In a vaguely hysterical frame of mind, a band of us descend the flight of roots into the forest, to see if Nature has kept her promise.

***

The air is warm and damp; it smells of leaf mould, and of summer, like fresh-cut runner beans. A monkey shakes the branches and cicadas syncopate about the trees as we weave our way down the slope. Along the way, we point out botanical curiosities to one another. Adriane looks wild-eyed as he consults each leaf and flower, while Pat and Regi read the forest through their camera lenses. Joko spots a wild banana thrusting out of the thicket, which none of us know. Its ripening sickle-shaped fruits are flushed purple and arranged sparsely along their sprout. Deki points out glimmers of mysterious life we'd easily miss, for example a green lizard that's wrapped itself around a branch, and sits mid-air, staring at nothing. Then, he delights in finding a giant pill millipede crossing our path. He encourages me to pick up the creature; it forms a heavy ball of plated armour on my palm. Standing back, he says, 'What do you mean?' Often Deki asks this, seeking confirmation that I like something, I think. Further on, we find a titan millipede the length of my forearm and thicker than a finger. I'm instructed to pet this brute as well, and it responds by releasing a foul-smelling compound that no amount of hand sanitizer can erase all day.

We reach a fork in the half-imagined path, and look to Al and Min Juanda who lead us to the right, down a more thickly forested slope. In little under an hour we identify twenty-six species without trying, including begonias, shell gingers (*Alpinia*), torch gingers (*Etlingera*), lipstick plants (*Aeschynanthus*), and the leafy parasol of *Amorphophallus gigas*. I write them all down in pencil; the names fill an entire page of my book. The riotous tangle of palms and ferns appears primeval. Immense, motionless trees run high into the heavens and we become enveloped by them, as if entering another existence; marching back to the beginnings of time.

Our path becomes obscured by a gargantuan strangler fig that has layered itself into vertical sheets, forming a great temple we have to clamber inside to pass. Light dances about its fluted collar and its mighty grey roots writhe along the floor fluidly over a great length. 'What do you mean?' asks Deki, as he slaps his hand on the arms of the tree, looking at me expectantly. I mirror his posture, connecting myself to the tree as well, and smile.

After a short, vertical scramble below the fig tree, we enter an open bowl of forest, and gasp. Before us sits this: a monstrous unopened specimen of *Rafflesia arnoldii*. It's far and away the largest bud any of us has seen. The bloated mass seems to be bulging almost in real time – it's several days away from opening but already threatens to exceed a metre when it does. In a feat of physics, its host vine has hoisted it up from the floor to our waists, as if pulled by apron strings in the canopy. Al and Min Juanda have knocked together a confusion of tree-poles beneath it, presumably to hold the mighty flower in position as it unfolds. It looks like a floating brain.

A battleship of cloud shifts across the canopy's gaps as we take turns to stroke the vital mass, glittering in the leaf-tempered light. It seems to glow red in the leafy penumbra. The thin cord of vine sustaining it looks meagre, deficient. Yet life is pounding through it imperceptibly, nourishing something obscenely vast; like a cuckoo in the nest. As I place my hand on the bud, I ponder silently on the sap, cells, and molecular forces that will summon the great unfolding in a few days' time: a million microscopic events ballooning as one. Deki watches me closely as these thoughts drift along the roots of my consciousness. 'Process,' he says, holding my gaze.

Clouds are gathering fast now, and the sky has turned a gunmetal grey. 'We don't have long,' says Joko, reading the air. 'Not if we want to find an open one.' So we leave the growing premonition, reinventing it in our minds as we go; making it bigger. We clamber over the shelves of root and vine, and reach another fork in the trees.

And this time I know which way to go without anyone telling me.

★★★

Good God!

We falter on our approach, cannonading into one another stupidly, lost in astonishment. The confrontational creature barring our path looks dangerous. Erupting from the freshly launched earth, he spans a metre. He seems mythological, predatory – like a dragon. His leathern wings are reclined upon the floor, resting. One is half-closed, poised. Another, oddly, has a seam of stitches running along the distal third; he's had a run-in with a falling branch, and Deki's friends have lovingly put him back together with a weave of grass. A wounded beast, resting but potent. Breathing. Watching.

'Wow,' says Adriane softly, and Deki giggles. We converge on the shaded slope, leaning on trees and making a show of being careful not to fall into the monstrous thing; or let it swallow us. In a crouched ring, we peer into his yawning mouth of fangs and run tentative fingers around the walls of the lightless core, or *cawan*, as Deki calls it – the black hole. Inside this, a forest of close-set pinnacles and protrusions feels rubbery yet brittle. I'm reminded of a suede brush. Pat and Adriane sex the flower with stretched arms and cupped fingers; he is indeed male, as we suspected (most *Rafflesia* flowers here are). 'He's a boy!' cries Pat.

There's a miasma that hangs about the flower like a spell – an aura around its supernatural centrality. There's also a whiff of meaty breath, like a cat's, although it's not strong. As we mutter a commentary about the flower's intricacies, its anatomy and so on, I run a finger over the brick-red petals, which are warm from the forest's eternal heat. Its warts are the largest I've seen. They've left punched impressions of themselves on the flower's exterior, like echoes, and they seem to possess a life all their own; those bubbling around the centre have multiplied, like Petri-dish colonies mid-fission. Like mould.

We stage photographs, starting with Adriane's. He pushes his hair back and stares into the abyss, then looks up and smiles meekly. He looks small and vulnerable beside the flower; susceptible to unknown forces. Next, Deki crawls down to the titan, crab-like, half-embracing it, and grinning like a lunatic. In turns, we creep, crouch, lounge and leap around it, in a growing field of madness, our passions let loose.

Al (left) and Min Juanda (right) with Rafflesia arnoldii in the interior of Bengkulu, Sumatra.

Al and Min Juanda go last. They look incurious, easy in its presence. But then this flower belongs to them, doesn't it? To them, its proportions are a common marvel.

'*I should have been fearful of mentioning the dimensions of this flower,*' Arnold had written, and now I understand. Perhaps he was already gripped by his fatal fever when he wrote this – had lost his grasp of the real? Because it isn't quite. Its existence is bewildering. I too have a weaker hold on reality after my encounters with mythical beasts across the archipelago, leading to this: the inconceivable. Serenity, joy, and love; sickness, fear, and pain: they've all been touched by the wheel of human emotion that's circled these forests; battered me senseless.

Oh, I know, once again I'm slipping the bonds of soundness; my sanity is shot, extorted by a flower. But it's *preposterous*!

Decades, I've spent dreaming about this moment. And now I feel a new impulse rising inside me, brought on by all this madness – a strange and irrepressible urge.

To laugh.

28.

'Kaur, *Kauuuur!*' we cry like a pack of wolves. We've all gone a bit mad now, I think. It's taken most of the day to get to Kaur, the southernmost regency of Bengkulu Province. The 190-kilometre drive and the thrill of finding *Rafflesia arnoldii* seem to have unleashed a frenzied excitement among the group; especially Deki, who's howling out of the car window.

We off-road the vehicle into the night, weaving bumpily around the inky-still coconut palms, to reach a terrace of wooden huts. Joko inspects our lodgings before we assign rooms – he does this whenever we stay somewhere new. He declares them 'basic but OK'. Deki wants to select my room personally. 'This one very-very good,' he says holding open the door, grinning. It's cell-like with green-washed walls and a bucket of water for bathing, in which I notice the twitching hyphens of mosquito larvae.

After a brisk, purse-lipped wash, I shake myself dry and meet the others by the van. We hunt for a place to eat along the road to Bintuhan under a wild and starry sky. Deciding on an open-sided café offering grilled fish, we file in, batting away looping insects seduced by the light. A blue fog of appetizing smells wafts over us as we seat ourselves around a bench-like table. Almost immediately after settling down, Pat rises again, and asks Adriane, Regi, and our driver to accompany him to the van, saying 'beer', casually over his shoulder.

'This normal in Philippine?' Joko asks me after they've gone. 'Always beer?' Then he adds, 'Anyway they won't find here – religious place.'

Twenty minutes later they return heavily laden with black bags divulging the contours of bottles. Adriane dutifully snaps the lid of one and pours. Regi, whom Pat has recently taken under his wing as a sort of protégé, is issued a particularly large glass just as a police car trundles along the road a few metres from us.

'They're coming for you, Regi,' whispers Pat.

As we sip and chat, I study the group's faces. There's a bright new static about us tonight; an ease with our own company. We jest, share photos on our phones, and trade stories from former adventures. Adriane tells us of his wild exploits in Kalinga, of inaccessible forests, and hunting for undiscovered begonias over landslips where one misstep could be fatal. He seems particularly animated tonight. Deki seems unconvinced; he turns to me and asks, not very quietly, 'Why Mr Adriane so serious?'

The trees torment my dreams again. As I wake to the sound of wailing prayers, the images slip through my fingers, but something disquieting lingers, like smoke. At first light, Deki and I wander along the crunchy ribbon of cowries, cone shells, coral, and plastic. Fishermen are casting their traditional boats, which have long, pole-like contraptions projecting from the sides, like stabilizers. Deki runs over to help push one out, giggling as he goes. When he returns, he opens a balled fist to reveal a small hermit crab he's picked up by the surf; then with the help of his app, he tells me that larger ones climb the palms here. We crouch to admire a bejewelled sea-urchin shell gleaming on the sand; a work of nature. Beyond it, we reach a lake of sun-rotted plastic. 'Many problem,' Deki says as we trudge through the crackling drift, chuckling to himself softly. Beyond the white swathe, he pauses under a palm and taps on his phone, then presents me with a translation: 'I'm happy here.' He looks at me expectantly and I nod to show him I understand; then we wander back quietly together along the firm wet sand.

The rest of the clan has assembled on plastic chairs outside our rooms. We join them to discuss the day's plans over bananas and coffee. We've travelled to Kaur to corner an exceptionally rare species called *Rafflesia bengkuluensis*, which hides in the low-lying forests in this area; although no one seems optimistic about us finding it.

Deki has mobilized a patrol of people across the region to hunt it down, so far without success. 'But you know, most of the lowland forest *Rafflesia* in Philippines have gone,' says Pat. Deki doesn't look up from his phone. 'Here trampling is a risk in lowland forest,' Joko adds; 'they are sensitive to this; under threat.' A butterfly lands on his hat as he says this, emphasizing his point with a kiss of living fragility. 'And what about the titan arums, Deki? Do they grow here?' I ask. The titan arum (*Amorphophallus titanum*), which I first wrote about some way back, is native to these parts; if we cannot find *Rafflesia*, a titan would make a decent stand-in. 'Titan no flower,' he says firmly, as if for some recondite reason. We sip our coffee ponderously, watched by patient dragonflies from their invisible shelves, as the sea sighs gently beyond the palms.

Deki looks up from his phone and announces: 'Found. *Rafflesia bengkuluensis* is today.' His face lights up as he basks in our approval. Gathering up our things, we prepare for the jungle to reabsorb us. It feels like shaking off a dream in reverse.

Back in the van, we slap Regi over the shoulder conspiratorially, congratulating him for last night's beer-drinking achievements. 'You must have one beer for every *Rafflesia* flower we find,' Pat says. 'But you know in Kemumu we saw thirty buds, Regi.' Regi laughs self-consciously with a furrow between his eyes. The parallel conversations revert to Indonesian and Tagalog, with the odd English word thrown in, such as 'blooming' or 'sim card'. In the villages we pass young men in black kopiah hats, sitting on plastic chairs by the road, smoking. A woman is raking coffee beans on a large plastic mat, while a boy – perhaps her son – pulls a small goat by a lead. By and by, the still, dark halls of forest return to us, rising steeply on both sides. Ferns abound: laddered fronds of *Nephrolepis* arch out of the thicket, and papery clumps of *Drynaria* throw themselves at the trees.

We enter a cage-like bridge over a great river slicing the hills. Sunlight pours over the steady frill, and a herd of buffalo are drinking from its shore. 'Padang Guci means, how-you-say, lawn. The thing for rich people,' Joko says. I'm about to seek clarification when we meet a great bull guarding the road at the other end of the bridge. He lowers his head and looks at us determinedly. 'Oh-kay,' says

Deki. 'Okay, Oh-*kay*,' then he leans out of the window and shouts 'Permissi, permissi!' This goes ungranted, but our driver manages to weave his way around the bull anyway, so we resume our journey west, deep into Kaur's interior.

We reach Ulak Bandung Moearasahoeng in the climbing heat of the day. The village is strewn about the red earth and trees. Filaments of smoke coil out from between the houses. It's hard to get a sense of how big or old the place is because it's half-consumed by foliage. We meet Dang (meaning 'older brother' in this district) Zul, the village leader, on a square of soaked grass. He has close-cropped hair and an athletic physique under sporty clothes; he looks less like a village leader than a PE teacher. 'Dang Zul is PE teacher,' Joko says, translating Dang Zul and Deki's exchange of consonants, serious looks, and vague gestures. Twice the word *Rafflesia* precedes a volley of synchronized nods.

Other men from the village appear as we gravitate towards the trees. Soon, a small village of us is converging on the forest under the silver sky. We walk ponderously across the fringe of civilization: an open, wet complexion of grass, gangly palms, and black heaps of rotting durian fruit rinds. I wonder what these men are thinking; what they make of the pale man in their midst. I wonder, too, what is their connection to this forest. The lives of trees are always intertwined with people's lives; trees outlive us and connect our generations – this is true everywhere. But here, the lines between forest and farm are blurred. Millions of people in forest-edge communities earn a living from domestic-scale palm-oil agriculture. Joko tells me the native forest we're about to enter is at risk of clearance for palm oil; not on an industrial scale, but by local people, to make ends meet. 'Slash and burn,' he calls it. Perhaps that's why I keep smelling smoke.

The vegetation thickens. Arborescent clubmosses spiral out of the grass and brush stiffly against our ankles like miniature Christmas trees, and great lichened trunks shoot into the sky. We reach a rocky stream escaping the forest at an awkward angle. It ponders briefly in a glassy pool, then obeys its contours fiercely again. Dang Zul wades barefoot into the pool, scattering white diamonds, and waits the other side. In a line, we're shepherded into the forest by an attentive Deki who stands like a sentinel on his mossy boulder. Then, after a short storm of leaves, the wilderness takes us in, enveloping us like the tide.

The world changes quickly. It's claustrophobic and smells of damp earth. Weak light strobes the sultry air. Spent leaves hang like seaweed and trees rise like spears in a thousand shades of green. A profusion of fern species – How many? Ten? Twenty? – all writhe over the rocks and up the trees. Then there's the shrill siren of a million unseen creatures leading connected little lives; their wild music.

We clamber over boulders into creepers like dropped rope, pushing through the spiky pandans (*Pandanus*), *Pinanga* palms, and Pacific lychee trees (*Pometia pinnata*) racing towards the sun. Deki plays with a large brown stick insect he's plucked from somewhere, then sets it free on a branch. The trek is gentle; still, I'm conscious of my breathing and the wet hair plastering my forehead. Half a mile in, we reach a stream that we help each other cross with stretched arms and wobbling steps. After the crossing, Dang Zul takes us into the vault of the forest under the thick, dark canopy. We enter a little enchanted grove set about the trees and mossy boulders. And here, he stops, pointing to the floor.

We stare at it, rapt, like it's a magician's trick: a pale vision issued from the forest's depths, brought forth from the underworld like an exorcism. We congregate quietly around the yawning apparition. Peering, probing, and sniffing, we try to make sense of what's before us: the new reality we've just entered. The flower is half a metre across and white, like a negative image of itself. In the uncertain light it's almost blue – as if glanced at by the moon. Far paler than any *Rafflesia* I've seen, that's for certain. The bloodless creature seems to emanate its own internal glow. Its smell is strong; awful – yes, but with a high, sweet note. Quite different to the last two flowers we've seen here. Like them it shares a bold line of descent from mythical beasts, only this species possesses its own preciousness; a pale fragility. Nuzzling its locus of earth and vine, it looks vulnerable. Ephemeral.

Adriane and I kneel before the flower as the others queue up behind us. Adriane looks at me sidelong. 'So white!' he says dreamily. I dragnet my brain for the appropriate attributes but all the words die in my mouth. Silently, I caress the flower lightly with two fingers,

Dang Zul with Rafflesia bengkuluensis in Kaur, south Bengkulu, Sumatra.

uploading colour and contour. A picture is quietly forming in my mind from the negative image before me, setting; a moment that will become fixed later in paint. It always begins this way.

In the background Deki is busy marshalling the group, whispering, as one might usher relatives to admire a newborn baby. He creeps up to us. 'Like your,' he says pointing to the flower, then to my skin, laughing. We ask Dang Zul to sit with it, so we can take his photograph with our trophy. Crouching behind it, he folds a well-muscled arm on a resting knee, then caresses the flower gently with his free hand. He stares, gazes at it fondly like a father, and we watch.

A dozen men fawning over a plant – you might think there's something faintly perverse about that, but there isn't: our feelings are true. If you were here, you'd know. Being with the plant is like I had anticipated only different, as in all those small, indiscernible ways not caught by words; like the imagined intimacy with a person finally realized. Today we baited probability and we won: it opened specially for us – and it *needed* to be seen.

But now it wants something back.

Don't paint what you see. Look at the colours and shapes in front of you – do that by all means; do what they tell you. But don't paint what you see. *Feel* it.

Feel the tingle down your spine. Feel it reach into your consciousness, travel along the nerves, then grab you by the scruff of your soul.

Now forget the colours and shapes, the details; they'll come; but for now, you must see beyond them: light and dark. Like a ghost. Let the world fall away from you for a moment and watch the paint creep down the canvas in lines.

As if it's in blood.

Dang Zul leads us through the village towards his back garden. Along the way I ask him to add the local name for *Rafflesia* to the list in my book. 'Titiau Bon,' he writes in careful letters, peering closely at the page. He explains, through Joko's translation, that the name means 'decayed fungus'. As we stroll, villagers call out from plastic chairs in their doorways; according to Joko they're asking why a tall, pale man has appeared in the village. Self-consciously I try to appear friendly but not overbearing as I smile at the growing line of spectators.

Dang Zul's back garden contains an assortment of things vying for sun, including tropical leaves, family washing, and a large red plastic mat sprinkled with coffee beans. A woman in a green headscarf sits by the front door watching our approach. Dang Zul directs us past her to a sort of enclosure made of propped-up palm stumps latticed with bright foliage. Projecting out of the contraption is a potted titan arum in bud. It seems Dang Zul is cultivating it as a sort of pet. The fat sprout rises to our shoulders – which is small for this species. *Rafflesia* boasts the world's largest flower, but the titan arum possesses the largest unbranched inflorescence (technically a group of many small flowers), which can rise to three metres; as I said earlier, people often confuse the two. 'MALNOURISH! MALNOURISH!' Deki cries, seemingly a little upset by the warped dimensions; odd that he should know this word. Once he's composed himself, we stage photos around the starved titan to a growing audience of villagers.

We have lunch in the netted shade of a gnarled old tree next to a concrete tank containing catfish. They look like small sharks circling. Using our hands, hungrily we eat *tempe* (soy bean), grilled chicken, and *Parkia speciosa* beans, with rice. A lady holding a doughy toddler appears at the side of the street; Deki wanders over to her, telling us the child is his nephew (although the child is a girl).

Anyway, such terms are fluid here – I'm already an uncle to several children here now, including Deki's daughter. 'Oh-*kay*,' Deki says when he returns to the table, looking at his phone. '*Rafflesia bengkuluensis* is again.'

Remarkably, another flower has been located in Kaur. And it's within reach.

★★★

'This is Yogi.' Deki ushers forward a young man who bows repeatedly like a nervous dove, each time with a small smile. 'This is leader,' he adds, still referring to Yogi. I write his name in my book.

'What's his surname?' I ask Joko.

'No surname. People in this village is only one name.'

Yogi is accompanied by two men and two women, all of similar age. Their names are said too quickly for me to catch. The women look shyly at their feet. They're well turned out, with a sheen of makeup and florid headscarves; not really dressed for the jungle. In a line we troop across a field of corn where the blackened stumps of trees rise out of the red earth like distant pinnacles of rock. Slash and burn – recent, from the look of things. But I mend it quickly in my mind – I will the fallen trees to spring back around me; paint them with imagination, in lichen, moss, and fern. Daft, I know, but I find myself doing this sometimes.

The forest is guarded by tall ranks of grasses which rustle like paper as we push through them. Beyond their threshold lies a dark and intimate space. It smells of leaf and fungus. Within moments we're assailed by mosquitoes despite our repellent. Clambering over the dark floor spattered with bright foliage, we reach a gentle rise. At the top of the slope – not twenty metres from the forest's shore, in a thicket of leaf and vine – sits our brazen flower.

This specimen is larger than this morning's, a full arm across. It, too, is pale, and the eye of the flower is small and black. 'Male again,' says Pat, diving into the mechanism and withdrawing his arm in one deft stroke, disturbing a wave of dreaming flies. Nearby, we find a spent flower, black with rot. Small white gnats are teeming over the septic mess like plankton. Buds too are bubbling up all over

231

Yogi with Rafflesia bengkuluensis *in Kaur, south Bengkulu, Sumatra.*

the place including a mature, lustrous one – ribbed and smooth, like an ornamental squash. We have to take care not to step on the smaller buds, which are half-buried in leaf-fall. Joko points them out with murmurs of caution as we creep about the place taking photos.

We ask Yogi questions about his interest in the plant. Adriane records the interview on his phone journalist-style, while Joko translates: 'As young person, I have the responsibility to conserve it. One of the most important flora make like campaign to, how-you-say . . . so all the people knows about *Rafflesia*.' He pauses, allowing Joko to catch up. We nod encouragingly. 'No incentive government but community make, like, incentive.' He bows awkwardly at the end of his uncertain little speech and we clap.

'You're doing an important job, Yogi,' I say, and I mean it. He's the plant's custodian. I can see how deeply he cares for it; and for this island of forest it's moored to, in a fast-rising tide.

'Mr Chris heppy?' asks Deki as we leave the forest. 'I'm happy,' I tell him. 'Oh-*kay!*' he says, and laughs. Then he takes my hand to lead me around the blackened stump of one of the decapitated trees. The sun must be setting now, because their shadows seem longer than when we arrived.

If the forests are broken, fix them. If the petals have torn, unite them. Conjure the plants with thought. Breathe life on the flowers in paint.
And watch.

Watch the petals form fists and retract. Feel the tears ride up your face. Let the thoughts fire backwards, and see?

The trees spring back in place.

29.

'Small problem,' says Deki, with arms stretched half a metre. 'Not many-big problem, small-big problem,' he adds quickly, reading my expression. Despite months of paperwork, letters of engagement, and written endorsement, the Ministry is unhappy we're here without a pre-arranged courtesy meeting. They've sent a message to Deki telling him as much.

'Will we go to jail?' asks Adriane. 'I've heard of researchers being sent to jail.'

'We're not collecting anything or doing anything illegal; just observation,' says Joko. Still, the barred doors of this office do look like jail.

Joko tells Adriane to wait in the car. Then Deki leads Joko, Pat, and me through the barred door, along a corridor past cell-like rooms, to a large office with brown leather sofas and papers quivering under an electric fan. Here we're met by a squat, sheriff-like man in a brown cotton uniform with a gold belt and badges. Joko directs preliminaries and we arrange ourselves awkwardly around a wooden table. Pat and I, who don't understand the conversation, nod tentatively, while Deki makes encouraging noises in the background. Joko smiles as he speaks and the sheriff nods gravely. 'Oxford' comes up, and I smile politely. Deki mimes 'OK' discreetly behind the sheriff. The meeting ends with a photo-shoot outside the office.

'No jail,' says Deki as we clamber back into the car, causing Adriane to look up from his phone. 'No *jail*,' Deki repeats to the trees through the window.

Back on course for the interior we stop at a roadside lake choked with ferns and pencil orchids to search for a pitcher plant (*Nepenthes mirabilis*). First, Deki takes my hand and leads me across the road, navigating a swarm of motorcycles with just three near misses. On the opposite side, he presents me with a wooden shack of dried fish strung up by their mouths and bags of water containing living eel-like specimens, gawping. They look like deep-sea monsters.

'*Gabus*,' he says, pointing at the eel. He points to my mouth, encouraging me to repeat it.

'It snek-head,' he adds. Then he identifies the dried creatures one by one: 'This is *Belut*. This is *Pelus* . . .'

By the time we return, the others have already found the pitcher plants sprawling around the shore. Deki beckons me to remove my socks and shoes, roll up my trousers, and follow him into the swamp. I sink up to my shins in the wet, vegetable warmth and mosquitoes nag my bare legs. A few metres from the road, we reach a pair of identical, fern-green pitchers hanging from red-splashed leaves on a creeping vine. One has sent a missile of purple flowers up into the sky. I smile – they're worth every bite.

'Careful Mr Chris,' says Deki as we wade back to the roadside. 'Sneks.'

We sit at a rickety table by the softly dimpled lake, smacking mosquitoes, and checking our legs for leeches. Deki wanders off periodically, returning with assorted items for me to examine, including a fresh coconut.

'This is,' he says, pointing at the cut lid of the fruit. 'This is,' he repeats, showing me the straw. Then he films me drinking from it.

Joko joins us and he and Deki have a serious-sounding conversation.

'What's wrong?' I ask, occupying myself with a blooming red mosquito bite on my ankle, gifted by the swamp. I'm still on edge from all the talk of jail.

'One of the men with us in Kemumu has malaria,' Joko says. 'We should not go back there this trip.'

***

Mr Holidin is a small, middle-aged man with an inquisitive face. He wanders up and down the forested slope in flip-flops, showing us plants he's propagated. Deki points to this and that behind him, chipping in with 'You know?' and 'This same. This not same.' As we pass an *Amorphophallus* corm breaching the earth, he says: 'This is, you know, dormant fossil.'

I peer curiously at the trees as he speaks.

'Piss-piss?' he asks, with an expectant look followed by a snake-like noise.

'No, Deki, I'm just observing.'

We're led over a disintegrating wooden bridge above a small ravine, into a wire-mesh shade frame. Here we're shown a brood of baby titan arums that Mr Holidin has coaxed out of black plastic pots. Later he'll plant them in the forest. When they bloom in years to come, weekend tourists will pay him a small fee to take selfies with them. This nursery is his business: ecotourism.

'You have a beautiful piece of forest here,' I tell him.

He bows, then stands on the roadside watching us leave, like we're family.

The site of *Rafflesia arnoldii* we visited a few days ago is just a short drive away, so we return to see if the giant bud is any closer to opening. As we change our shoes by the van, Deki pulls out from under my seat a loose plastic box with holes punched into the lid. I don't know how long it's been there. He opens the lid and probes the box with a metre-long stick, and when he withdraws it a small green snake has knotted itself around the end. Flourishing the viper like a wand, Deki extracts another polished brown specimen, which begins coiling around his arm.

'This is Mr Chris . . .' he says, grappling with the brown one. 'Cat snek. And this is . . .' he continues, placing the brown specimen back in its box, to refocus on the green one, 'pit veeper.' He rolls the r with gusto.

'Deadly,' he adds, nodding gravely. Then he stows the box safely back under my seat.

The bud spans over half a metre now. It might break a world record when it opens. It's expanding, almost perceptibly, as the dark

Deki with Rafflesia arnoldii in bud in the interior of Bengkulu, Sumatra.

forest seethes around it. The men say it will open in two days' time – Thursday – which is when we're due to leave Sumatra. I ask to revisit the open specimen.

'Gone,' the men say, shaking their heads; still, I'd like to see for myself. They point me in the right direction and I find it soon enough, a little way down the slope; it's strange to be back here again, alone.

There's a keening sound that seems to rise from around the flower. It's gone of course, like they said; not the shell, but the *essence* – the part that, depending on your view of things, is either mortal or immortal.

***

Adika and Agung plod along the mud road in matching black boots, their skin glistening in a bath of heat. They pass the nursery of hopeful potted shoots, ready for planting, then they kick through the spoil of palms. Some of the orange fruits have been missed by the pickers; they gleam in the fibrous heap like embers. The fruits need processing within forty-eight hours of harvesting, so these will be useless now. They slip into the forest's dark embrace. Not a big forest – only three hectares, but it's theirs.

As they walk, the brothers talk of their hopes for the children. Adika wants his daughter to go to university; Agung wants his son to work in business – finance, IT, or something like that. Together they chart their undetailed map to a brighter future. Like their parents did for them – only their parents had next to nothing, so you can hardly compare.

The more trees they plant, the more income they'll make: that's just business.

But there's an important choice to be made.

***

Honey-gold light pours over the land as we drive back to Kota Bengkulu, giving the hills a mournful glow. A girl in a green gown sits watching her father shovelling earth. An old woman scatters seed for small chickens that I first mistake for pigeons;

one lies on its back like a dog as another one pecks it. There's the sound of a pneumatic drill somewhere far away and smoke wafts in on the warm breeze. A woman in a mauve headscarf tends to the edible plants in her garden as five passing children proceed to climb a tree. People are going about their business here quietly in tune with the land.

Sunset. We spot a woman selling fruit from a sagging shack at the side of the road and decide to stop. Fast-moving insects orbit an electric bulb crazily. Joko selects a large fruit called *cempedak*, which the woman uses a long knife to slice. Peculiar yellow growths spool out of the dissected orb like new life. The slimy flesh has a pleasant, nutty flavour. Next we sample durian – a heavy, prickly brown fruit resembling a rugby ball, dubbed the 'king of fruits'. It's renowned for its strong, gassy smell, which piques the interest of rainforest beasts including elephants, tigers, pigs, deer, tapir, rhinoceros, monkeys, and squirrels. And people – although its antisocial smell has seen it banned from most major public transport systems and buildings. We hand round the half-moons of fruit, scooping out the pale flesh, laughing at the mess it makes of our hands and faces. It's greasy like an avocado, and tastes of custard with just a hint of garlic.

Recently, Joko and I co-authored a paper on durian cultivation in Southeast Asia with other foresters in Indonesia and Malaysia.[66] Of the thirty described species of durian (*Durio*), about a third produce edible fruits, but only one (*Durio zibethinus*) is grown on a commercial scale. Traditionally, durian trees are grown sustainably in smallholdings, along streets, or intercropped sparsely in native forests; just today we saw them planted this way.

But in recent years there's been a 'durian boom' – people across Asia and beyond want more of it; more than the natural forest can supply. Intensive 'durian farms' are cropping up: they're a new threat to the forests of Southeast Asia. And unlike with palm oil, we don't even know the extent of this one.

★★★

Rubber or palm? That's the question. The family has grown both since the 1990s, when they were supported by a government scheme to establish the farm. Whichever you grow, the devil's in the detail, but Adika and Agung know the ropes. Rubber needs harvesting five times a week – and theirs is a small family; they don't have the labour to expand. Palms need fertilizer so there are additional running costs to consider; but there's a good market for the oil, and that doesn't look likely to change anytime soon. On balance, palm oil is less risky says Adika.

Anyway, Agung is *anak bawang* – the onion child. He needs direction from the outer layers – his brothers. Adika's the eldest. He has the casting vote.

★★★

Back in town, Deki's family is preparing a feast. They usher me towards a prayer mat and we sit cross-legged in a ring, while mother-in-law Masita and sisters-in-law Adinda, Mentan, and Chairunisa set out bowls of 'Delicacy from West Sumatra' in the middle of the floor. The flavours are sublime. There are clove-scented chicken legs, cubes of root vegetable in a spinach-like confection, diced watermelon, and assorted battered creations like tempura. I sample a bright pink wafer with a satisfying crunch. 'This one very-cracker,' says Deki, laughing, 'very-cracker'.

As we eat, I'm asked questions as quickly as Google Translate will allow.

'How-long-your-flight-take-five-hour?' asks Indra, Deki's father-in-law.

'How many cousin you have?' asks Masita. She also asks me for foreign coins to add to her collection of 'hand fruit' – souvenirs, I think.

Then we retire to the sofas under the porch where Deki serenades us with 'Apa kabar Sayang' on the household karaoke system, and his daughter Momoi zooms about in her remote-controlled toy car.

Deki, Regi, and I are given mattresses for the floor. Deki shows me a photograph on his phone depicting the silken fruits of a kapok tree (*Ceiba pentrandra*) from which the mattresses are made, he says.

There's an awkward moment when I begin taking off my clothes as Masita strolls past and has to avert her eyes with a shocked gasp; in the end I lie on the mattress fully clothed like Deki and Regi in the heavy heat. Deki seems to want to say something to me before we turn in. As he fiddles with his phone, I find myself wondering again why he wanted me to come. What does he need from me? What does the forest need from him?

'Mr Chris, do you heppy?'

'Yes, Deki, I'm happy.'

'Yes,' he says, then pauses. 'I am proud you are my friend.'

***

There's one last site Deki wants us to see. It's an eight-hour drive to the north of Bengkulu Province. Along the way, Deki, Pat, and I sing along to Westlife and compare local names for the trees we see. We stop to eat *tempe* and *mochi* – little green-stained coconut balls with a rich sugary-brown filling. Back on the road, we pass pitcher plants creeping down the ferny banks, and whiskery white flowers of a plant that Deki tells me is used by people here to ease backache.

The plants vanish as we drive through mile after mile of naked hills. In one of the valleys, insect-like yellow diggers are mining the blood-red earth. The land is being ploughed for palm oil and rubber on an industrial scale. I've seen deforestation in the Philippines; goodness knows I have. But there the scars were made decades before I was born. Here the wounds are fresh; they're on our watch. Hesitantly we take photographs through the window, but none of us says anything. Perhaps we're worried it might upset Deki.

Anyway, eventually the forest returns and silently we agree to pretend it never left us.

***

Adika and Agung pause in the hissing heat, re-evaluating their plans over balls of *mochi*. The dry season is still three months away. That's when Adika says they'll do the burn. They won't publicize this because people are against the practice. But how else could they clear such large trees? How else can they make a living? *Their* forest, their choice. No one can argue with that.

Only they will. Because there's another issue at stake, besides slash and burn: *Bunga Padma*. It's always grown here – Adika vaguely remembers being shown the plant as a child; a mere curiosity then. But things are different now: people want to visit the *Sekedai* cup, take selfies, broadcast it over Facebook. Then *menerobos* happens – more people come, beating a path to the flower. And with *menerobos* comes forest protection. *Bunga Padma* is a problem to be solved, and that's just business.

***

Mounds of grey shingle flicker between the palms. 'Bangau River,' says Deki. It looks like a series of small lakes; as if the river's heart isn't really in it. Above the water on the opposite side of the river rises a dark curtain of foliage. This is a place so wild that Sumatran elephants and tigers still roam here. We park on the shingle shore and change our clothes behind a tree. Deki finds a man to ferry us over the river in his small green motorboat. The boat can only fit four so he takes us in two trips. The mineral air is cool and fresh on my face, and lazy brown water slaps the sides of the boat. We clamber up a mounded bank of grass and breadfruit trees to reach a plain containing a mighty elephant. Although native to this forest, it's the product of a breeding programme that's been established here in recent decades – a desperate effort to ward off extinction. A decade ago, the Sumatran elephant was promoted from 'Endangered' to 'Critically Endangered' because of a population in freefall. All the usual reasons. Still, at least people are trying to save them, I suppose.

'Aggressif,' Deki says, wandering off to slap the creature hard on the back.

We reach a line of sky-blue wooden huts on stilts. One has on it a fresco. 'I paint,' says Deki; he must spend quite a lot of time here, despite the long drive and the boat crossing required to reach the place. We're taken into one of the huts where we meet an earnest vet in her late twenties, and a man in late middle age with a kindly face. Seemingly unaware that we're here to look for *Rafflesia*, they cite a list of facts about elephants for us – how many there are, how often they breed, and so on. 'How long do they live?' I ask, keen to show interest. 'About fifty or sixty,' says the vet. 'Same as human.'

Then there's a long exchange between the staff, Deki and Joko, followed by a pause. They look troubled by something. I look at Joko expectantly. 'So actually,' he begins hesitantly, 'there is no *Rafflesia* today.' But Deki was certain – he said the buds were seen here just a few days ago. He was *certain* there was a flower for us.

Something's not right.

I smell smoke. Pictures drift through my consciousness like half-remembered dreams: a falling book; a forester; a fight. Naked hills. A wondrous flower. A knife.

There's a rising hum, like tinnitus. The hairs on my arm stand on end and the voices in my thoughts begin to scream . . .

'It was destroyed.'

And then they stop. Dead.

★★★

Adika holds the knife. Agung is hesitant, but Adika insists. They have their children's futures to consider, he says. Every parent wants the best for their children.

30.

It is raining hard again. And have you been careful?

Now I have brothers, we will work together. *Rafflesia* will exist for my children, Sir. Yes?

People must know if the forest is sick.

But who will tell them?

31.

They scatter the floor in a formation, like a cryptic code. I'd forgotten their witchery. We converge around the flowers with eyes fixed to the floor; bowing over them. Then we look up to the dream in the sky from where they fell. The jade vine is suspended several metres above our heads: a ringing blue glow in the canopy. One of the young foresters in the group, called Edwin, crouches to gather the fallen treasure, sorting the flowers through finger and thumb. 'Butterflies, Sir,' he says, and I laugh in agreement; they do resemble butterfly wings, I suppose. 'No, look.' He arranges a pair side by side in the palm of his hand, then presents them to me. The united flowers are reborn as a perfect butterfly.

A soapy fragrance wafts down from the trees – it's unclear which – and their talons clamp to rock like witches' hands; above them, happy ferns spiral over the path. A fig tree forms a waterfall of roots and the gentle *hish* of insects starts and stops around us. I let the forest of Mount Makiling seep into me again.

Horses strapped with vegetables, a dog on a parked motorcycle, chickens, glinting scraps of foil, and all the other signs of human life evaporate as the mountain track narrows under the steep jungled slope. Our band of foresters falls quickly into file – uniform T-shirts, black hair, and gleaming necks – marching, bobbing, obeying the wavering contours. Along the way we allow ourselves occasional distractions: a wild tea bush that Pat finds in the thicket; an overhead bower of coral tree; one of Adriane's wild gingers – but we move on quickly every time, bound by purpose.

Rafflesia panchoana is declared and we disband our foraging line like disturbed ants. We approach the flower in pairs, awkwardly constrained by giant ferns and knotted brown figs, blossoming like crazy formations of coral. Adriane and I crouch to peer at it side-long through the floating vines. It looks so small after the mythical beasts of Sumatra. Adriane sexes it deftly. Female. I cup my hand and extend a middle finger into the cramped, rubbery crevice, but I'm so concerned about damaging it that I struggle to locate the vital organs. Adriane guides my hand.

'Your fingers are too big,' he says.

We locate another flower further up the slope. This one is male; Adriane squints at the bead of pollen on his fingertip. It looks just like soft butter. The flower looks dipped in ink around one half, and blotched on the other, like a spoiled banana. Nothing lasts long here.

We set to work. Pat, Adriane, and I instruct the team of nodding foresters as to the requirements, indicating the necessary dimensions and attributes of the vine with spaced arms and fingers. We form breakout groups among the trees. A contender is located by one of the young foresters, and we converge around him as he begins to unsnarl the vine. 'Gentle, gentle,' Glen whispers over him. But the line bends sharply and vanishes into the floor; we can't get a purchase on it. We abandon the failed attempt and begin extricating another, like electricians unravelling cables. But again, we fail – it can't be undone from the forest's morass; will not be relinquished. So we move up the slope, persisting with the unrelenting chaos in a growing urgency about us, bordering on frenzy. To fail is unthinkable.

There's a restless murmur in the trees, like a beehive. Clouds shift over the gaps in the canopy and a tropical bird calls overhead. Below, oblivious, eleven men scrabble about the floor with wild eyes and mud-stained knees. There's an anxious pause as with a mud-streaked hand one of the foresters presents a loosened length of vine to Pat, who holds it up to the sky. We crouch and look up at him, like children waiting for a magician's trick. Then the bird stops singing and a broken beam of light falls through the trees. 'Yes,' says Pat. 'This will be our scion.'

At night, I sleep with the vines beside my bed.

Pat and the foresters selecting the scion on Mount Makiling, Luzon.

★★★

I look about as I stretch my legs. Things have changed up at the Land Grant. Gangs of men are scurrying around a small village of scaffolds by the lake in a gale of shouting, knocking, and sawing. The wind has changed too. There's a warm wet breeze that feels fresh on my face; it whips the canopy, then skitters off into the forest.

We set off down an old logging road in the leaf-coloured light. It smells of cut grass. The foresters and guards form a band at the front; Kuya Dante is entrusted with our precious sack, which he's holding at a slight distance, as if the vines were vipers. Pat, Adriane, Ana, and I stride a little way behind them, in a tailwind of anticipation. Swiftly we squelch through canyons of wet mud, hopping up onto the drier shelves of clay when they're offered. I glance covertly at our reunited family as we trek side by side: at Pat's bright smile; at Ana's considered, slightly mournful look; and the glimpse of the former child in Adriane's wide-eyed face. We've come to know one another quite well now, I think.

Stooping under dripping branches, Ana tells me of recent perils at the Land Grant: of the forester who was bitten recently by a venomous snake and now has a bad back; of illegal poaching, logging, and guns. She says that some of the roadside shacks selling potted ferns and orchids harbour more specimens than their own nursery. I sigh and shake my head at the floor, but not too hard. Like all my kind, I know I'm quick to judge; to define the problem with lofty words – words that speak louder than actions.

'Many people are reliant on this forest,' Ana continues in her monotone voice, pushing a tendril of wet hair from her face. 'But there is a solution.'

I look up.

'We are teaching the community here to propagate rare plants. So that they can make more; sell them, without poaching from the forest.'

There's a pause in the conversation as we gather together along a clearing. The breeze is singed; something's burning upwind. Tree ferns form black silhouettes like locked snowflakes against the brilliant cloud. Beneath them, softly forested peaks march along the horizon like a hidden kingdom.

'The ridges,' says Ana.

'Beautiful,' I murmur. I say this a lot here.

'But this is an illegal clearing,' she adds, still looking at the view. 'It was made by people to plant these coconut palms.'

She makes a sweeping gesture over the symmetrical rows of twinkling trees. I swallow hard. Threats, everywhere I look.

'But see, Chris?' Ana points to the spaces between the palms. 'Last year we planted native species too.'

Lanky teenage trees are spiralling out of the palms' embrace, like rising hopes. Already some are up to my shoulder.

'So that the forest can recover,' she says quietly.

The mud-road concedes to a path, then gives up altogether in a clearing of trodden clay and bright weeds under a wall of jungle. At its foot nestles a wooden shack.

'This is the bunk house,' says Pat, disappearing inside.

The slats have been knocked together jaggedly, nailed in places with corrugated squares of rust. Inside, hammocks have been strung up along both sides in the striped shade.

'The guards sleep here at night to listen out for chainsaws,' Ana says.

At the far end of the shack, an old man is tending a cauldron, bathing in a blue fog that's creeping out through the slats. Beside the wood fire, four large pans have been filled with black river snails, like marbles. Outside, we pick our way over timber, pots, and pans, squinting at the humid sun. Time hasn't quite left this place.

Clouds are moving fast now, and the air sparkles with possibility. We cross a pebbly stream bed leading into a forest with no path. Kuya Dante and the guards wait for us under a steep rise of lush vegetation; then wielding their knives, they stoop and slash a way up. A few steps behind, the rest of us push into the riot of fern and vine, moving crabwise up the slope. The ground is a loose drift of fallen leaf and lace – it's hard not to slip. Creepers hang from the sky like loose string; I pull at one and it falls without a fight. Creamy light lances the trees and the air has a high, sharp note like bracken. Everything is flourishing out of the rot, weaving across an ever-changing canvas at the speed of logic: ecology; connectivity; life after death. You can never cross the same forest twice.

Kuya Dante stops halfway up the slope and rests his knife – he's been briefed by Pat and Ana. This is the place: the blank slate.

Once everyone has caught up, we examine the mother vine from our cramped positions among the ferns. We run fingers along her swooping tresses, tracing them to the ground. Three tributaries are mapped, and we settle on the strongest.

'Adi,' snaps Pat.

Dutifully, Adriane unpacks a trowel and scalpel, and lays the scion along the floor. Like a surgical team, we're poised, each ready to play our part. And we're bound by a quiet intimacy; you can almost hear us breathe in time with the purr of crickets. Next, Adriane takes out a sheath of clear plastic labelled BAWANG, garlic wrapper; he must have bought garlic in Indonesia especially. I leaf through my notes from the workshop in Bogor, lingering over the mud-stained symbols and annotated diagrams, like a gardening spell book. Then, in Tagalog, Pat instructs Kuya Dante, who begins marking a trench in circles with the tip of his sword-like knife. Like a mandrake gathering, we've magic on our hands here.

Pat hands me the scion. The life-bearing thread looks unprepossessing, like a length of old rope.

'You cut,' he says.

'Me?'

'Yes.'

Adriane hands me the scalpel. I check my notes again, reread what I already know by heart. I cleave the end in one swift stroke and I'm pleased with the cut. Only, when I hold it to the light, it's not quite straight – and it must be. There's a knot beneath the bark; a glitch. I make another attempt but there's little improvement and soon I'll be down to the wick. I hand the scion to Kuya Dante – surely he's good with a knife? He improves the line but it's still not plumb – any imperfection will lead to an air space; a bubble in the feed line. Kuya Dante relays the scion to Adriane, who pauses, cocks an eye, then whittles the end as if striking a match, and hands it back to Pat. Pat holds it to the light, and squints.

'Yes,' he says smiling. '*Yes.*'

I push the scalpel into the mother vine. It's woody and resistant – like overgrown ivy, but I'm firm with the knife and it cuts deep. We insert the enchanted key into its lock and it fits: the union, separated by the thickness of a shadow. I press the pieces in place while Adriane unravels the garlic wrapper. Faces in the group draw close; all eyes are on the vine, on my fingers. Holding the ropes with reptilian calm as Adriane bandages them together, I sense a life pass through solid matter. Although the voices have gone away now.

We rise awkwardly from the ground, brushing away the ferns and creepers. The wind has dropped and a gentle shower patters the canopy. Adriane packs away the clinking surgical instruments and Kuya Dante begins throwing earth over the work like a gravedigger. Rain falls on my open book and wrinkles the paper, but the pencil holds. I scan the last passage of notes.

'We've forgotten to bless the vine!' cries Pat.

Kuya Dante pauses his gardening and we all look up at Pat. We fidget among the leaves in a crackle of anticipation. Pat steadies himself with a loop of vine and considers the floor for a moment.

'Gods of the forest, bless this vine,' he says.

We resume what we were doing, then quietly leave the forest; but not the same way we came.

References

Prologue

1 C.J. Thorogood, L. Teixeira-Costa, G. Ceccantini, C. Davis, S.J. Hiscock (2021). 'Endoparasitic plants and fungi show evolutionary
   convergence across phylogenetic divisions'. *New Phytologist* 232 (3):
   1159–1167.
2 L. Cai, B.J. Arnold, Z. Xi, D.E. Khost, N. Patel, C.B. Hartmann, S. Manickam, S. Sasirat, L.A. Nikolov, S. Mathews, T.B. Sackton, C.C. Davis
   (2021). 'Deeply altered genome architecture in the endoparasitic
   flowering plant *Sapria himalayana* Griff (Rafflesiaceae)'. *Current Biology* 8; 31 (5): 1002–1011.e9.

Main Text

1 D.P. Bebber, M.A. Carine, J.R. Wood, A.H. Wortley, D.J. Harris, G.T.
   Prance, G. Davidse, J. Paige, T.D. Pennington, N.K. Robson, R.W.
   Scotland (2010). 'Herbaria are a major frontier for species discovery'.
   Proceedings of the National Academy of Sciences USA 21; 107 (51):
   22169–22171.
2 A. Akira and Y. Okuno. 'Flight of a Samara, *Alsomitra macrocarpa*'
   (1887). *Journal of Theoretical Biology* 129: 263–274.
3 C. Neinhuis and W. Barthlott (1997). 'Characterization and distribution of water-repellent, self-cleaning plant surfaces'. *Annals of Botany*
   79 (6): 667–677.
4 F. Box, A. Erlich, J.H. Guan, C.J. Thorogood (2022). 'Gigantic floating
   leaves occupy a large surface area at an economical material cost'.
   Science Advances 8 (6): eabg3790.
5 C.R. Darwin (1875). *Insectivorous Plants*. D. Appleton and Co., New
   York.

6   C.M. Clarke, U. Bauer, C.C. Lee, A.A. Tuen, K. Rembold, J.A. Moran (2009). 'Tree shrew lavatories: a novel nitrogen sequestration strategy in a tropical pitcher plant'. *Biology Letters* 5: 632–635.

7   L. Chin, J.A. Moran, C.M. Clarke (2010). 'Trap geometry in three giant montane pitcher plant species from Borneo is a function of tree shrew body size'. *New Phytologist* 186: 461–470.

8   T.U. Grafe, C.R. Schöner, G. Kerth, A. Junaidi, M.G. Schöner (2011). 'A novel resource–service mutualism between bats and pitcher plants'. *Biology Letters* 7: 436–439.

9   J.G. Morilla, N.H.N. Sumaya, H.I. Rivero, R.S.B. Madamba (2014). 'Medicinal plants of the Subanens in Dumingag, Zamboanga del Sur, Philippines'. International Conference on Food, Biological and Medical Sciences, Bangkok (Thailand).

10 G. Chomicki, C.J. Thorogood, A. Naikatini, S.S. Renner (2019). '*Squamellaria*: Plants domesticated by ants'. *Plants, People, Planet* 1: 302–305.

11 G. Chomicki and S.S. Renner (2016). 'Obligate plant farming by a specialized ant'. *Nature Plants* 2: 16181.

12 A. Dejean, P.J. Solano, J. Ayroles, B. Corbara, J. Orivel (2005). 'Arboreal ants build traps to capture prey'. *Nature* 434: 973.

13 J.L. Morris, M.N. Puttick, J.W. Clark, D. Edwards, P. Kenrick, S. Pressel, C.H. Wellman, Z. Yang, H. Schneider, P.C.J. Donoghue (2018). 'The timescale of early land plant evolution'. *Proceedings of the National Academy of Sciences USA* 115 (10): E2274–E2283.

14 M.N. Puttick, J.L. Morris, T.A. Williams, C.J. Cox, D. Edwards, P. Kenrick, S. Pressel, C.H. Wellman, H. Schneider, D. Pisani, P.C.J. Donoghue (2018). 'The interrelationships of land plants and the nature of the ancestral embryophyte'. *Current Biology* 28 (5): 733–745.e2.

15 A.J. Hetherington, C.M. Berry, L. Dolan (2016). 'Networks of highly branched stigmarian rootlets developed on the first giant trees'. *Proceedings of the National Academy of Sciences USA* 113 (24): 6695–6700.

16 C.K. Boyce, T.J. Brodribb, T.S. Feild, M.A. Zwieniecki (2009). 'Angiosperm leaf vein evolution was physiologically and environmentally transformative' (2009). *Proceedings of the Royal Society B: Biological Sciences* 276 (1663): 1771–1776.

17 B.T. Drew, J.G. González-Gallegos, C. Xiang, R. Kriebel, C.P. Drummond, J.B. Walker, K.J. Sytsma (2017). '*Salvia* united: The greatest good for the greatest number'. *Taxon* 66: 133–145.

18 C.C. Davis, M. Latvis, D.L. Nickrent, K.J. Wurdack, D.A. Baum (2007). 'Floral gigantism in Rafflesiaceae'. *Science* 315 (5820): 1812.

19 R.D. Lasco, R.G. Visco, J.M. Pulhin (2001). 'Secondary forests in the Philippines: Formation and transformation in the 20th century'. *Journal of Tropical Forest Science* 13(4): 652–670.

20 T.B. Moya and B.S. Malayang (2004). 'Climate variability and deforestation – reforestation dynamics in the Philippines'. *Environment, Development and Sustainability* 6: 261–277.

21 G.J. Perez, J.C. Comiso, L.V. Aragones, H.C. Merida, P.S. Ong (2020). 'Reforestation and deforestation in northern Luzon, Philippines: Critical issues as observed from space'. *Forests* 11 (10): 1071.

22 S.K. Papworth, R. Rist, L. Coad, E.J. Milner-Gulland (2009). 'Evidence for shifting baseline syndrome in conservation'. *Conservation Letters* 2: 93–100.

23 M.C. Press and G.K. Phoenix (2005). 'Impacts of parasitic plants on natural communities'. *New Phytologist* 166: 737–751.

24 C.C. Davis (2008). 'Floral evolution: dramatic size change was recent and rapid in the world's largest flowers'. *Current Biology* 18 (23): R1102-4.

25 Z. Xi, Y. Wang, R.K. Bradley, M. Sugumaran, C.J. Marx, J.S. Rest, C.C. Davis (2013). 'Massive mitochondrial gene transfer in a parasitic flowering plant clade'. *PLoS Genetics* 9 (2): e1003265.

26 L. Cai, B.J. Arnold, Z. Xi, D.E. Khost, N. Patel, C.B. Hartmann, S. Manickam, S. Sasirat, L.A. Nikolov, S. Mathews, T.B. Sackton, C.C. Davis (2021). 'Deeply altered genome architecture in the endoparasitic flowering plant *Sapria himalayana* Griff. (Rafflesiaceae)'. *Current Biology* 31 (5): 1002–1011.e9.

27 M. Bendiksby, T. Schumacher, G. Gussarova, J. Nais, K. Mat-Salleh, N. Sofiyanti, D. Madulid, S.A. Smith, T. Barkman. 'Elucidating the evolutionary history of the Southeast Asian, holoparasitic, giant-flowered Rafflesiaceae: Pliocene vicariance, morphological convergence and character displacement'. *Molecular Phylogenetics and Evolution* 57 (2010): 620–633.

28 P.B. Pelser, D.L. Nickrent, J.R.C. Callado, J.F. Barcelona (2013). 'Mt. Banahaw reveals: The resurrection and neotypification of the name *Rafflesia lagascae* (Rafflesiaceae) and clues to the dispersal of *Rafflesia* seeds'. *Phytotaxa* 131 (1): 35–40.

29 P.B. Pelser, D.L. Nickrent, B.W. van Ee, J.F. Barcelona (2019). 'A phylogenetic and biogeographic study of *Rafflesia* (Rafflesiaceae) in the Philippines: Limited dispersal and high island endemism'. *Molecular Phylogenetics and Evolution* 139: 106555.

30 F.P. Schiestl and S. Cozzolino (2008). 'Evolution of sexual mimicry in the orchid subtribe orchidinae: The role of preadaptations in the attraction of male bees as pollinators'. *BMC Evolutionary Biology* 8:27.

31 B.K. Ehlers and J.M. Olesen (1997). 'The fruit-wasp route to toxic nectar in *Epipactis* orchids?' *Flora* 192: 223–229.

32 R.D. Bardgett and W.H. van der Putten (2014). 'Belowground biodiversity and ecosystem functioning'. *Nature* 515 (7528): 505–511.

33 M.Y. Siti-Munirah, N. Dome, C.J. Thorogood (2021). '*Thismia sitimeriamiae* (Thismiaceae), an extraordinary new species from Terengganu, Peninsular Malaysia'. *PhytoKeys* 179: 75–89.

34 M.I. Disney, M. Boni Vicari, A. Burt, K. Calders, S.L. Lewis, P. Raumonen, P. Wilkes (2018). 'Weighing trees with lasers: Advances, challenges and opportunities'. *Interface Focus* 8 (2): 20170048.

35 C. Schmitt, P. Parola, L. de Haro (2013). 'Painful sting after exposure to *Dendrocnide* sp: two case reports'. *Wilderness and Environmental Medicine.* (4): 471–473.

36 C. Parker (2009). 'Observations on the current status of *Orobanche* and *Striga* problems worldwide'. *Pest Management Science* 65: 453–459.

37 C.J. Thorogood, J.R. Witono, S. Mursidawati, A. Fleischmann (2022). 'Parasitic plant cultivation: examples, lessons learned and future directions'. *Sibbaldia: The International Journal of Botanic Garden Horticulture* 21: 109–136.

38 K. Akiyama, K. Matsuzaki, H. Hayashi H. (2005). 'Plant sesquiterpenes induce hyphal branching in arbuscular mycorrhizal fungi'. *Nature* 435 (7043): 824–827.

39 H. Bouwmeester, C. Li, B. Thiombiano, M. Rahimi, L. Dong (2021). 'Adaptation of the parasitic plant lifecycle: germination is controlled by essential host signaling molecules'. *Plant Physiology* 185 (4): 1292–1308.

40 C.J. Thorogood and S.J. Hiscock (2010). 'Compatibility interactions at the cellular level provide the basis for host specificity in the parasitic plant *Orobanche*'. *New Phytologist* 186 (3): 571–575.

41 W. Meijer (1997). 'Flora Malesiana – Series 1'. *Spermatophyta* 13 (1): 20–21.

42 Ibid: 19–20.

43 Ibid: 19.

44 Ibid: 20.

45 W. Meijer (1984). 'New species of *Rafflesia* (Rafflesiaceae)'. *Blumea* 30: 209–215.

46 S. Harris (2021). *Roots to Seeds: 400 Years of Oxford Botany*. Bodleian Library Publishing, Oxford.

47 S. Lawrence (2020). *Witch's Garden: Plants in Folklore, Magic and Traditional Medicine*. Kew Publishing, London.

48 C.J. Thorogood, S.J. Hiscock (2019). *Oxford Botanic Garden: A Guide*. Bodleian Library Publishing, Oxford.

49 *Henry VI Part Two*, Act III, Scene 2, in A.J. Carter (2003). 'Myths and mandrakes'. *Journal of the Royal Society of Medicine* 96 (3): 144–147.

50 B.A. Adnan, S. Hadisusanto, P. Purnomo (2021). '*Rafflesia patma* Blume in Pananjung Pangandaran Nature Reserve, West Java: population structure, distribution patterns, and environmental influences'. *Journal of Tropical Biodiversity and Biotechnology* 06: 03: jtbb64800.

51 Y.W.C. Kusuma, O. Noerwana, Y. Isagi Y. (2020). 'New evidence for flower predation on three parasitic *Rafflesia* species from Java'. *Tropical Conservation Science* 11: 1–6.

52 R.S. Beaman (1988). 'Pollination of *Rafflesia* (Rafflesiaceae)'. *American Journal of Botany* 75 (8): 1148–1162.

53 B.J.D. Meeuse (1978). 'The physiology of some sapromyophilous flowers', in A.J. Richards (ed.), *The Pollination of Flowers by Insects*, 97–104. Linnean Society Symposium, Series 6, Academic Press, London.

54 C.C. Davis, P.K. Endress, D.A. Baum (2008). 'The evolution of floral gigantism'. *Current Opinion in Plant Biology* 11 (1): 49–57 (49).

55 Ibid: (54).

56 J. Ollerton, R.A. Raguso (2006). 'The sweet stench of decay'. *New Phytologist* 172 (3): 382–385.

57 A. Jürgens, S. Dötterl, U. Meve (2006). 'The chemical nature of fetid floral odours in stapeliads (Apocynaceae-Asclepiadoideae-Ceropegieae)'. *New Phytologist* 172: 452–468.

58 A. Susatya, S.N. Hidayati, S. Riki (2017). '*Rafflesia kemumu* (Rafflesiaceae), a new species from Northern Bengkulu, Sumatra, Indonesia'. *Phytotaxa* 326 (3): 211–220.

59 C.J. Thorogood, L. Teixeira-Costa, G. Ceccantini, C. Davis, S.J. Hiscock (2021). 'Endoparasitic plants and fungi show evolutionary convergence across phylogenetic divisions'. *New Phytologist* 232 (3): 1159–1167 (1164).

60 L.A. Nikolov, P.B. Tomlinson, S. Manickam, P.K. Endress, E.M. Kramer, C.C. Davis (2014). 'Holoparasitic Rafflesiaceae possess the most reduced endophytes and yet give rise to the world's largest flowers'. *Annals of Botany* 114 (2): 233–242.

61 W. Meijer (1997). 'Flora Malesiana – Series 1', *Spermatophyta* 13 (1): 18.

62 R. Brown (1821). 'An account of a new genus of plants named *Rafflesia*'. Reprinted from the *Transactions of the Linnean Society* XIII: 201–234, in *The Miscellaneous Botanical Works of Robert Brown* (2015), pp. 367–398. Cambridge University Press.

63 D.J. Mabberley (1999). 'Robert Brown on *Rafflesia*'. BLUMEA 44: 343–350.

64 W. Meijer (1997). 'Flora Malesiana – Series 1'. *Spermatophyta* 13 (1): 21.

65 W.H. de Vriese (1853). *Memoire sur les Rafflesias Rochussenii et Patma, d'apres les recherches faites aux iles de Java et de Noessa Kambangan, et au jardin de l'universite de Leide; dedie Son Excellence M.J.J. Rochussen, Ministre d'état ancien gouverneur-general des Indes Orientales Néerlandaises*. Anz & Co., Leiden & Dusseldorf, p. 9.

66 C.J. Thorogood, M.N. Ghazalli, M.Y. Siti-Munirah, D. Nikong, Y.W.C. Kusuma, S. Sudarmono, J.R. Witono (2022). 'The king of fruits'. *Plants, People, Planet* 4 (6): 538–547.

Index

malaria, 212, 235

Malaysia, 33, 46–7, 139

Mande, Kuya, 8, 16, 26, 44, 45, 55, 57, 59–61; at Amro River, 78, 92; in Balbalasang–Balbalan forest, 108; and drive to Kalinga, 97, 98, 104, 106

mandrake (*Mandragora officinarum*), 183–4

Marge (fern specialist), 7, 16, 21

Margotia species, 80

mathematics, 41

medicine: herbal remedies, 46, 47–51; nature and mental health, 30; traditional in Iraq, 47–51; traditional in Southeast Asia, 7, 20, 46–7

Medinilla genus, 33–4, 45, 89, 91

Meijer, Willem, 179, 213–14

mental health, impact of nature on, 30

millipedes, 218

Missan, Kuya, 96, 114, 127, 134, 140–41, 142, 146, 147

mistletoe, 114

monitor lizards, 26, 28, 77

monkeys, 15, 28, 85, 185, 186–7, 197, 218

mosses, 66, 67, 71, 72

moths, 53, 191

mountains, 15–16, 26, 28, 63, 100; Cordillera Central (Luzon), 117; Sierra Madre range (Luzon), 26, 44, 52–4, 55–7, 63, 76, 106, 116, 117, 120 *see also* Banahaw, Mount (Luzon); Makiling, Mount (Luzon)

Munirah, Siti, 139

Mursidawati, Sofi (Curator of *Rafflesia* at Bogor), 166, 168–71, 177–8, 183, 186, 198, 199

Nepenthes genus/pitcher plants, 15, 36–7, 38–42, 82–3, 191, 235, 241

Ngatari, Mr, 164–5, 166, 167–70, 169, 183

Nikong, Dome, 139

Ollerton, Jeff, 194

Orbea variegata (stapeliad), 195

orchids: *Agrostophyllum* genus, 45; *Androecium sesquipedale* (Madagascan comet), 191; in Balbalasang–Balbalan forest, 113, 114, 128, 129–30, 132, 133–4, 138, 140; bee orchids, 130–32, 195; *Bulbophyllum* orchid, 53; Christmas orchid (*Calanthe triplicata*)., 46; conservation at Land Grant, 36, 45–6, 248; epiphytic, 73; and evolutionary science, 128, 130–32, 133–4, 191, 195; 'flying duck orchid' (*Caleana major*), 132; ghost orchid (*Epipogium roseum*), 140; helleborine (*Epipactis*), 132–3; moth orchids, 46, 191; North European, 132–3; pencil orchids, 235; *Phalaenopsis lueddemanniana*, 45–6; Philippine ground orchids (*Spathoglottis plicata*), 81, 138; and pseudobulbs, 114; sex life of, 128, 130–34, 191, 195; strapped to trees, 27, 36, 45–6

Osmoxylon genus, 121

Oxford Botanic Garden, 2, 11, 19, 37–8, 41, 54, 71–2, 160, 184, 192, 204

Oxygyne genus, 138–9

paint, self-cleaning, 18–19

palaeontology: *Cooksonia* (fossil plant), 67; fossils in coal, 69; and genetics, 66–7, 119; Scotland's

Rhynie Chert, 66; sudden appearance of flowers in fossil record, 69

Palawan (Philippine island), 120

palm-oil plantations, 33, 204, 205, 217, 240, 241

pandans (*Pandanus*) genus, 52–3, 142, 227

Pangandaran (Java), 180, 183, 184–6

parasitic plants: *Balanophora*, 160; broomrape (*Orobanche*), 118–19, 154, 157, 158, 159–60; CT's research on, 2–3, 77–8, 80, 118–19, 154–5, 157–61; *Cytinus*, 70, 80, 160; and evolutionary science, 2, 3, 70–71, 80, 114, 117–19, 154–5, 158–61, 191–4, 203; and genetics, 3, 70; growing/cultivating of, 57, 119, 157–8, 159, 160–61, 164–71; hemi-parasites, 114; holo-parasitism, 114; host resistance against, 159–60; and host specificity, 119, 158, 160; International Parasitic Plant Society (IPPS), 154–6; mycoheterotrophs, 138–9; Rafflesia as, 2–3, 70; reproduction of, 22, 158–9, 161, 177–8, 190–94, 197, 203; seeds of, 119, 157, 158–9, 160–61, 177–8; speciation in, 119; and strigolactones, 158–9, 161; war on agriculture by, 155, 156, 157, 159; witchweed (*Striga*), 155, 156, 157, 159

Parker, Chris, 154–5, 156

Philippine warty pigs (*Sus philippensis*), 28

Philippines: Amro River Basin, 76, 77–80, 81–93; bandits in, 76; the Cordillera, 108; deforestation, 31–2, 63, 99–100, 104, 120, 177, 217; geological history of, 120; invasive species in, 181–2; Mount Banahaw as sacred place, 60, 106; mountain-climbing, 63; species unique to, 12, 44–5, 59–60; Tagalog (national language), 10, 12, 55; United States Exploring Expedition (1841), 11; *see also* Balbalasang–Balbalan forest (Kalinga); Banahaw, Mount (Luzon); Kalinga Province (Luzon); Luzon Island; Makiling, Mount (Luzon)

photosynthesis, 2, 3, 19, 114

pigs, 28

Pinanga palms, 227

pitcher plants/*Nepenthes*, 15, 36–7, 38–42, 82–3, 235, 241

plants: ancient origins of, 65–6; carnivorous, 15, 36–41, 82–3, 191, 235, 241; charophytes, 66; and communication, 112, 158–9, 161, 195; 'discoveries' of bestowed upon Western explorers, 46–7, 211; epiphytes, 27, 29–30, 45, 73; farmed by ants, 54–5; four main lineages of, 66, 67; gymnosperms, 68, 204; Horizontal Gene Transfers (HGTs), 3; houseplants, 33, 44, 46, 83; in Iraq, 47–51; lycophytes, 67–8, 69, 72, 113; mycoheterotrophs, 138–9; poisonous, 9, 49, 111, 124, 145; principle of self-cleaning, 18–19; scientific names, 17; and strigolactones, 158–9, 161; vascular, 66, 67–8; Victorian plant hunters, 37 *see also* ferns; flowering plants (angiosperms); parasitic plants; trees and entries for individual plants

reproduction: *Alternation of Generations*, 71–2; asexual, 71–2; double fertilization, 72; flying seeds, 18; negative frequency-dependent selection, 194; of parasitic plants, 22, 158–9, 161, 177–8, 190–94, 197, 203; Rafflesia's use of flies, 22, 70–71, 190–94, 197, 203; sexual, 70–72, 191–4; wind, 18, 131, 158

Rhynie Chert (Scotland), 66

roots, 18, 27, 30, 45, 48, 157–8; in fossil lycophytes, 69; mandrake, 183–4; and propagation of *Rafflesia*, 166–8; of strangler fig, 16–17, 187, 218–19; used by parasites, 158–60

rose grape (*Medinilla* species), 33–4, 45

rosemary, 70

rubber plantations, 200, 204, 240, 241

Ryukyu Islands of Japan, 138–9

sage, 70

Salak, Mount (Java), 176–7, 179

satin pothos (*Scindapsus pictus*), 44

seeds, 54–5; in Carboniferous period, 68–9; Corner's definition, 68; evolution of, 72; gymnosperms, 68, 204; of parasitic plants, 119, 157, 158–9, 160–61, 170–71, 177–8; of *Rafflesia*, 160–61, 170–71, 177–8; winged/flying, 18

shell gingers (*Alpinia*), 218

Sierra Madre mountain range (Luzon), 26, 44, 52–4, 55–7, 63, 76, 106, 116, 117, 120

Sigillaria (lycophyte), 68

snakes, 96, 236, 248

social media, 43

soil communities, 138

staghorn fern, 30, 33

stapeliads (starfish flowers), 194–5

stoneworts, 66

Sumatra, 8, 17, 179, 199, 200–205, 214–16; 'Bangau River', 242; deforestation, 241–3; Kemumu, 201, 205–9, *208*, 235; *see also* Bengkulu province (Sumatra)

Sumatran elephant, 242–3

Sunandar, Regi, 201, 202, 206, 207, *208*, 218, 223–4, 225, 240–41

Sunda porcupines, 190

sundews, 37, 39

Susatya, Professor, 201–3

syconia (structures of figs), 11

Talyantan (species of *Leea*), 52

Tangkuban Perahu, Mount (Java), 182

taro (*Colocasia esculenta*), 30

taxonomy, 17, 70, 136, 177, 211

Teijsmann, Johannes Elias, 165–6

Tetrastigma vine, 57, 167–70, 205, 245–51

Thapsia genus, 9

Thorogood, Chris (CT): in Amro River Protected Landscape, 76, 77–80, 81–93; in Balbalasang–Balbalan forest, 108–10, 113–16, 120–25, 126–30, 132, 133–8, 139–47; at Bogor Botanic Garden, 164–71, 173–5, 177, 183, 250; in Borneo, 43; carnivorous plant research, 37–9, 41–2; childhood, 1–2, 15, 37, 43, 109, 143, 148, 211–12, 216; dreams of the forest, 15, 43, 111–12, 148, 210–11, 224; drive to Kalinga, 97–100, 101–8; and earthquake in Java, 174–6; field diary of, 101; finds *Rafflesia arnoldii*, 219–22, 223; finds *Rafflesia banaoana*, 148–52, 161–2; finds *Rafflesia bengkuluensis*, 227–30, 231–3;